THE *MAYFLOWER*
AND HER PASSENGERS

THE *MAYFLOWER* AND HER PASSENGERS

Caleb H. Johnson

To order additional copies of this book, contact:
Xlibris Corporation
1-888-795-4274
www.Xlibris.com
Orders@Xlibris.com
29152

CONTENTS

ACKNOWLEDGMENTS

I would first like to thank my wife Anna for her extreme patience with this extraordinarily time-consuming project. Her support made this book possible. One of the precursors to this book was our 1170-page *Complete Works of the Mayflower Pilgrims*, now out of print. That book, which my wife greatly helped me type, organize, and proofread, was also instrumental in making research for this book much more efficient.

Special thanks are due to Mike Haywood, who graciously painted the gorgeous cover artwork, "Mayflower's Dawn," especially for my book. It depicts the *Mayflower*, anchored off the tip of Cape Cod, on the morning of arrival, 11 November 1620.

Researching records in England, especially records like the High Court of Admiralty and the Customs Books of the Exchequer that are written in Latin, is very expensive and time consuming. Thanks is therefore due to the following individuals who donated some of the needed money to make the research possible: Ben B. Johnson, MD; Carolyn Rust; Peter Ansoff; Elsie J. Wagner; Henry B. Stevens; John F. Hoffman; George A. Hall; Bryce Stevens; Deborah Saller; Michael Mott; Karri Samson; H. J. Dalton Jr.; Sammy Lee Ehrnman; and Andrew McClellen.

The researcher who carried out most of my projects in English records was Simon Neal, who deserves much credit for his thorough and careful work. Without him, many of the discoveries and findings would not have been possible. In the course of this project, he provided translations and transcriptions of more than a hundred pages of requested documents, from the Public Records Office to the British Library to local county records offices across England. I would also like to thank Leslie Mahler and David Greene for occasional correspondence regarding ongoing *Mayflower* research, and for sharing unpublished research, especially on the Billington and Allerton families. Leslie Mahler has also supplied me, on many occasions, with copies of records, especially from parish registers and probates, some of which I have used in this work.

Thanks is also due to Alicia Crane Williams and the Alden Kin Search Project, and to Frank Soule and the Soule Kindred in America, who supplied funds in support of research into the Mullins family of Dorking, and the Soule family, respectively.

PREFACE

The story of the Pilgrims and the voyage of the *Mayflower* has been told and retold in seemingly countless books. Generally, *Mayflower* passengers have been treated as a collective unit. There have certainly been a few biographies written about some of the more notable passengers, the leaders of the colony, such as William Brewster, William Bradford, and Edward Winslow. But for the most part, the names and lives of the other hundred passengers remain almost unknown. Many were just ordinary men, women, and children for whom not enough historical material could ever be gathered to write a full biography. Nonetheless, each Pilgrim family was unique. Understanding who the Pilgrims were as individuals is necessary to more fully understand them as a collective group.

With the few scant records available, I have attempted to write short biographies of each family group or individual that came on the *Mayflower*, whenever possible, tracing their lives from baptism to burial through England, Holland, and America. Additionally, I have attempted to put together a biography of the ship itself, using Admiralty Court and customs records to trace the ship's movements and the business dealings of her owners.

During the course of the eight years it took to compile and research all the material found in these biographies, I managed to make several new discoveries. Some of my more significant discoveries have already been published, including the English origins of *Mayflower* passenger Stephen Hopkins, and the English origins of *Mayflower* passenger Peter Browne. Several other English origins are published here for the first time, including the origins of John Hooke, John Crackston, and the probable origins of Thomas Williams.

We know who all the *Mayflower* passengers were because William Bradford, governor of Plymouth, recorded a list of them all in his manuscript history *Of Plymouth Plantation*. But for some of the passengers, that enumeration in the passenger list is the only record of their existence. Some passengers are known only by name. And if the name is "Richard Clarke," for example, there are literally thousands of men with that name living in England during the early seventeenth century. There is no practical way to identify such passengers. Nonetheless, a surprising number of *Mayflower* passengers have been conclusively identified, many discovered in the last few decades as computer-assisted searching and genealogical research techniques have matured.

WILLIAM BRADFORD'S
MAYFLOWER PASSENGER LIST

8	Mr. John Carver. Katherine, his wife. Desire Minter; & 2 man-servants John Howland Roger Wilder William Latham, a boy. & a maid servant, & a child that was put to him called, Jasper More	2	William Bradford, and Dorothy his wife, having but one child, a son left behind, who came afterward.
		6	Mr. Isaac Allerton, and Mary his wife; with 3 children Bartholomew Remember, & Mary; and a servant boy, John Hooke.
6	Mr. William Brewster. Mary his wife, with 2 sons, whose names were Love, and Wrestling and a boy was put to him called Richard More; and another of his brothers the rest of his children were left behind & came over afterwards.	2	Mr. Samuel Fuller; and a servant, called William Butten. His wife was behind & a child, which came afterwards.
		2	John Crackston and his son John Crackston.
5	Mr. Edward Winslow Elizabeth his wife, & 2 men servants, called George Soule, and Elias Story; also a little girl was put to him called Ellen, the sister of Richard More.	2	Captain Myles Standish and Rose, his wife
		4	Mr. Christopher Martin, and his wife; and 2 servants, Solomon Prower, and John Langmore

5	Mr. William Mullins, and his wife; and 2 children Joseph, & Priscilla; and a servant Robert Carter.	2	Francis Cooke, and his son John; But his wife, & other children came afterwards.
6	Mr. William White, and Susanna his wife; and one son called Resolved, and one born a-shipboard called Peregrine; & 2 servants, named William Holbeck, & Edward Thompson	2	Thomas Rogers, and Joseph his son; his other children came afterwards.
		2	Thomas Tinker, and his wife, and a son.
		2	John Rigsdale, and Alice his wife.
8	Mr. Stephen Hopkins, & Elizabeth his wife; and 2 children, called Giles, and Constanta a daughter, both by a former wife. And 2 more by this wife, called Damaris, & Oceanus, the last was born at sea. And 2 servants, called Edward Doty, and Edward Leister.	3	James Chilton, and his wife, and Mary their daughter; they had another daughter that was married came afterward.
		3	Edward Fuller, and his wife; and Samuel their son.
1	Mr. Richard Warren, but his wife and children were left behind and came afterwards.	3	John Turner, and 2 sons; he had a daughter came some years after to Salem, where she is now living.
4	John Billington, and Ellen his wife: and 2 sons, John, & Francis.		
4	Edward Tilley, and Ann his wife; and 2 children that were their cousins: Henry Sampson, and Humility Cooper.	3	Francis Eaton, and Sarah his wife, and Samuel their son, a young child.
3	John Tilley, and his wife; and Elizabeth their daughter.		

10

Moses Fletcher
John Goodman
Thomas Williams
Degory Priest
Edmond Margesson
Peter Brown
Richard Britteridge
Richard Clarke
Richard Gardinar
Gilbert Winslow

1

John Alden was hired for a
cooper, at Southampton where
the ship victualed; and being
a hopeful young man was much
desired, but left to his own
liking to go, or stay when
he came here, but he stayed,
and married here.

2

John Allerton, and Thomas
English were both hired, the
later to go Mr. of a shallop here,
and the other was reputed as
one of the company, but was
to go back (being a seaman) for
the help of others behind. But
they both died here, before the
ship departed.

2

There were also other 2 seamen
hired to stay a year here in the
country, William Trevore; and
one Ely; but when their time was
out they both returned.

There being about a hundred
souls came over in this first ship;
and began this work, which God
of His goodness hath hitherto
blessed; let his holy name have
praise.

And seeing it hath pleased Him
to give me to see 30 years
completed, since these beginnings.
And that the great works of his
providence are to be observed. I
have thought it not unworthy my
pains, to take a view of the
decreasings, and increasings of
these persons, and such changes as
hath passed over them, & theirs, in
this thirty years. It may be of
some use to such as come after;
but however I shall rest in my own
benefit.

I will therefore take them in order
as they lie.

Mr. Carver and his wife, died the
first year, he in the spring, she in
the summer; also his man Roger,
and the little boy Jasper, died before
either of them, of the common
infection. Desire Minter, returned
to her friend & proved not very
well, and died in England. His
servant boy Latham after more than
20 years stay in the country went
into England; and from thence to
the Bahama Islands in the West
Indies; and there with some others
was starved for want of food. His
maid servant married, and died a
year or two after here in this place.
His servant John Howland married
the daughter of John Tilley,

15

Elizabeth, and they are both now living; and have 10 children now all living and their eldest daughter hath 4 children And their 2 daughter, one, all living and other of their children marriageable so 15 are come of them.

4

Mr. Brewster lived to very old age; about 80 years he was when he died, having lived some 23 or 24 years here in the country & though his wife died long before, yet she died aged. His son Wrestling died a young man unmarried; his son Love, lived till this year 1650, and died, & left 4 children, now living. His daughters

2

which came over after him, are dead but have left sundry children alive;

4

his eldest son is still living, and hath 9 or 10 children, one married who hath a child, or 2. Richard More, his brother died the first winter; but he is married, and hath 4 or 5 children, all living.

2

Mr. Ed. Winslow, his wife died the first winter; and he married with the widow of Mr. White, and hath 2 children living by her marriageable,

8

besides sundry that are dead. One of his servants died, as also the little girl soon after the ships arrival. But his man George Soule is still living, and hath 8 children.

4

William Bradford, his wife died soon after their arrival; and he married again; and hath 4 children, 3 whereof are married.

8

Mr. Allerton his wife died with the first, and his servant John Hooke. His son Bartle is married in England but I know not how many children he hath. His daughter Remember is married at Salem & hath 3 or 4 children living. And his daughter Mary is married here, & hath 4 children. Himself married again with the daughter of Mr. Brewster, & hath one son living by her but she is long since dead. And he is married again, and hath left this place long ago. So I account his increase to be 8 besides his sons in England.

2

Mr. Fuller, his servant died at sea; and after his wife came over, he had two children by her; which are living and grown up to years. But he died some 15 years ago.

0

John Crackston died in the first mortality; and about some 5 or 6 years after his son died, having lost himself in the woods, his feet became frozen, which put him into a fever, of which he died.

4

Captain Standish his wife died in the first sickness; and he married again, and hath 4 sons living, and some are dead.

Mr. Martin, he, and all his, died in the first infection; not long after the arrival.

15 Mr. Mullins, and his wife, his son, & his servant died the first winter. Only his daughter Priscilla survived, and married with John Alden, who are both living, and have 11 children. And their eldest daughter is married & hath five children.

7 Mr. White, and his 2 servants died soon after their landing. His wife married with Mr. Winslow (as is before noted) His 2 sons are married, and Resolved hath 5 children; Peregrine two, all living. So their increase are 7.

3

4 Mr. Hopkins, and his wife are now both dead; but they lived above 20 years in this place, and had one son, and 4 daughters born here. Their son became a seaman, and died at Barbados, one daughter died here and 2 are married, one of them hath 2 children, & one is yet to marry. So their increase, which still survive, are 5. But his son Giles is married, and hath 4 hildren.

12 His daughter Constanta, is also married and hath 12 children all of them living, and one of them married.

4 Mr. Richard Warren lived some 4 or 5 years, and had his wife come over to him, by whom he had 2 sons before died; and one of them is married, and hath 2 children So his increase is 4 but he had 5 daughters more come over with his wife, who are all married; & living & have many children.

8 John Billington after he had been here 10 years, was executed, for killing a man; and his eldest son died before him; but his 2 son is alive, and married, & hath 8 children.

7 Edward Tilley, and his wife both died soon after their arrival; and the girl Humility their cousin, was sent for into England, and died there. But the youth Henry Sampson, is still living, and is married, & hath 7 children.

John Tilley, and his wife both died, a little after they came ashore; and their daughter Elizabeth married with John Howland and hath issue as is before noted.

8 · 4

Francis Cooke is still living, a
very old man, and hath seen
his children's children have
children: after his wife came over,
(with other of his children) he
hath 3 still living by her, all
married, and have 5 children
so their increase is 8. And his
son John which came over
with him, is married, and hath
4 children living.

6

Thomas Rogers died in the first
sickness but his son Joseph is still
living, and is married, and hath 6
children. The rest of Thomas
Rogers came over, & are married, &
have many children.

Thomas Tinker, and his wife, and
son, all died in the first sickness.

And so did John Rigsdale, and his
wife.

10

James Chilton, and his wife also
died in the first infection. But their
daughter Mary is still living
and hath 9 children; and one
daughter is married, & hath a child;
so their increase is 10.

4

Edward Fuller, and his wife died
soon after they came ashore; but
their son Samuel is living, &
married, and hath 4 children or
more.

John Turner, and his 2 sons all died
in the first sickness. But he hath a
daughter still living at Salem, well
married, and approved of.

4 · 1

Francis Eaton, his first wife died in
the general sickness; and he married
again, & his 2 wife died, & he
married the 3 and had by her
3 children; one of them is married,
& hath a child; the other are living,
but one of them is an idiot. He
died about 16 years ago. His son
Samuel, who came over a sucking
child is also married, & hath a child.

Moses Fletcher
Thomas Williams
Degory Priest
John Goodman
Edmond Margesson
Richard Britteridge
Richard Clarke
    All these died soon after their
arrival in the general sickness that
befell. But Degory Priest had his
wife & children sent hither
afterwards, she being Mr. Allerton's
sister. But the rest left no posterity
here.

Richard Gardinar, became a
seaman, and died in England, or at
sea. Gilbert Winslow after divers
years abode here, returned into
England and died there.

6

Peter Brown married twice; by his
first wife he had 2 children, who are
living, & both of them married; and
the one of them hath 2 children
by his second wife, he had 2 more;
he died about 16 years since.

Thomas English; and John Allerton
died in the general sickness.
John Alden married with Priscilla,
Mr. Mullins his daughter, and had
issue by her as is before related.

Edward Doty, & Edward Leister,
the servants of Mr. Hopkins:
Leister after he was at liberty, went
to Virginia, & there died; but
Edward Doty by a second wife hath
7 children and both he and they are
living.

Of these 100 persons which came
first over, in this first ship together,
the greater half died in the general
mortality; and most of them in 2
or three months time. And for
those which survived though some
were ancient & past procreation; &
others left the place and country;
yet of those few remaining are
sprung up above 160 persons; in
this 30 years. And are now living in
this present year 1650. Besides
many of their children which are
dead, and come not within this
account.

And of the old stock (of one, &
other) there are yet living this
present year 1650 near 30 persons.

Let the Lord have the praise;
who is the High Preserver of men.

Meat for the Fishes

Loving friend,

    My most kind remembrances to you and your wife; . . . whom in this world I never look to see again; for besides the eminent dangers of this voyage, which are no less than deadly; an infirmity of body hath seized me, which will not in all likelihood leave me till death; what to call it I know not, but it is a bundle of lead, as it were, crushing my heart more and more these 14 days, as that although I do the actions of a living man, yet I am but as dead; but the will of God be done.

    Our pinnace [the *Speedwell*] will not cease leaking, else I think we had been halfway at Virginia; our voyage hither hath been as full of crosses, as ourselves have been of crookedness. We put in here [Dartmouth] to trim her, and I think, as others also, if we had stayed at sea but 3 or 4 hours more, she would have sunk right down. And though she was twice trimmed at Hampton, yet now she is as open, and leaky as a sieve; and there was a board a man might have pulled off with his fingers 2 foot long, where the water came in, as at a mole hole; we lay at Hampton 7 days in fair weather waiting for her, and now we lie here waiting for her in as fair a wind as can blow, and so have done these 4 days, and are like to lie 4 more, and by that time the wind will happily turn as it did at Hampton. Our victuals will be half eaten up, I think, before we go from the coast of England; and if our voyage last long, we shall not have a month's victuals when we come in the country. Near £700 hath been bestowed at Hampton, upon what I know not, Mr. [Christopher] Martin saith he neither can, nor will give any account of it; and if he be called upon for accounts, he crieth out of unthankfulness for his pains and care, that we are suspicious of him, and flings away, and will end nothing. Also he so insulteth over our poor people, with such scorn and contempt as if they were not good enough to wipe his shoes. It would break your heart to see his dealing, and the mourning of our people; they complain to me, and alas I can do nothing for them; if I speak to him, he flies in my face, as mutinous and saith no complaints shall be heard, or received but by himself, and saith they are froward and waspish discontented people, and I do ill to hear them.

Friend if we ever make a plantation, God works a miracle; especially considering how scant we shall be of victuals, and most of all ununited amongst ourselves, and devoid of good tutors, and regiment . . . . If I should write to you of all things which promiscuously forerun our ruin, I should overcharge my weak head, and grieve your tender heart; only this I pray you prepare for evil tidings of us every day; but pray for us instantly, it may be the Lord will be yet entreated one way or other to make for us. I see not in reason how we shall escape even the gasping of hunger-starved persons, but God can do much, and His will be done. It is better for me to die, than now for me to bear it, which I do daily, and expect it hourly; having received the sentence of death, both within me and without me. Poor William Ring and myself do strive who shall be meat first for the fishes.

Remember me in all love to our friends, as if I named them, whose prayers I desire earnestly, and wish again to see, but not till I can with more comfort look them in the face; . . . That which I have written is true, and many things more which I have forborne; I write it as upon my life, and last confession in England; what is of use to be spoken of presently, you may speak of it, and what is fit to conceal, conceal. Pass by my weak manner, for my head is weak, and my body feeble; the Lord make me strong in Him, and keep both you and yours.

Your loving friend,

Robert Cushman
Dartmouth, Aug. 17, 1620.[1]

MAYFLOWER OF LONDON

Master Christopher Jones of Harwich, co. Essex, England, acquired the 180-ton *Mayflower* about 1608, apparently in a trade with Robert Bonner for Jones's 240-ton ship the *Josian*, named after his wife. While Christopher Jones became the *Mayflower*'s master, he was only a quarter owner of the ship: the other owners were Robert Childe, Christopher Nichols, and Thomas Short.[2] Christopher Nicholls, incidentally, was one of the signatories of the Second Virginia Charter of 23 May 1609. Somewhat later, John Moore would purchase an interest in the *Mayflower*, buying out either Christopher Nicholls's or Thomas Short's share.[3]

Christopher Jones's first voyage of record in the *Mayflower* would prove unforgettable. Andrew Pawling, a 46-year-old London merchant, hired the *Mayflower* to freight a cargo of hemp, hats, salt, vinegar, hops, and wine to Trondheim, Norway. Pawling and Jones signed a fairly standard shipping contract, known as a charter party, which stipulated that Jones would depart on 22 August 1609 with the cargo that Pawling would load, "being no more than the said ship could reasonably stow and carry over and besides her victual, tackle, and apparel, and over and above such goods as she could carry in the gunroom and forecastle.[4]" Jones was to sail to Trondheim, Norway, and remain there twenty-one days for the cargo to be unladed and for a return cargo to be purchased and loaded. He was then to return to the port of London, where he would remain for ten days to allow the return cargo to be unladed. The freight charge would come to £125, plus thirty shillings for each day the *Mayflower* had to remain in port over and above the stipulated time periods in the agreement.

What Christopher Jones did not know when he signed the charter-party was that merchant Andrew Pawling was on the verge of bankruptcy. Pawling owed Bevill Mouldsworth £120, half of it due on August 26, and half of it due October 26. Master Jones and the *Mayflower* departed for Norway just four days before his first debt payment came due. Pawling's plan was to find some way to delay the August 26 payment, and then use the profits from the return cargo to pay off his debts. Pawling managed to do just that: he negotiated a new loan with Mouldsworth, so that he now owed £200 instead of the original £120, but with the due date extended to November 25. With the *Mayflower* scheduled to return sometime in October, he would be able to make his debt payment from the sale of the goods she carried back.

But the November 25 payment date rolled around, and the *Mayflower* was nowhere to be seen. She was more than a month overdue. Pawling offered the cargo of the unarrived *Mayflower* to Mouldsworth as payment for his debts, but Mouldsworth would not accept payment of nonexistent goods: he had his doubts that the ship would ever return. When Pawling failed to make his debt payment on November 25, Mouldsworth had him arrested: Pawling was jailed at the Kings' Bench for failure to make a debt payment.

In the meantime, Moudsworth himself went bankrupt—he owed the state nearly £2000. Because his various debtors, including Pawling, were not paying their debts to him, he was unable to make good on his own debt payments. Unable to pay, Mouldsworth turned all his bonds over to the king for collection. Now it was England, in the name of the king, that was bound to collect Mouldsworth's debts.

Mouldsworth was not the only person to whom Pawling owed money. There was also Thomas Rudd, a salter. Unlike Mouldsworth, Thomas Rudd did not have Pawling jailed for his failure to pay up, but he did go to visit Pawling in prison to request his debt be paid. Pawling offered him the contents of his house as payment, but the twenty-seven-year-old Rudd, on his seventy-four-year-old father's advice, turned down the offer because they did not feel the contents of his house were worth £50. So, to satisfy Rudd, Pawling transferred the £50 debt to Richard Nottingham with a £100 bond, moving the due date of the bond out to March 6. Now, Pawling was indebted to Nottingham.

But where was the *Mayflower*? She had departed London on August 22 for Norway, and should have been back in October.

Andrew Pawling had sent Andrew Samson with the ship to act as his agent: the man responsible for unloading and selling the cargo and purchasing and reloading the ship for the return voyage. But instead of taking twenty-one days to sell off and reload the cargo as specified in the charter party, it actually took Samson more than two months to accomplish the task. When the *Mayflower* was finally able to depart Norway, well behind schedule, she was caught up in a severe North Sea storm, blown three hundred miles off course, and nearly lost at sea.

A relative of Christopher Jones, twenty-four-year-old mariner Thomas Thompson (probably a nephew), recalled what happened next:

> [The *Mayflower* was] by contrary and tempestuous weather, driven leeward at least one hundred leagues . . . and brought into such danger by the extremity of the foul weather, that the Master, [myself], and company thought they should all have perished, and therefore to lighten the ship for safeguard of their lives, the Master Christopher Jones did cast overboard into the sea a cable, hawser, and about a hundred deal boards . . . to lighten the ship and make way for their more safety in that extremity. [5]

John Cowbridge was the *Mayflower*'s boatswain for this fateful voyage, and he recalled:

> [B]y the way [we] met with such tempestuous and foul weather, that [I] was informed to lighten the ship and cast overboard a cable and a hawser, an iron pot, a pair of mustard querns of the ship's provision, and about fourscore or one hundred deals of the merchant's, to save ship and goods and men's lives. [6]

But John Cowbridge and Thomas Thompson also reported something else: They saw Andrew Samson, the man responsible for loading Pawling's goods, filling some of the herring and tar barrels only half full. When Christopher Jones and the crew questioned him about it, he responded, "What is that to you, if I should [decide to] lade stones?" So, not only did Pawling's agent take significantly longer than he was supposed to for the reloading of the ship, but he was also filling many of the barrels only half full.

Finally, on the night of December 6, the beaten, battered, and long-delayed *Mayflower* sailed into London and anchored off Ratcliff Mill. Certainly, Master Jones was not happy with all the delays: if he had gotten back on time, he would have been able to see his new baby daughter, Josian, born just a few days before her baptism on November 12.

While lying in custody, it would appear that Pawling had grown bitter towards Mouldsworth, and hatched a plan to prevent his getting any of the money—apparently not realizing that Mouldsworth's debt had been turned over to the king. Pawling was going to pay off all his other debts, even those that were not due yet: he would make sure that there was nothing left for Mouldsworth! When word of the *Mayflower*'s arrival reached Pawling on the night of December 6, he sprung into action. Accompanied by prison guard Thomas Horne and a young merchant friend, twenty-two-year-old Yorkshire-native Henry Somerscales, he went to the office of Thomas Grey, notary public of King's Bench in Southwark. There, he drew up a bill of sale, signing over all the goods on the *Mayflower* to Richard Nottingham for £150. The bill of sale was drawn up that night, and signed at 7:00 AM the next morning. Within an hour, Richard Nottingham had arrived at the *Mayflower*, paid the freight charge of £125, and taken physical custody of the goods.

Pawling turned around and used that £150 to pay off his debt to Thomas Rudd, along with several alleged debts to Richard Nottingham, leaving him with nothing left. Mouldsworth would later come to believe that Pawling and Nottingham were conspiring together to fabricate debts in an effort to prevent him from receiving any money.

By 11:00 AM, Mouldsworth got wind of the arrival of the *Mayflower*, and had a court officer, William Smith, sent to arrest the goods for payment of his debt.[7] Unfortunately for Mouldsworth, the goods no longer belonged to Pawling, they belonged to Richard Nottingham. The goods were taken into custody, nonetheless, on suspicion of a fraudulent transaction, and the case went to trial before the High Court of Admiralty. Nottingham argued that the goods were his because his bill of sale was signed prior to the court order to arrest the goods, and he had physically taken custody of the goods prior to the officer's arrival. The attorneys, in the name of the king, argued

that the bill of sale and some of the debts claimed by Pawling were
fraudulent, and were merely attempts designed to avoid paying his
bonds, now owed to the king.

For five weeks, the ownership of the goods was disputed in court.
Christopher Jones was not happy at all: with ownership of the goods
in question, the cargo was not unloaded, and he could not prepare his
ship for the next voyage. According to the charter party, Pawling had
agreed to pay thirty shillings per day for every day that he went over
and above their agreed-upon time frame. With the month delay in
Norway and the five weeks of delays in London, Christopher Jones
was owed a lot of money: Jones calculated the demurrage fees at £160—
more than the entire freight charge, and nearly the value of the entire
cargo that was shipped!

Back at the High Court, testimony and depositions were taken
from many people. Thomas Gray, the notary public, testified to the
time of the signing of the bill of sale[8]; Henry Somerscales testified on
his knowledge of Pawling's debts to Rudd and Nottingham, and as a
witness to the signing of the bill of sale.[9] Thomas Haddon and Peter
Fenton, guarantors on Pawling's loan from Mouldsworth, testified that
they thought the Nottingham debts were fraudulent.[10] Thomas Rudd
Sr. and Jr. both testified on their £50 debt to Pawling.[11] Nottingham
and Pawling both testified about their debts, and testified that at the
time of the bill of sale they had no idea that Mouldsworth had turned
his debts over to the king.[12]

The court asked John Whitehall to inventory and value the goods
on the *Mayflower*, which was done on January 3. He valued the total
cargo at £187 and 16 s as follows[13]:

> 3000 deal boards of Norway pine, £108
> 120 barrels of tar, "whereof twelve are empty," £63
> 42 barrels of herring, "rusty and very bad," £16 and 16 s.

Jacob Lister, an ironmonger, testified that he overheard appraiser
John Whitehall say that Nottingham asked him to undervalue the
inventory[14], but Whitehall testified this was not true, saying that the
low valuation was because many barrels were not full, and the herring
was "rotten and little worth." He stated he originally thought the herring
to be worth more, but later found none of the fish had been oiled.[15]

In the end, admiralty judge Richard Trevor concluded that Pawling's bill of sale to Richard Nottingham was legal, and the goods belonged to Nottingham.[16]

Christopher Jones then sued Pawling for the £160 demurrage fee he was owed[17], but the outcome of the lawsuit was not recorded, and it may have been settled out of court.

Master Christopher Jones appears to have learned two valuable lessons from this episode. He would never again reserve the entire ship to carry the cargo of just one merchant, and he would never again take the *Mayflower* into the North Sea.

Master Christopher Jones

Christopher Jones was born about 1570, the son of Christopher and Sybill Jones of Harwich, co. Essex, England. He was raised in a house "in the High Street of Harwich next the water with the quay." When he was eight, in 1578, his father Christopher died. His father, in his will, bequeathed "all that my part of the ship called the *Marie Fortune* . . . to my eldest son Christopher Jones at 18 years." Christopher's younger brother Roger received an "eighth part and stock of the new ship called the *Centurion*" when he turned eighteen. On 20 September 1579 in Harwich, Christopher's mother remarried to Robert Russell.

On 27 December 1593, Christopher Jones married a girl who lived across the street from him, Sarah Twitt, the daughter of Thomas Twitt, a relatively wealthy merchant in Harwich. Their first son, Thomas, was baptized on 1 December 1595, but was buried just a few months later on 17 April 1596. In 1597, Christopher's brother Robert died, apparently while on a sea voyage. Roger Jones left his brother Christopher his astrolabe, a navigational instrument. Father-in-law Thomas Twitt died in 1599, leaving to Christopher and Sarah Jones a twelfth share in the ship *Apollo*.

Christopher's wife Sarah did not live for much longer—she was buried in Harwich on 23 May 1603. Christopher remarried six months later to Josian, the young widow of Richard Gray, and the daughter of Thomas Thompson. Richard Gray and Thomas Thompson were both ship owners and merchants of Harwich.

By 1604, Christopher Jones's life and career were starting to come together. He had already amassed a decent-sized estate and stock in various ships which he obtained by inheritance from his father Christopher, his brother Roger, his first father-in-law Thomas Twitt, and from his second wife Josian (who had received much of the estate of her first husband Richard Gray). Christopher Jones was one of thirty-two citizens of Harwich named in the city's renewed charter of that year. And he and Josian had their first child together, whom they named Christopher, on 14 October 1604.

The next year, 1605, Christopher Jones had a ship of his own built, a brand-new 240-ton ship which he named the *Josian* after his wife. Like the first voyage in the *Mayflower*, Jones's first voyage in the *Josian* would also be one that he would remember for some time to come. He had taken the *Josian* to the port of Bordeaux, France, in 1607. There, he made an agreement with "a certain Batteleir," an agent for London merchant James Campbell, to transport to London a cargo of fifteen tons of Damascan prunes. However, after delivering the prunes in good condition, James Campbell failed to pay the twenty-five shillings and six pennies per-ton freight charge. After a couple of years of trying to get his money, Christopher Jones finally sued him in the High Court of Admiralty.[18]

The Admiralty Court issued an arrest warrant for James Campbell on 6 March 1610/11, and he was brought to court to answer the charges six days later.[19] Campbell made a £30 bail payment, and presented two sureties—Edmund Scott, a grocer, and Thomas Harrison, an ironmonger—to guarantee his appearance at the court session to be held in April 1611. Campbell didn't show up on his court date, however, and Jones's attorney asked that Campbell be found guilty and fined.[20] Campbell was apparently located, however, and on May 6, he and his attorney Richard Holman filed a petition with the High Court of Admiralty, claiming that Jones was using the Admiralty Court to harass him. He argued that the High Court did not have jurisdiction in the matter since the freight agreement was made in Bordeaux, France. The High Court of Admiralty only had jurisdiction over shipping contracts made within England, or on the high seas. He asked that Christopher Jones be ordered not to sue him in the High Court for this or any future plea. The High Court agreed: "And it is granted to him.[21]"

Around 1608, Christopher Jones appears to have traded away the *Josian* for the smaller and older *Mayflower*, which he would own jointly with three other men.

French Wine Trade

After the Pawling/Nottingham cargo was finally unloaded from his ship, Christopher Jones took the *Mayflower* to the Charente coast of France, and returned to London in April 1610 with 177½ tons of French wines and cognac, which were bought up by twelve different merchants, buying in quantities ranging from half a pipe to thirty tons.[22]

The Customs Books of the Exchequer, often referred to as the Port Books, provide some insight into the voyages of the *Mayflower*. From 1610 through 1620, she was used almost exclusively in the French wine trade. The typical voyage consisted of a stop at either Bordeaux or La Rochelle, France, traveling outbound from England with cargos containing English trade goods such as cloth, pewter, iron, stockings, rabbit and fox furs, and tobacco, and returning with various types of French wines, and occasionally some vinegar and Bay salt. In April 1613, the *Mayflower* unloaded about one hundred tons of French wines from Bordeaux.[23] And in May 1615, Christopher Jones returned from La Rochelle and unloaded 181¼ tons of French and cognac wines.[24]

In 1614, the *Mayflower* took a year-long hiatus from the wine trade and made two voyages to Hamburg, Germany, bringing English cloths, and returning with various European fabrics including taffeta, satins, sarcenets, and lawns.

One other voyage that was slightly out of the ordinary occurred in August 1615, when the *Mayflower* went not only to Rochelle, France, but also made a stop in Malaga, Spain, a port the ship had not previously visited. Someone else was in Malaga at the time as well—a Patuxet Indian named Tisquantum, who had been one of twenty-four captured near Cape Cod by Captain Thomas Hunt, who had brought them to Spain to be sold into slavery. Tisquantum was taken in by some Catholic friars who thwarted Captain Hunt's attempt at profit. The *Mayflower* and "Squanto" were but strangers passing in the Spanish night: five years later, they would meet again.

The years immediately preceding the *Mayflower*'s voyage to America were relatively uneventful, though in 1616 a young sailor named Edward Baillie accidentally fell overboard and drowned while the ship was anchored in London. John Cawkin, the officer sent to investigate the death, helped himself to the ship's cargo of wine a little too freely, got drunk, and tried to start a mutiny amongst the crew—for which

Christopher Jones sued him in Admiralty Court for £100. But for the most part, the ship simply made its routine voyages to Bordeaux and La Rochelle: a voyage they performed several times each year.

In January 1619/20, the *Mayflower* returned from France and unloaded a cargo of 160 tons of French wines.[25] The ship then returned to France a few months later, arriving back in London in May 1620, where she began unloading her cargo. On May 15, she unloaded fifty tons of French wine for William Speight, and nineteen tons of wine for John Crabbe. On May 19, John Crabbe took another hogshead.[26]

Right at this time, the Pilgrims' business agents in London, including Thomas Weston and Robert Cushman, were trying to locate a ship to carry the colonists to Northern Virginia. Robert Cushman, writing in a letter in June 1620 to John Carver, wrote: "Mr. Crabbe, of whom you write, he hath promised to go with us; yet I tell you I shall not be without fear till I see him shipped." Perhaps this "Mr. Crabbe" is the John Crabbe who purchased the nineteen tons and one hogshead of wine from the *Mayflower*, and perhaps that is the way that Cushman and Weston came to learn of the ship's availability. By June, Christopher Jones and the *Mayflower* had been hired for the task.

THE VOYAGE

"Wednesday the sixth of September, the wind coming east-northeast, a fine small gale, we loosed from Plymouth, having been kindly entertained and courteously used."

And so began the now-famous voyage of the *Mayflower* across the Atlantic, departing from Plymouth, England, on 6 September 1620. At the truly chelonian pace of somewhat under two miles per hour, the passengers and crew onboard would cover the twenty-seven hundred miles in just over two months.

"A Prosperous Wind," painting courtesy of Mike Haywood.

Robert Cushman and William Ring, who feared they were destined to be meat for the fishes, got their chance to quit the voyage about two weeks after Cushman's letter, when the *Mayflower* and *Speedwell* made yet another failed attempt to leave England. The *Speedwell* was just too leaky for the voyage, and there was no more time to waste trying to fix it. About two dozen frustrated passengers, including the Cushman and Ring families, used the opportunity to disembark. The others crammed onto the already crowded *Mayflower* for the voyage.

Sixty-six days was a long time to be sardined onto the gun deck of the *Mayflower* with 102 passengers (including three pregnant women). Luckily, about a quarter of the passengers were children, who wouldn't have required quite as much space. Unluckily, because of all the delays caused by the *Speedwell*, everyone had already been living shipboard for more than two months before they had even departed England; and more unlucky still, many of the passengers, particularly the women and children, would remain living aboard the ship for four or five more months after they had arrived in America.

Layout of the Ship

The gun deck, where most of the passengers rode out the voyage, had a living space of about fifty feet by twenty-five feet, with a ceiling probably about five feet high.[27] Following the gun deck back to the stern of the ship, there was a small step downward that led to the gun room, which was generally off limits to the passengers and their cargo. The gun room held the powder and ammunition for the ship's cannons, and any guns and other weapons belonging to the ship. It also could have housed a pair of stern chasers—cannons used to fire out the back of the ship at anyone that may be in pursuit. The *Mayflower* was a merchant vessel, and the master and crew needed to be prepared to defend themselves against pirates and privateers. The ship and crew also needed to be ready for military conscription should the king or queen of England ever need to use the ship in battle.

Beneath the gun deck was the cargo hold, where the passengers stored the majority of their provisions and supplies. There were barrels of wheat flour, oats, peas, barley, rice, sugar, beer, wine, cider, aqua vitae, biscuit, salt pork and bacon, dried fish, dried beef, pickled vegetables, butter, salad oil, cheese, and vinegar. There were chests full of clothing such as canvas and cloth suits, waistcoats, stockings, shoes, and boots; and cloth and canvas for making additional clothing and bedding. There were sets of armor, muskets, gunpowder and shot, swords, and bandoliers. Then, there were the work tools—shovels, axes, picks, hoes, handsaws, hammers, spades, hatchets, chisels, augers, grindstones, and nails. For cooking, there were iron pots, bronze kettles, gridirons, skillets, pewter platters, wooden trenchers (plates) and spoons, and spits upon which roasting meats could be rotated over a fire.[28]

To go above the gratings, to the main deck above, the passengers would have had to climb up a wooden or rope ladder. On the main deck, toward the front of the ship, was a small structure called the forecastle, where the ship's cook prepared the meals for the crew. The forecastle was likely also the place where the ordinary sailors slept in hammocks or bunks when not on duty.

At the back of the ship was the steerage room, where the *Mayflower* was controlled by a whipstaff—not a wheel, as in later sailing vessels. The steerage room would have housed the ship's compass, and is likely where the ship's officers slept.

Continuing on through the steerage room to the back of the ship was the Great Cabin, which belonged to the ship's master. The *Mayflower*'s master, Christopher Jones, would have been the only person onboard with a room all his own, though it measured little more than ten feet by seven feet.

Above the steerage room and master's cabin was the poop deck, upon which was the poop house. Despite its funny-sounding name, this room had nothing to do with a toilet—that duty was handled either by a chamber pot or a stroll up to the front of the ship, where the men at least could climb out onto the beakhead. The poop house may well have been available for the passenger's use, either as additional sleeping space or cargo space, though during normal merchant voyages it was most likely a chartroom, and perhaps a cabin for the master's mates.[29]

The *Mayflower*'s Crew

Master Jones and the *Mayflower* had never been across the Atlantic before. Their stormiest seas were those of the North Sea off Norway in 1609, and their longest voyage was just to Malaga, Spain, and back in 1615. To bring on some experienced hands, two men were hired, John Clarke and Robert Coppin, to be master's mates and pilots. Both had been to the New World before.

Robert Coppin had been an early investor in the Virginia Company, buying a share of stock for £12 and 10 s; he was named on the Second Virginia Charter of 23 May 1609. He quite possibly was from a Coppin family found in Harwich, the same hometown as Christopher Jones. He appears to have had some experience in whaling and may have spent time in Newfoundland; he had some knowledge of the New England coastline and had been to the region at least once previously. Otherwise, very little is known about him.

Much more is known about Master's Mate John Clark—his adventures in Virginia could fill an entire book. John Clark had been a ship's pilot since 1609, but his first experience with the New World came in March 1611, when he left London piloting a three-hundred-ton ship to Jamestown, Virginia. Along with the ship that he was piloting, there were two other ships: one 150 tons and one 90 tons, all under the command of Sir Thomas Dale. In all, the ships brought three hundred men to the Jamestown colony, then in its fourth year. The voyage lasted two and a half months, although they made brief stops in Dominica and on the "island of Nevis" to the north-northwest before reaching Jamestown.

Once in Virginia, John Clark piloted the ships into the mouth of the James River, to Point Comfort—the farthest point up the river that large ships could sail. For many weeks after arriving, he piloted barges back and forth between Point Comfort and the Jamestown fort, unloading the six hundred barrels of flour, fifty barrels of gunpowder, and other supplies that had been brought to the colony, and loading the ships back up with timber and sassafras for the return voyage to England.

After living and working in the Jamestown colony for about forty days, John Clark noticed a Spanish ship enter the mouth of the James River. The ship sent out a longboat with about thirteen men to the small English fort at Point Comfort. Three men got out of the longboat—one of which John Clark recognized as an English pilot he had seen in Malaga, Spain, in 1609. The three men informed the English that they were seeking a Spanish ship that had gotten lost on the coast. The English captain at Point Comfort sent for the governor, who came down from Jamestown on a barge to speak with the men. The governor informed them that their ship was not anchored in a safe place in the bay—they should bring it in closer to the fort. The Spanish replied that they did not have a capable pilot to do that. So the governor had the three Spanish men remain on shore and ordered John Clark and a couple others to take the longboat out to the Spanish ship and then pilot the ship into safer harbor.

When John Clark arrived at the Spanish ship with the longboat, he informed the ship's master, Don Diego de Molina, that he was to pilot the ship into a safer harbor near Point Comfort. But Don Diego was leery of a trap and refused, saying he would not sail in until the Spanish men onshore were returned to his ship. John Clark was taken captive, and tied up for good measure. The next day, still bound, he was carried over the shoulder by one of the Spanish mariners onto the longboat, and with the master of the Spanish ship, they went to speak with the English. Don Diego demanded the return of their three men in exchange for Clark. The English at Point Comfort said they would have to consult with the governor at Jamestown first, before they could make such a decision. But the governor was many hours away. Fearing the English would send out some of their ships to attack, the Spanish, with captive John Clark, fled back to their ship and sailed away. They ended up taking him as their prisoner to the Spanish settlement at Havana, Cuba.

John Clark remained in Spanish custody in Havana, where he was interrogated on his knowledge of the English settlements in Virginia, and English plans to colonize the region. After two years, he was transferred to Madrid, where he was again interrogated by Spanish authorities.[30] Finally, in 1616, after having been in Spanish custody for five years, he was freed in a prisoner exchange with England.

It was not long before John Clark was back in the piloting business. In 1618, he found himself working for Captain Thomas Jones, an English sometime pirate who happened, in this case, to be taking a load of cattle to Jamestown in his ship the *Falcon*. Shortly after his return, Clark was hired to be a pilot for the *Mayflower*'s voyage to America.

The *Mayflower* carried a crew of about thirty men, though the exact number is not known. In addition to master's mates Robert Coppin and John Clark, there was Giles Heale, the ship's surgeon.

The ship's surgeon was exempt from all regular crew duties—his only job was to tend to the sick and injured. Giles, who lived on Drury Lane in the parish of St. Giles in the Field, London, had just finished his apprenticeship with the Barber-Surgeons the previous year, and the *Mayflower*'s voyage to America may well have been his first "real" job. On 10 February 1620/1, he received a book entitled *Annotations Upon the Book of Psalms*, written by Henry Ainsworth, as a gift from *Mayflower* passenger Isaac Allerton (the book, with inscription, is now in the collections of the Library of Virginia in Richmond); and eleven days later, Giles was a witness to the nuncupative will of *Mayflower* passenger William Mullins. Giles Heale survived the first winter, and returned with the *Mayflower* to London in April 1621, where he continued as a surgeon, practicing on Drury Lane until his death in 1653.[31]

The ship's cooper, responsible for tending and maintaining the ship's barrels, was twenty-one-year-old Harwich native John Alden, who appears to have been a distant relative of Master Jones. It may seem odd to have a crewmember whose only duty was tending to the barrels, repairing and mending their leaks, but when the barrels hold your only source of food and drink while you are at sea, the critical nature of the job becomes apparent. The cooper had to be rather trustworthy too—many of the barrels contained beer, wine, cider, and aqua vitae. Because the *Mayflower*'s cooper decided to remain at Plymouth rather than return with the ship to London, he is also classified as one of the passengers.

The master gunner was the person in charge of the ship's cannons. He was also responsible for watching over and maintaining the ship's guns, ammunition, and powder. The name of the *Mayflower*'s master gunner is not known, but he went out on one of the explorations on 6 December 1620. One of the passengers remembered that the gunner was "sick unto death (but hope of trucking made him to go) and so remained all that day, and the next night"; the master gunner died later that winter.

The ship's carpenter was responsible for stopping leaks, caulking, splicing masts; basically, fixing anything that broke. He was also responsible for maintaining the supplies and tools necessary to carry out his carpentry activities, including a store of nails, cinches, hatchets, saws, and rudder irons. The name of the *Mayflower*'s carpenter is unknown, but his services were certainly needed during the voyage, as will be seen.

The boatswain was in charge of the ship's rigging, rope, tackle, and sails, as well as the ship's anchors; he (or his mate, if he had one) was also in charge of the ship's longboat. William Bradford, one of the passengers and later the governor, remembered that "the boatswain . . . was a proud young man, who would often curse and scoff at the passengers, but when he grew weak they had compassion on him and helped him." Despite the passenger's help, the unidentified boatswain died the first winter.

The four quartermasters were in charge of maintaining the cargo hold and setting and maintaining the shift and watch hours. The quartermasters were also responsible for fishing and maintaining the fishing lines, fish hooks, and harpoons. Though the names of the *Mayflower*'s quartermasters are unknown, it is known that three of the four died the first winter.

The ship's cook was responsible for preparing the crew's meals and for maintaining the food supplies and cook room, which was typically located in the forecastle of the ship. Like the master gunner, boatswain, and three quartermasters, the *Mayflower*'s cook also died the first winter.

The swabber, perhaps the lowliest position on the ship, was responsible for cleaning the decks. By tradition, each Monday a new crewmember was appointed the liar—the first person caught telling a lie the previous week. The crew would gather around the main mast and yell "a liar, a liar, a liar" to the poor soul, who for that week would be under the command of the swabber. Typically, the swabber would appoint the liar to clean the ship's beakhead, which doubled as the crew's toilet.

Voyage Events

Very little is actually known about what happened on the *Mayflower*'s two-month voyage; only one written account of the journey has survived, and that was just a few paragraphs written by William Bradford about ten years after the fact. Luckily, a few journals survive from some other early voyages to New England, from which we can learn a little more about life at sea and the day-to-day experiences of the voyage. Francis Higginson wrote a journal of his voyage on the three-hundred-ton *Talbot*, carrying nineteen cannons and thirty crewmembers, which sailed to New England in April 1629.[32] John Winthrop kept a similar journal of his voyage on the 350-ton *Arbella* in 1630.[33] That ship carried twenty-eight cannons and fifty-two seamen. And John Josselyn recorded in his journal his voyage to New England in April 1638 onboard the three-hundred-ton ship *Nicholas*, which had twenty cannons and forty-eight crewmembers.[34] While those ships were all about twice as big as the *Mayflower*, the experiences these men had at sea were undoubtedly very similar to the experiences had by the *Mayflower* passengers.

After leaving behind the English Channel, one of the first experiences the passengers encountered was rather unwelcome:

Higginson: "Wednesday [13 May 1629] . . . [we] left our dear native soil of England behind us; and sailing about ten leagues further, we passed the isles of Scilly, and launched the same day a great way into the main ocean. And now my wife and other passengers began to feel the tossing waves of the western sea, and so were very sea-sick."

Winthrop: "[11 April 1630] . . . The sickness of our minister and people put us all out of order this day, so as we could have no sermons . . . [April 12] In the afternoon less wind, and our people began to grow well again. Our children and others that were sick and lay groaning in the cabins we fetched out, and having stretched a rope from the steerage to the mainmast, we made them stand, some of one side and some of the other, and sway it up and down till they were warm, and by this means they soon grew well and merry."

Sailing on the *Mayflower*, the passengers would have seen a wide variety of sea animals. Francis Higginson, on his voyage, reported seeing "many porpoises playing in the sea, which they say is a sign of foul weather." He also saw "abundance of grampus fishes, two or three yards long, and a body as big as an ox." On June 3, he reported: "This day myself and others saw a large round fish sailing by the ship's side, about a yard in length and roundness every way. The mariners called it a sun-fish." It was a large jellyfish. The next day, he wrote: "This day I saw a fish very strange to me, they call it a carvel, which came by the ship's side, wafting along the top of the water. It appeared at the first like a bubble above the water, as big as a man's fist; but the fish itself is about the bigness of a man's thumb; so that the fish itself and the bubble resembleth a ship with sails." On June 9, he recorded: "This day we saw a fish called a turtle, a great and large shellfish, swimming above the water near the ship."

John Josselyn reported on 8 May 1638: "Two mighty whales we now saw, the one spouted water through two great holes in her head into the air a great height, and making a great noise with puffing and blowing . . . In the afternoon the mariners struck a porpoise . . . with a harping iron, and hoisted her aboard, they cut some of it into thin pieces, and fried, it tastes like rusty [rancid] bacon, or hung beef, if not worse; but the liver boiled and sauced sometime in vinegar is more grateful to the pallet." And on June 20, he reported: "We saw a great number of sea-bats, or owls, called also flying fish, they are about the bigness of a whiting, with four tinsel wings, with which they fly as long as they are wet, when pursued by other fishes . . . in the afternoon we saw a great fish called the vehuella or sword fish, having a long, strong and sharp fin like a sword-blade on the top of his head, with which he pierced our ship, and broke it off with striving to get loose, one of our sailors dived and brought it aboard."

Pirates and privateers were always a concern. English ships were routinely targeted by Spanish, French, and Turks. Francis Higginson reported that on 4 May 1629 his ship spotted "six or seven sail of Dunkirkers [Spanish pirates] wafting after us. But it seemed they saw our company was too strong for them, for then we had with us three or four ships that went for the Straits; so they returned back from pursuing us any longer." On Sunday, May 17, the church services were disturbed "by the approach of a Biscayner's ship [French pirates] . . . that made towards us, and manned out his boat to view us; but finding us too strong for him, he durst not venture to assault us, but made off." John Winthrop reported that in April 1630 on his voyage to America, they saw eight ships heading toward them, and thinking they were Dunkirkers, they tore down their cabins and prepared their cannons, armed everyone with muskets, and took the women below deck for additional safety. Winthrop noted of his fellow passengers: "It was much to see how cheerful and comfortable all the company appeared, not a woman or child that showed any fear, though all did apprehend the danger to have been great." The ships would turn out to be friendly.

Strong Atlantic storms, quite frightening to passengers inexperienced with sea travel, was another element common to all New England voyages. Higginson recorded in his journal on May 27:

> [A]bout noon there arose a south wind which increased more and more, so that it seemed to us, that are landmen, a sore and terrible storm; for the wind blew mightily, the rain fell vehemently, the sea roared, and the waves tossed us horribly; besides, it was fearful dark, and the mariners' mate was afraid, and noise on the other side, with their running here and there, loud crying one to another to pull at this and that rope. The waves poured themselves over the ship, that the two boats were filled with water, that they were fain to strike holes in the midst of them to let the water out. Yea, by the violence of the waves the longboat's cord, which held it, was broken, and it had like to have been washed overboard, had not the mariners, with much pain and danger, recovered the same.

John Winthrop reported that on his voyage, on May 22, 1630:

> [M]uch wind and rain. Our spritsail laid so deep in as it was split in pieces with a head sea at the instant as our captain was going forth of his cabin very early in the morning to give order to take it in . . . About 10 in the morning in a very great fret of wind it chopped suddenly into the west as it had done divers times before, and so continued with a small gale and stood north and by west. About 4 in the afternoon there arose a sudden storm of wind and rain, so violent as we had not a greater. It continued thick and boisterous till well in all the night . . . Still cold weather.

Even though Winthrop's voyage was in the middle of spring, he thought it "good to note that all this time, since we came from the [Isle of] Wight, we had cold weather, so as we could well endure our warmest clothes."

John Josselyn reported on 9 May 1638, that "about two of the clock in the afternoon, we found the head of our main mast close to the cap twisted and shivered, and we presently after found the fore-top-mast cracked a little above the cap."

Storms, cracking masts, and torn sails were not the only danger out at sea; accidentally falling was always a danger: and accidentally falling overboard could be fatal. On Francis Higginson's voyage, Thomas Goffe's "great dog" fell overboard and could not be recovered. Thomas Goffe was, incidentally, one of the investors in the Pilgrims' joint-stock company. On John Winthrop's voyage, "a maid of Sir R. Saltonstall fell down at the grating by the cook room, but the carpenter's man (who occasioned her fall unwittingly) caught hold of her with incredible nimbleness and saved her. Otherwise, she had fallen into the hold."

As if storms and accidents were not enough to worry about, there was another major concern of the passengers: disease. Francis Higginson's daughter died of smallpox on the voyage, as did several others. He reported on May 19: "This day, towards night, my daughter grew sicker, and many blue spots were seen upon her breast, which affrighted us. At the first we thought they had been the plague tokens; but we found afterwards that it was only a high measure of the infection of the pocks, which were struck again into the child; and so it was God's will the child died about five of the clock at night, being the first in our ship that was buried in the bowels of the great Atlantic sea; which was a grief to us her parents, and a terror to all the rest, as being the beginning of a contagious disease and mortality."

And there was a smallpox outbreak on John Josselyn's voyage as well, with several passengers dying. On May 12, Josselyn wrote: "The party that was sick of the smallpox now died, whom we buried in the sea, tying a bullet (as the manner is) to his neck, and another to his legs, turned him out at a port-hole, giving fire to a great gun." Others would die of smallpox and tuberculosis later on during the voyage.

Almost every voyage seemed to have a "profane seaman" who got his just desserts in the form of an untimely death by a grievous disease. Francis Higginson relates on 18 June 1629: "This day a notorious wicked fellow, that was given to swearing and boasting of his former wickedness, bragged that he had got a wench with child before he came this voyage, and mocked at our days of fast, railing and jesting against Puritans; this fellow fell sick of the pocks, and died." John Winthrop reported a similar story on 27 May 1630: "In the *Jewel* also one of the seamen died, a most profane fellow, and one who was very injurious to the passengers."

Unlike a typical merchant or fishing voyage, crossing the Atlantic for several months with a group of passengers had another unique circumstance: the presence of women and girls. While men were often more free to move about the ship, women were often confined—for their better safety—to the parts of the ship that were below deck, especially during storms or when any unknown ships were spotted. Because of this, sea sickness tended to affect women much more than the men. And because the voyages could easily last several months, women would occasionally end up giving birth while at sea. On John Winthrop's voyage, one of the women in the *Arbella* went into labor. He recorded: "A woman in our ship fell in travail, and we sent and had a midwife out of the *Jewel*. She [the *Jewel*] was so far ahead of us at this time . . . as we shot off a piece and lowed our topsails, and then she brailed her sails and stayed for us." But traveling pregnant was hard on women's bodies, and miscarriages were not uncommon. Winthrop noted later in his journal on June 7: "A woman was delivered of a child in our ship, stillborn."

With passenger ships carrying a hundred or more passengers and thirty or more crewmembers, disciplinary actions were often necessary. Typically, the ship's master was responsible for the discipline of the crew, and an appointed or elected governor was responsible for the disciplining of the passengers. Punishments were often severe. Winthrop reported on April 1-2: "In the time of our fast, two of our landmen prized a rundlet of strong water and stole some of it, for which we laid them in bolts [leg irons] all the night, and the next morning the principal was openly whipped, and kept with bread and water that day." On another occasion, "Complaint was made to our captain of some injury that one of the under-officers of the ship had done to one of our landmen. He called him and examined the cause, and commanded him to be tied up by the hands and a weight to be hanged about his neck, but an intercession of the governor (with some difficulty) he remitted his punishment." On another occasion, "We set 2 fighters in the bolts till night, with their hands bound behind them. A maidservant in the ship, being stomach sick, drunk so much strong water that she was senseless and had near killed herself. We observed it a common fault in our young people that they gave themselves to drink hot waters very immoderately."

John Josselyn reported that on his voyage "a passenger was ducked at the main yards arm (for being drunk with his master's strong waters which he stole) thrice," and a few days later recorded "Martin Ivy, a stripling, servant to Captain Thomas Cammock, was whipped naked at the capstan, with a cat and nine tails, for filching 9 great lemons out of the surgeon's cabin, which he ate rinds and all in less than an hour's time."

But do all these accounts of other early voyages to New England adequately depict what may have occurred on the *Mayflower*'s voyage in 1620? While, of course, the exact details will be somewhat different, the general events would have been very similar. And indeed, by reading the only firsthand account of the *Mayflower*'s voyage, one quickly begins to see the commonalities. So, without further ado, here is the full text of the only firsthand account of the *Mayflower*'s voyage, written by passenger William Bradford, who would later become the colony's governor:

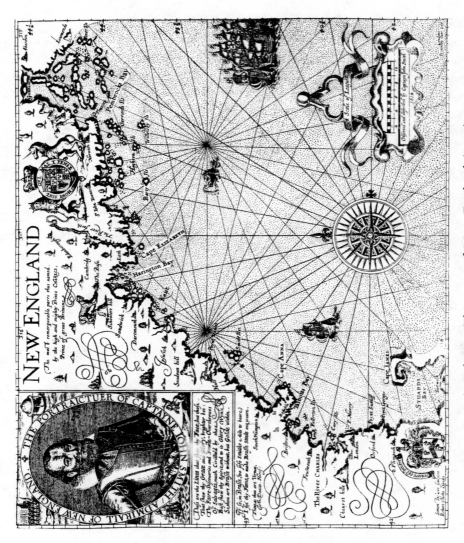

Captain John Smith's map of New England (1614).
The Pilgrims had access to this map and likely used it while exploring.

September 6 [1620]. These troubles being blown over, and now all being compact together in one ship, they put to sea again with a prosperous wind, which continued divers days together, which was some encouragement unto them; yet according to the usual manner many were afflicted with seasickness. And I may not omit here a special work of God's Providence: there was a proud and very profane young man, one of the seamen, of a lusty, able body, which made him the more haughty; he would always be condemning the poor people in their sickness, and cursing them daily with grievous execrations; and did not let to tell them, that he hoped to help to cast half of them overboard before they came to their journey's end, and to make merry with what they had; and if he were by any gently reproved, he would curse and swear most bitterly. But it pleased God before they came half seas over, to smite this young man with a grievous disease, of which he died in a desperate manner; and so was himself the first that was thrown overboard; thus his curses light on his own head; and it was an astonishment to all his fellows, for they noted it to be the just hand of God upon him.

After they had enjoyed fair winds, and weather for a season, they were encountered many times with cross winds, and met with many fierce storms, with which the ship was shroudly shaken, and her upper works made very leaky; and one of the main beams in the midships was bowed and cracked, which put them in some fear, that the ship could not be able to perform the voyage. So some of the chief of the company (perceiving the mariners to fear the sufficiency of the ship, as appeared by their mutterings) they entered into serious consultation with the master, and other officers of the ship, to consider in time of the danger; and rather to return, than to cast themselves into a desperate, and inevitable peril. And truly there was great distraction, and difference of opinion amongst the mariners themselves; fain would they do what could be done for their wages' sake (being now half the seas over) and on the other hand they were loath to hazard their lives too desperately. But in examining of all opinions, the master and others affirmed they knew the ship to be strong, and firm under water, and for the buckling of the main beam, there was a great iron screw the passengers brought out of Holland, which would raise the beam into his place; the which being done, the carpenter, and master affirmed that with a post put under it, set firm in the lower deck, and other ways bound he would make it sufficient. And for the decks and upper works they would caulk them as well as they could, and though with the working of the ship they would not long keep staunch, yet there would otherwise be no great danger, if they did not overpress her with sails; so they committed themselves to the will of God, and resolved to proceed.

In sundry of these storms the winds were so fierce, and the seas so high, as they could not bear a knot of sail, but were forced to hull, for divers days together; and in one of them as they thus lay at hull in a mighty storm, a lusty young man (called John Howland) coming upon some occasion above the gratings, was with a seele of the ship, thrown into sea; but it pleased God, that he caught hold of the topsail halyards, which hung overboard, and ran out at length, yet he held his hold (though he was sundry fathoms under water) till he was hauled up by the same rope to the brim of the water; and then with a boat hook, and other means got into the ship again and his life saved; and though he was something ill of it, yet he lived many years after, and became a profitable member, both in church and commonwealth.

In all this voyage there died but one of the passengers, which was William Butten, a youth, servant to Samuel Fuller, when they drew near the coast. But to omit other things (that I may be brief) after long beating at sea, they fell with that land which is called Cape Cod; the which being made, and certainly known to be it, they were not a little joyful.

William Bradford also noted at the end of his *History* that Elizabeth Hopkins had given birth on the voyage to a young boy they named Oceanus. A few days after arriving, Susanna White gave birth to a son they would name Peregrine, meaning "traveler to foreign lands." Later in February, still living aboard the *Mayflower* as the houses remained under construction, Mary Allerton gave birth to a stillborn son.

At anchor in Cape Cod Harbor shortly after arrival, one passenger remembered "And every day we saw whales playing hard by us." And later in early December, about a month after arrival, and while the Pilgrims were still out exploring for a place to settle, Dorothy Bradford accidentally fell overboard and drowned.

Seasickness, a profane seaman dying a terrible death, frightful storms, splitting masts, accidentally falling overboard, women giving birth, disease and the occasional death of a passenger, whales and other sea creatures—the *Mayflower*'s voyage seems to have been fairly typical.

JOHN ALDEN

John Alden was a member of the *Mayflower*'s crew, but since he stayed at Plymouth rather than returning with the ship, he can also be considered a passenger. He was hired in Southampton, England, to be the ship's cooper, responsible for tending and repairing the ship's barrels—an important job given that the barrels were holding everyone's food and drink.

The English origins of John Alden have been a matter of much speculation and research.[35] The currently prevailing theory is that he was from an Alden family located in Harwich, Essex, England. Members of this Alden family of Harwich have connections, if somewhat distant, to the *Mayflower*'s master Christopher Jones. Based on a deposition in which he gave his age[36], and a broadside published at his death that also gave his age[37], we know that John Alden was born about 1598.

Wherever John Alden may have originated from, he somehow found himself in July 1620, at the age of about twenty-two, working as a cooper onboard the *Mayflower*, preparing for a voyage to America with a group of religious separatists. William Bradford recorded that "John Alden was hired for a cooper, at Southampton where the ship victualed; and being a hopeful young man was much desired, but left to his own liking to go, or stay when he came here; but he stayed, and married here." Alden was one of the forty-two men who signed the "Mayflower Compact" on 11 November 1620, his signature falling directly after that of Myles Standish. After arrival, John Alden's carpentry skills were no doubt put to good use building the first structures and houses in Plymouth.

Around 1622 or 1623, John Alden married fellow *Mayflower* passenger Priscilla Mullins, who had been orphaned in Plymouth after the first winter when her parents William and Alice, and her brother Joseph all died. Their exact marriage date is not known, but it was either the second or third marriage to occur at Plymouth—the first being that of Edward Winslow to the widowed Susanna White on 12 May 1621, and the fourth being that of William Bradford to Alice Carpenter on 14 August 1623.

A story of the romance of John Alden and Priscilla Mullins, and another suitor, Myles Standish, was made famous by the Henry Wadsworth Longfellow poem, "The Courtship of Myles Standish," published in 1858. Wadsworth's poem was based on an earlier anonymous poem by the same title published in 1843, which in turn was based on a family tradition first published in Rev. Timothy Alden's *American Epitaphs* (1814).[38] Longfellow, incidentally, was a direct descendant of John and Priscilla—but it should be remembered that he was born nearly two hundred years after the *Mayflower*'s arrival and he had little or no knowledge about actual events. In the poem, the young John Alden has a secret interest in the young and beautiful Priscilla; and his world is turned around when his best friend, Myles Standish, says he wants to marry Priscilla and asks John for help—by actually going to Priscilla and asking for her hand in marriage on Standish's behalf. John pushes back his own desire for Priscilla, in order to fulfill the request of his best friend. He tries to convince Priscilla of Standish's many virtues:

> Heir unto vast estates, of which he was basely defrauded,
> Still bore the family arms, and had for his crest a cock argent
> Combed and wattled gules, and all the rest of the blazon.
> He was a man of honor, of noble and generous nature;
> Though he was rough, he was kindly; she knew how during the winter
> He had attended the sick, with a hand as gentle as a woman's;
> Somewhat hasty and hot, he could not deny it, and headstrong,
> Stern as a soldier might be, but hearty, and placable always,
> Not to be laughed at or scorned, because he was little of stature;
> For he was great of heart, magnanimous, courtly, courageous;
> Any woman in Plymouth, nay, any woman in England,
> Might be happy and proud to be called the wife of Myles Standish!

> But as he warmed and glowed, in his simple and eloquent language,
> Quite forgetful of self, and full of the praise of his rival,
> Archly the maiden smiled, and, with eyes overrunning with laughter,
> Said, in a tremulous voice, "Why don't you speak for yourself, John?"

Into the open air John Alden, perplexed and bewildered,
Rushed like a man insane, and wandered alone by the sea-side;
Paced up and down the sands, and bared his head to the east-wind.

Alden went to Priscilla to propose on behalf of his best friend, but in the end succeeded only in getting permission for himself. Standish ended up being so furious that he stormed off to fight Indian wars. When John and Priscilla were finally married, Standish made a surprise appearance at the wedding:

Why does the bridegroom start and stare at the strange apparition?
Why does the bride turn pale, and hide her face on his shoulder?
Is it a phantom of air,—a bodiless, spectral illusion?
Is it a ghost from the grave, that has come to forbid the betrothal?
Long had it stood there unseen, a guest uninvited, unwelcomed;

* * *

Boldly there in his armor Myles Standish, the Captain of Plymouth!
Grasping the bridegroom's hand, he said with emotion, "Forgive me!
I have been cruel and hard, but now, thank God! It is ended."

But back to the real story of John Alden. In 1623, the Plymouth colonists divided up their land, each family receiving an acre of land per family member who came over. Unfortunately, the document is damaged right in the spot where it states the number of acres assigned to John Alden. His plot was described as lying "on the north side of the town next adjoining to their gardens which came in the *Fortune*." Adjoining his property on the one side was apparently John Crackston, whose father had died the first winter at Plymouth; he was probably nearing adulthood himself. On the other side was the orphaned thirteen-year-old Mary Chilton, whose parents both died the first winter. On the other side of Mary was Myles Standish. [39]

By May 1627, John and Priscilla had just begun to raise their family. They already had two children, Elizabeth and John, and a third child, Joseph, was only a few months away. That month, the Plymouth Colony had decided to divide up the responsibility (and profits) of the cattle, which had, to that point, been owned collectively. John, Priscilla, and their two children Elizabeth and John were grouped together with the Howland family, which also included few singletons, including William Wright, Clement Briggs, Edward Doty, and Edward Holman. All the family groups, including the Howland/Alden group, drew lots to see which of the cattle they would be required to care for. To the Howland/Alden group fell a heifer named Raghorn, who had arrived on the ship *Jacob* in 1624. Oddly, their lot was the only one that did not include two goats. Either Raghorn was one great heifer, or they drew one of the shorter straws.[40]

John and Priscilla appear to have started out their family in pretty good financial condition. When Priscilla's father, mother, and brother all died the first winter, she came into the possession of nearly all her family's American land entitlements, a large amount of money, £40 worth of shoes and boots, a number of shares in Plymouth Colony's joint-stock company, and all of the family's household goods.[41]

In 1626, the joint-stock company that was supporting Plymouth was deep in debt, and in turn, so were all the planters in Plymouth who owned shares and were employed by the company. It was decided the best way to handle the situation was for a few men at Plymouth to purchase the entire company from everyone else. They would then become the owners of the company, along with several trading boats, trading houses, and land patents, along with all the company's tools and equipment. They would run the company, hoping to pay off all its debts, and perhaps even make a profit for themselves. Eight men from Plymouth were the primary purchasers of the company: Governor William Bradford, Captain Myles Standish, Isaac Allerton, Edward Winslow, Elder William Brewster, John Howland, Thomas Prence, and John Alden.[42]

Despite his apparently "simple" roots as a seaman and cooper, John Alden rose quickly through the ranks of Plymouth Colony, becoming one of the most prominent and influential men in the colony. It would seem to have been due to a combination of his wife's inheritance and family's social status, along with his own industriousness and honesty. He must have been very well respected by his fellow planters. The court records of Plymouth Colony do not begin until January 1632/3, but in that year John Alden was one of seven men elected by the freemen of Plymouth to the governor's council.[43] Alden had been involved in the Plymouth government even before the official records commence, however; for example, Governor John Winthrop of the Massachusetts Bay Colony happens to mention that Alden was a court assistant at Plymouth in February 1631/2.[44]

The governor and his council attended the four court sessions held each year, and attended to such business as hearing and judging civil lawsuits, confirming land deeds and other property transactions, recognizing marriages, enacting new laws, and assessing fines and penalties for law breaking.

At the first court in January 1632/3, for example, Alden and his fellow council members heard the lawsuit of William Bennett against Edward Doty, in which Bennett felt he was defrauded in a trade when the bacon he purchased turned out to be worth only half the claimed value. In addition, Bennett had sold a parcel of boards to Doty and had not received payment. Bennett won both cases. The court sentenced a servant, Thomas Brian, to be privately whipped for running away from his master for five days. Servant Robert Barker complained that his master John Thorp was not providing him suitable clothing, which the court judged to be true; they ordered he either be properly appareled or transferred to another person who could better support him. Dr. Samuel Fuller and one of his patients, Peter Browne, had a dispute about their accounts, and the court assigned two arbitrators to adjudicate. Francis Eaton sold property to Kenelm and Josias Winslow, which was confirmed by the court. Stephen Deane requested permission to set up a water work upon the brook adjoining Plymouth, to grind corn, and the court agreed and created a set of terms by which he would be allowed to operate it. In addition, the court assessed everyone a tax. The tax was to be paid in corn before the last day of November, at the rate of five shillings per bushel—failure to do so would result in a court officer confiscating twice that value. Alden, who was himself one of the twelve appointed tax assessors, was taxed £1, 4ss—placing him in the top-15 of the highest taxed men in Plymouth.[45]

By the April court, the dispute between William Bennett and Edward Doty had continued, and Bennett now sued Doty for slander. The case was heard by a jury, and Doty was fined fifty shillings, thirty shillings of which went to William Bennett. John Holmes was fined twenty shillings and ordered to sit in the stocks for drunkenness. John

Hewes and his wife Jane, along with John Thorp and his wife Alice, were sentenced to sit in the stocks because the couples had conceived children before they had been married.[46]

Alden was reelected to the Plymouth Court each year through 1639. Court sessions were held from four to seven times a year. Court officials did not run for office, and were not compensated—it was considered mandatory public service. In fact, failing to fulfill the duties to which you were elected was cause for an enormous £10 fine[47]— that's almost five times as much as the fine for conceiving a child out of wedlock!

Whether Alden enjoyed or wanted to be a public servant year after year cannot be known; certainly, he had other things he could be doing, which would have been a greater benefit to himself and his growing family. He and his wife Priscilla added five more children during the 1630s, namely Priscilla, Jonathan, Sarah, Ruth, and Mary: bringing the total number of children in their family to eight.

Based on recent dendrochronological evidence, also known as tree-ring dating, it appears that in 1629, John Alden first begin building a small 38 feet x 10½ feet house in what would become the town of Duxbury, just north of Plymouth.[48] The house included a 6½-foot-square root cellar that was about 7½ feet deep. The house site and cellar were excavated in 1960 by a small team of archaeologists led by Roland Wells Robbins, and the results of the excavations were published in 1969. The archaeologists uncovered the foundation and a number of artifacts, including hand-wrought nails, glass and pottery shards, knives and spoons, scissors, clothing buttons and buckles, gun fragments, fishing hooks, and clay pipe fragments.[49]

In April 1632, John Alden, along with Myles Standish, Jonathan Brewster, and Thomas Prence, agreed with the Plymouth Court to reside inside of Plymouth during the winters, "that they the better repair to the worship of God." But the formation of auxiliary towns within the Plymouth Colony was inevitable. By October 1633, the town of Plymouth reclaimed the now-vacant lots of those, including Alden and Standish, who had moved north; and about a year later, the "ward" of Duxbury had formed its own church, led by Pastor Ralph Partridge. The Plymouth Colony would not formally recognize Duxbury as a separate town until 1637.

As one of the purchasers of the joint-stock company, Alden also continued to work for the company, and was involved in establishing the fur trade with the Indians on the Kennebec River. It was there, in 1634, that a trading rights dispute with neighboring Englishmen erupted into a deadly conflict. The Plymouth men, led by John Alden and John Howland, had established a trading post on the Kennebec River to trade with the Indians up the river. Then, along came John Hocking with two other men and a boy from a small trading settlement established to the north in Piscataqua. The joint-stock company, now owned by Alden and the other purchasers at Plymouth, had a legal patent that provided them exclusive rights to trade on the Kennebec River, so when Hocking moved his boat up the river to intercept the trade before it could reach them, they had to act. The company was already heavily in debt, due to some questionable deals arranged by Isaac Allerton: they could not suffer the potential loss of the Kennebec trade.

John Howland went up to Hockings and his men, and asked them to leave. They refused. Howland stated he would not allow them to remain. Hocking remained defiant with "foul speeches." Howland then ordered three of his men, John Irish, Thomas Savory, and William Reynolds, to cut the anchor lines that were holding Hocking's barge in place—the strength of the river's current would then wash Hocking and his men out of their position. Howland's men were only able to cut one of the cables; however, the river's current prevented them from getting into a good position to cut the others. So, they sent Moses Talbot in a canoe to finish the job. As Talbot was cutting the cables, Hocking stormed across the deck of his barge with guns in hand, and shot Moses in the head at point-blank range, killing him instantly. Then, "one of his fellows which loved him well could not hold, but with a musket shot Hocking, who fell down dead and never spake a word." Alden was present with Howland during the whole episode, as they were the two men in charge of the trade on the Kennebec.[50]

Soon after the incident, John Alden took a small shallop to bring some trade goods to the Massachusetts Bay Colony: but the Bay Colony led by Governor Winthrop had received accounts of what had happened from the Piscataqua Colony, and had become enraged at the events that had transpired. So, they arrested John Alden and put him in prison, pending Plymouth Colony's answer to the state of affairs. Plymouth Colony was quite angered by the jailing of John Alden—not only did the Massachusetts Bay not have any jurisdiction over the events that transpired, but John Alden was more of an onlooker than participant in the events that transpired. Plymouth's governor at the time, Thomas Prence, wrote letters to the Bay Colony leaders, insisting they had no right to jail Alden, nor any right to adjudicate the matter in their courts. Prence also sent Captain Myles Standish to the Bay Colony to negotiate and procure Alden's release from prison.

While Standish managed to procure Alden's release from prison, the matter was not dropped immediately. Eventually, after many frustrating disagreements between the two colonies, they agreed to have the dispute arbitrated at a hearing—but when the representatives for the allegedly-aggrieved Piscataqua Colony decided not to show up, the matter was all but decided in Plymouth's favor.

In the late 1630s, John Alden started to amass various properties north of Plymouth. In 1636, he was granted "a parcel of land containing a knoll, or a little hill, lying over against Mr. Alden's lands at Bluefish River." In 1637, he was granted "certain lands at Green's Harbor." And in 1638, he and Myles Standish were granted three hundred acres of upland "lying on the north side of the South River, the breadth whereof to begin at the easterly side of the Beaver Pond, (the said pond being included) unto the westerly side of the little brook next Scituate Path over the South River, and to range in length upon a norwest line on both sides, up into the land, and all that tract of meadow lying within or at the end of the forementioned breadth.[51"]

As John Alden entered his forties, life was pulling him farther away from Plymouth, to the new town of Duxbury, where fellow settlers Myles Standish, Thomas Prence, Jonathan Brewster, and others had now moved. The Duxbury church was founded about 1635, and the town was formally recognized in 1637. In 1641, Alden was elected as a council member and representative for Duxbury to the Plymouth Court, and he would continue to represent Duxbury throughout the 1640s.[52]

In 1642, the Plymouth Colony, which now included a number of townships including Duxbury, Scituate, Sandwich, Taunton,

Barnstable, Yarmouth, and Marshfield, was threatened by a neighboring Indian group, the Narragansett, who were thought to be in a conspiracy to drive out or kill all the English settlers. John Alden served as one of eight representatives for Duxbury on the Council of War that was held by the Plymouth Court in September 1642. The council would meet several times more, in October 1643 and June 1646, to discuss the situation, share intelligence, and decide on the defensive and offensive measures to be taken. One of the things the committee decided to do was to take a census of all men aged sixteen to sixty, in all the townships, who were capable of carrying a gun for defense: John Alden and his two eldest sons John (about seventeen years old) and Joseph (about sixteen years old), were enumerated under the town of Duxbury.[53] The Narragansett threat would ultimately subside after several very tense years. John Alden also spent time on other court-related appointments. In 1645, he was on a committee that was appointed to revise some laws "for redress of some present abuses, and for preventing of future[54] "; that same year, he was also appointed to a committee that was to decide how to handle the Kennebec trade, along with fellow Kennebec trader John Howland and three others. The next year, Alden and Howland were appointed to provide the treasurer an audit of the Kennebec trade for the previous year. Alden would serve again on the committee for Kennebec trade in 1649, and again in 1655.[55]

Time spent performing public service was not the only thing increasing for John Alden in the 1640s: so was his family. His ninth child Rebecca was born about 1640, and son David came a couple years later, finishing out his family of ten children—six daughters and four sons. It must have been quite crowded in their small 38-x-10½-foot house! Alden family tradition suggests the family built a bigger house about 1653, a short distance away, reusing many of the timbers from their old house constructed in 1629. This later Alden house, with substantial eighteenth through twentieth century additions and renovations, is still standing today in Duxbury, and is operated by the Alden Kindred of America.

Beginning in 1650, John Alden was again regularly elected as an assistant to the Plymouth Court—he would be reelected to the position every year thereafter, until his death thirty-six years later. In addition to being a court assistant, he also again participated on several councils of war, on another committee to revise laws, and on another committee to authorize Kennebec trade. And if that were not enough, he was also elected to be the Plymouth Colony treasurer from 1656-1658.[56]

All the unpaid time spent in government service at Plymouth, combined with the cost of caring for his large family of ten children and the poor return of all his early investments in the Plymouth joint-stock company, began to take a heavy financial toll on John Alden and his family. His eldest daughter Elizabeth was married in 1644, and his other children would soon be following suit. His sons, especially, would need some land from their father to get themselves and their future families started, but Alden did not have too much in the way of land to give out. Recognizing his financial situation, the Plymouth Court in 1657 allowed John Alden to "look out a portion of land to accommodate his sons withal, and to make report thereof unto the court, that so it may be confirmed unto him.[57]" And again in 1660, "in regard that Mr. John Alden is low in his estate, and occasioned to spend much time at the courts on the country's occasions, and so hath done this many years, the court have allowed him a small gratuity, the sum of ten pounds, to be paid by the treasurer.[58]" The court would grant him additional lands in 1665 at Nemasket; and again in 1673, he was granted one hundred acres at Teticutt.[59]

At the Plymouth court session held in March 1665, John Alden served as deputy governor of Plymouth Colony due to the temporary absence of Governor Thomas Prence. As deputy governor, he attended a number of issues at his court. He oversaw several probates, including that of an Irishman named Cornelius More, as well as Thomas Lambert, Ann Vinall, and Gowin White. Elisha Hedges was forced to forfeit sixteen gallons of liquor after failing to give notice of what liquors he had brought into the town of Yarmouth. George Allen and Richard Chadwell had a dispute about a highway; the court ordered the dispute be arbitrated. The court authorized several men to purchase some land in Barnstable that the Indians there were willing to sell. The court ordered "Harry the Indian" to pay £4 damages to Gabriel Fallowell for catching his cow in one of his deer traps, which injured the cow enough that it had to be killed. Alden was apparently tentative about handing down sentences of corporal punishment: Thomas Cushman was fined £5 for "committing carnal copulation with his now wife before marriage but after contract," but the court ordered "for the latter part of the law, referring to imprisonment, is referred to further consideration." Thomas Totman was fined £10 for the same offense, but the fine was double because he could not prove the copulation occurred after he had become engaged. Again, no physical punishment was inflicted, as was normally customary in such cases. William Randall was fined three shillings for "poking or striking Jeremiah Hatch with a hoe pole." Thomas Summers was fined five shillings for being drunk.[60] And Alden heard from a couple of Rehoboth coroner juries, one on the death of Rebecca Sale (apparent suicide), and the other for Elizabeth Walker (a two-and-a-half-year-old girl who was "sent to school" and was later found "accidentally drowned" in the river). All in all, a pretty typical court session.

Alden would fill in as deputy governor one other time in his life, at the October 1677 session of the Plymouth Court, standing in for the temporarily absent governor, Josiah Winslow. The October 1677 court was quite a bit more serious—it would decide whether or not to sentence Ambrose Fish to death for "wickedly and contrary to the order of nature, on the twelfth day of July last past before the date hereof, in his own house in Sandwich, in this colony of New Plymouth, by force carnally know and ravish Lydia Fish, the daughter of Nathaniel Fish, of Sandwich aforesaid, against her will." Although eligible for the death penalty, the jury hearing the trial instead sentenced him to "suffer corporal punishment by being publicly whipped at the post." John Alden's youngest son David was on the jury.[61]

Now in his seventies, John Alden began the process of deeding his land holdings off to his four sons John, Joseph, Jonathan, and David. In 1674, he gave his lands at Rooty Brook in Middleboro to youngest son David.[62] In 1679, he deeded his lands in Bridgewater to son Joseph.[63] And in 1685, he deeded his upland in Duxbury to son Jonathan.[64]

By 1687, John Alden had become quite old for his time—about eighty-eight years old. That year, he deeded one hundred acres of land at Peckard's Neck to his eldest son John[65], and five additional acres of salt marsh to sons Jonathan and David.[66]

John Alden died at Duxbury on 12 September 1687, having nearly reached the age of ninety. His death occasioned Rev. John Cotton to pen the following words[67]:

Upon the Death of that Aged, Pious, Sincere-hearted Christian,
John Alden, Esq.
Late Magistrate of New Plymouth Colony, who died
Sept. 12th 1687.
Being about eighty nine years of age.

He came one of the first into this land,
And here was kept by God's most gracious hand.
Years sixty seven, which time he did behold
To poor New England mercies manifold:
All God's great works to this His Israel
From first implanting what to them befell:
Of them he made a serious observation,
And could of them present a large narration,
His walk was holy, humble, and sincere,
His heart was filled with Jehovah's fear.
He honored God with much integrity,
God therefore did him truly magnify.
The hearts of Saints entirely did him love,
His uprightness so highly did approve,
That whilst to choose they had their liberty
Within the limits of this Colony
Their civil leaders, him they ever chose.
His faithfulness made hearts with him to close.
With all the Governors he did assist;
His name recorded is within the list
Of Plymouth's Pillars to his dying day.

*   *   *

On dying bed his ails were very great,
Yet verily his heart on God was set.
He bare his griefs with faith and patience,
And did maintain his lively confidence:
Saying to some, The work which God begun,
He would preserve to its perfection.
His mouth was full of blessings till his death
To ministers and Christians all: his breath

Was very sweet by many a precious word
He uttered from the Spirit of his Lord.
He lived in Christ, in Jesus now he sleeps:
And his blest soul the Lord in safety keeps.

John Alden had already distributed his land to all his sons, so he did not bother to make out a will. His estate was administered by son Jonathan Alden. His most valuable assets were £13 worth of livestock, including cattle, sheep, swine, and one horse; £5 worth of bedding; and £18 worth of goods that included a horse bridle and saddle, books, cash, and wearing clothes. The estate also included two chairs, beds, chests, andirons, pot hooks, tongs, brassware, cooper and carpentry tools, gridiron and dripping pans, pewter ware, two old guns, table linens, a spit, an axe, a case of trenchers (dinner plates), a winch, a bit of linen cloth, a marking iron, and some old lumber.[68]

Having had ten children, John and Priscilla Alden have numerous descendants. Among the more recognizable are presidents John Adams and John Quincy Adams, who were descendants of John's daughter Ruth. Marilyn Monroe and Orson Welles both descend from John Alden's eldest daughter Elizabeth, as does poet Henry Wadsworth Longfellow. Poet William Cullen Bryant descends from son Jonathan.

Isaac Allerton

and his wife Mary (Norris), and children Bartholomew, Remember, and Mary

Isaac Allerton was born about 1586-1588, based on his age given in several depositions.[69] Recently discovered evidence, in the form of a 1609 Blacksmith's Company of London apprenticeship record, suggests he may have been the son of Bartholomew Allerton, tailor of Ipswich, Suffolk.[70] The record indicates that Isaac Allerton was apprenticed to James Glyn on 12 June 1609, for the period of seven years. The belief that Allerton originated from co. Suffolk is further supported by the records of the New Netherlands colony, which give his origins as from Suffolk.[71] And that is also the county where his son Bartholomew would later take up residence.

Records from Leiden, Holland, refer to him as a tailor from the London area, the same occupation as Bartholomew Allerton of Ipswich mentioned in the Blacksmith's record.[72] Also living in Leiden was his sister Sarah, as well as a man named John Allerton who quite likely was a brother. Sarah had been married to a man named John Vincent prior to 1611, by which time she was a widow.

Isaac Allerton and his sister Sarah (Allerton) Vincent, had a double marriage in Leiden on 4 November 1611, with Sarah "of London" marrying future *Mayflower* passenger Degory Priest, and Isaac "of London" marrying Mary Norris of Newbury, Berkshire. No Mary Norris of Newbury has been identified, but five miles northwest of Newbury is the town of Welford, where a Mary Norris was baptized on 9 March 1592, daughter of John. This would seem to be a reasonable match, though perhaps a tad younger than would be expected. Additional research is definitely needed in identifying the origin of Mary.

Isaac and Mary Allerton had their first son, Bartholomew, born in Leiden about 1613. Isaac became an official citizen of Leiden on 7 February 1614, with guarantors Roger Wilson and Henry Wood. And the following year, on 16 November 1615, he was a guarantor for brother-in-law Degory Priest's citizenship request. About that year, Isaac and Mary had their second child, a daughter named Remember; a second daughter, Mary, came about two years later. From 1617 through 1619, Isaac and wife Mary were witnesses to the betrothals and marriages of a number of members of the Leiden congregation. Mary was a witness for Prudence Grindon in her marriage to John Reynolds on 18 August 1617. Isaac accompanied Edward Winslow in his betrothal on 27 April 1618, with Mary being a witness for the bride, Elizabeth Barker. Mary witnessed the marriage of Daniel Fairfield and Rebecca Willett on 4 August 1618. And Isaac was a witness for Roger Wilkins in his marriage to Margaret Barrow on 5 October 1619. On 5 February 1620, Isaac and Mary Allerton buried a child, name not recorded and probably an infant, at St. Peter's in Leiden.

Isaac Allerton appears in a couple of other Leiden records as well during this time period. On 18 June 1618, he made a deposition with Nicholas Claverly regarding the value of a crimson-grey coat. In that record, Allerton's occupation is given as a tailor, and he states he is about thirty years old.[73] And on 8 January 1619, tailor Isaac Allerton took on a young apprentice, twelve-year-old John Hooke, for the period of twelve years.[74]

As the Leiden congregation prepared to uproot itself and venture to Northern Virginia to establish a colony, Isaac Allerton had become one of the more prominent members of the church. With John Carver and Robert Cushman in England negotiating with the Virginia Company and the merchant adventurers who were going to buy stock in the joint-stock company that they would create to fund the voyage, Isaac Allerton and other leading members such as William Bradford, Edward Winslow, and Samuel Fuller, frequently exchanged letters and helped Carver and Cushman to make business decisions. One of the biggest controversies occurred in June 1620, when Robert Cushman gave in to demands by the London merchants that the colonists work for the company Monday through Saturday, instead of Monday through Friday as originally agreed; and that their personal dwellings, built before the liquidation of the company seven years later, would be the property of the company, and would not belong to the individual or family that built it. Allerton, along with Bradford, Winslow, and Fuller, wrote a letter to Cushman insisting that these terms were not acceptable, and that Cushman had not even been authorized to make such concessions. As it would turn out, Cushman would agree to the terms on behalf of the Leiden congregation, but the passengers would steadfastly refuse to agree; and so they sailed away to America without having come to agreement on their working contract.

Many of the *Mayflower* passengers had left behind wives and children, thinking the difficulties of establishing a new colony would be too hard on the bodies of women and children. Isaac Allerton apparently had no such qualms: he brought his son Bartholomew (age seven), his two young daughters Remember (age five) and Mary (age three), and his wife Mary, who at the time of the Atlantic crossing was entering the last trimester of a pregnancy.

After arriving off the tip of Cape Cod, somewhat north of their intended destination at the mouth of the Hudson River in modern-day New York, and outside the bounds of their land patent from the Virginia Company, they decided to draw up an agreement amongst themselves to establish a government there, now called the Mayflower Compact. Allerton was among the first five signers of the document, made on 11 November 1620. The Pilgrims would spend the next month trying to find a place to build their colony, during which time everyone continued to live aboard the damp, overcrowded ship. On December 11, on the third expedition set out by the Pilgrims, the men returned with great news—they finally found an area they liked where they could build a colony. By December 21, they had finally decided on the exact location, but then a storm kicked up and prevented them from doing anything for several days.

On the morning of December 22, with the storm still continuing, Mary Allerton gave birth, but her son was stillborn. As the Pilgrim men went ashore to begin the long and laborious process of building the colony, the women, children, and the sick remained aboard the *Mayflower*. December turned to January, and January into February, and finally the first few houses and storage sheds were taking shape. But the cold weather, scarce and stale provisions, and close quarters afforded on the *Mayflower* allowed disease to spread. By late February, barely a day went by when one of the passengers did not die. On February 25, Isaac's wife Mary Allerton died, leaving Isaac to care for his three young children.

Throughout the month of March, the Plymouth residents had their first initial contacts with the Native Americans, meeting Samoset and Tisquantum (i.e. "Squanto") for the first time. On March 22, the colony received its first visit from the leader of the Wampanoag himself, Massasoit, and his brother Quadequina. Massasoit and sixty of his men stood on a hill overlooking Plymouth, so Edward Winslow was sent with Squanto to bring gifts and to see what he wanted. Winslow was kept as a "hostage" while Massasoit and later his brother went into Plymouth to meet with Governor John Carver. That night, the Wampanoag slept in the woods on the other side of Town

Town brook in Plymouth.

Brooke, and the next morning several of them informed Plymouth that Massasoit wanted them to come visit him: "Captain Standish and Isaac Allerton went venturously, who were welcomed of him after their manner: he gave them three or four ground nuts, and some tobacco."

In April 1621, Governor John Carver died while planting corn seed. William Bradford was elected governor, and Isaac Allerton was appointed to assist him. Allerton would be an assistant to the governor for the next ten years. His early house in Plymouth was located east of the highway on the south side of the main street, sandwiched between the houses of John Billington on the west and Francis Cooke on the east. In the 1623 division of land, he received seven acres of land. Later that year, his sister Sarah, with her new husband Godbert Godbertson, and stepchildren Mary and Sarah Priest, arrived on the ship *Anne*. Given the shortage of housing in Plymouth, they probably all lived together.

In 1624, Isaac Allerton and Edward Winslow went to England and there took charge of some goods bought by the London investors, including "some cattle, cloth, hose, shoes, leather, etc." They brought the goods to Plymouth, where they were to be sold to the company.

About 1625, Isaac married Fear Brewster, the daughter of Plymouth Colony's church elder William Brewster, and they had a daughter they named Sarah about a year later—which must have made the Allerton-Godbertson family somewhat confusing with three Sarahs (Mrs. Sarah Godbertson, Sarah Allerton, and Sarah Priest).

With a business trip to England under his belt in 1624, Isaac followed up with another business trip in 1626. Allerton was sent to purchase supplies for the colony and to negotiate with the London merchants for the purchasing of the company away from them. Allerton was also authorized to seek out some loans to help get the business underway. In England, the best Allerton could get was a £200 loan at a 30 percent interest rate, but that was far better than the 40 and 45 percent interest rates they had gotten in previous years. From the £200, Allerton purchased provisions "which goods they got safely home, and well conditioned, which was much to the comfort, and content of the plantation." He also managed to negotiate for the sale of the joint-stock company, getting all the remaining London stockholders to agree to its sale for £1800, to be paid in £200 increments each year, from 1628 through 1637. If payment was not made at the appointed day each year, a thirty-shilling per week penalty would accrue. The deal, signed on October 26, was taken by Allerton back to Plymouth to be approved and signed by the men of Plymouth, who would bind themselves to make the £200 yearly payment.

In the May 1627 division of cattle, the Allerton and Godbertson families, along with singlemen Edward Bumpass and John Crackston, were allotted the "great black cow came in the *Anne* to which they must keep the lesser of the two steers, and two she goats."

Allerton was sent back to England in late 1627 with the approved and signed document, closing the transfer of the company into the control of the leading men at Plymouth. They also invited four men of London to join with them in the purchase of the company, who had been friendly and helpful to the colony since its inception. They were James Shirley, John Beauchamp, Richard Andrews, and Timothy Hatherley, and those men became the company's agents, authorized to do business for them in London. Allerton then made the first £200 payment in London, and managed to procure a general patent, giving them trading rights to the Kennebec River. With business concluded, Allerton returned again to Plymouth in late 1628 with the fishing ships, bringing "a reasonable supply of goods" without the great interest rates.

Thanks to Isaac Allerton, business was looking good. The company was now owned and controlled by the leading men of Plymouth and a few friends of the colony in London. The company had just £400 of foreign debts on the books, and outside of that small debt they simply had to make their yearly £200 payments. The company had land and trading patents for Plymouth Harbor and Cape Cod, and now the Kennebec River trade was theirs as well.

William Bradford reported: "Hitherto Mr. Allerton did them good and faithful service." But Allerton would not remain in the good graces of Governor Bradford and Plymouth for much longer. He had already raised a few eyebrows by bringing over a minister for the colony without consulting anyone about it. The minister proved to be "crazed in his brain," and the company had to pay all his expenses to return him. Bradford noted that "Mr. Allerton was much blamed that he would bring such a man over, they having charge enough otherwise." And Allerton had also used his business trips to England to buy goods with his own money and sold them in Plymouth. But as the quantities were small and he was otherwise performing his duties well, the matter was overlooked.

Allerton, perhaps overly enthused about his success as a merchant and negotiator of business deals, and his appetite whetted by his small attempts to turn a profit by buying and selling his own goods in Plymouth, took good advantage of the next opportunity in 1629, when he was sent by the company into England to once again conduct business in London. For this trip, he was given the task of enlarging the Kennebec patent, which the Plymouth men thought was too vague and nonspecific. He was instructed not to bring back any goods, except for £50 in shoes, hose, linen cloth, and some basic trade goods. He was also to finalize plans and costs involved in transporting the remaining church members from Leiden who had yet to make their voyage to the new colony—an expense the company was willing to incur.

In England, however, Allerton went out on his own. Without consulting anyone at Plymouth, he decided it was in the company's best interest to be formally recognized as a corporation, as the Massachusetts Bay Colony just had done. So he spent his time socializing with the elite, getting a patent from the Earl of Warwick and Sir Ferdinando Gorges. But when Allerton tried to have customs duties exempted for a period of time, his proposal got sent to the council table for later review. Allerton spent days and days sitting in council waiting for a chance to read his petition, but never got a chance to read it before he had to return to Plymouth. So he left the unfinished task in the hands of a solicitor. He never did work on the Kennebec patent he was sent to deal with.

Allerton purchased the £50 of goods he was requested to obtain, but he also purchased a large amount of goods for himself to sell in Plymouth and elsewhere. But due to time constraints, he had his goods and the colony's goods, all bundled or barreled up together. When Allerton arrived, he then had to sort out what belonged to whom, and in the process many felt he claimed the best and highest quality goods for himself, leaving the company with the remainder. And the remainder contained very little in the way of goods that could be traded for beaver and otter furs—which Allerton explained was because the company spent so much money, £550, to transport over the remaining members of the Leiden congregation.

Failure to buy decent trade goods and mixing them up with his own personal goods, and time wasted on officially incorporating the company, were just the tip of the iceberg, however. Isaac Allerton and James Shirley engaged the company's assets in another business venture—they joined in partnership with a man named Edward Ashley, who obtained a patent at Penobscot. He would be supplied by the company, and the company would share in his profits. But most of the Plymouth men did not particularly care for Ashley to begin with, and they could barely afford to buy trading goods for themselves, let alone for another, less trustworthy man. And in fact, when Ashley's trading post was established, Shirley and Allerton provided him with better trading supplies than they had received at Plymouth.

And as if that were not enough, Allerton had one more surprise in store for his fellow business partners at Plymouth: he brought back with him a man named Thomas Morton to work as his personal secretary. Thomas Morton had been to the Massachusetts Bay previously, and had been a part of an attempted colony. After the colony had fairly well disbanded, Morton remained behind, ousted the man who was left in charge, and collected around him a bunch of mutinous servants. Morton and his band drank heavily, named their homestead "Merrymount," and erected a maypole for dances with Indian women—activities which the neighboring Separatists and Puritans found entirely inappropriate. They had captured him once and banished him to an island, but he was rescued by some Indians, and he returned to his old haunts. When he began selling weapons to the Indians in trade, and defied Plymouth's requests to stop, they had had enough. Plymouth sent ten armed men, led by Captain Myles Standish, to arrest him. Morton refused to give up, and when the arrest party arrived, he had barricaded himself and his servants inside a house and was prepared to defend it in a bloody firefight with Standish and the others who had come to arrest him. Luckily for Standish, Morton's party of merry men was too drunk to be of much use in defending the house, and Morton was taken into custody after a brief standoff. All the surrounding colonies raised a special tax to send him to England for prosecution in the courts. So, a year after all this had transpired, this was the man that Isaac Allerton chose to bring back with him to Plymouth to be his own personal business scribe.

As if to rub more salt in the wound, Isaac Allerton also brought with him a letter from James Shirley in London, which asserted that Allerton was making progress in obtaining the patents and was doing the company a great amount of good, and urged the Plymouth men to return him again the next year to continue his work.

In light of James Shirley's letter, pressing for Allerton's return and the company's need to get the incorporation and the Kennebec patent processes completed now that so much time and money had already been invested in it, they felt obligated to send Allerton back to complete the job the following year, in the autumn of 1630. According to Bradford, Isaac Allerton "gave them fair words and promises of well performing all their businesses according to their directions, and to mend his former errors." Bradford also admits they kept sending Allerton back for a "more secret cause," namely "Mr. Allerton had married the daughter of their Reverend Elder, Mr. Brewster, a man beloved and honored amongst them and who took great pains in teaching and dispensing the Word of God unto them, whom they were loath to grieve or any way offend."

In England, Allerton again decided to take company business into his own hands. He and James Shirley agreed to use company money to send out a fishing vessel called the *Friendship*, and outright purchased another ship called the *White Angel* that was to be used for bass fishing, and for transporting trade goods. By now, the company's debts had tripled. Without any consultation with the other men of Plymouth, Allerton had engaged them in a trading post at Penobscot led by Ashley (who now appeared to be cheating them), set out a fishing expedition, and purchased an entire ship.

In Plymouth, they had expected some kind of resupply in the spring of 1631—resupplying their trading goods was one of Allerton's main duties. It never came. Allerton did return in June in the *White Angel* with decent supplies—but he went only to Ashley's trading post in Maine, not to Plymouth. The *Friendship* was intended to resupply Plymouth while on its fishing expedition, but it was battered at sea for eleven weeks and was forced back to England at great cost to the company. The *Friendship* made another voyage attempt in mid-May and finally arrived in Boston Harbor on 14 July 1631. By the time of her arrival, most of the provisions and goods had spoiled, and all that was left for Plymouth were some bundles of rugs and six gallons of metheglin, a fermented herbal drink. Allerton and the *White Angel* finally reached Boston on July 22, where he was "rebuked . . . very much for running into these courses." But Allerton insisted that the *White Angel* did not belong to the company yet, only if they wanted it. Otherwise, it was to be just a private venture between him and James Shirley. Allerton sold off some of his goods to the company, which included some useful provisions, and went about his bass fishing with the *White Angel*.

Timothy Hatherley had been sent by the four men in London to see firsthand how trading was going, and was given a tour of Plymouth and of the trading posts at Kennebec and in Penobscot, and according to Bradford he "saw plainly that Mr. Allerton played his own game and ran a course not only to the great wrong and detriment of the Plantation who employed and trusted him, but abused them in England also in possessing them with prejudice against the Plantation." Apparently, Allerton had been telling the London men that Plymouth would never be able to repay their debts unless they would engage in other projects, and that is why they so readily accepted taking on additional businesses like Ashley's trading post and the fishing expeditions.

At this time, Isaac Allerton was relieved of his duties as the agent for Plymouth, and the company refused to accept the charges (or potential profits) related to the *Friendship* and *White Angel* adventures. Edward Winslow then became Plymouth's agent in England. Winslow returned to Plymouth in June 1632 with "a large supply of suitable goods ... by which their trading was well carried on." Ashley had died in the meantime, and so with Allerton discharged of his duties, the business seemed to be back on track. Bradford summed up Allerton's business dealings with Plymouth by quoting 1 Timothy 6:9-10, "They that will be rich fall into many temptations and snares ... for the love of money is the root of all evil." He added: "God give him to see the evil in his failings, that he may find mercy by repentance, for the wrongs he hath done to any and this poor Plantation in special."

Even out of his job as agent, Allerton still found ways to cause problems. He had made such good acquaintance with James Shirley in London that he managed to get the company's cargo freighted on his own ship at the rate of £4 per ton, whereas the going rate for such cargo was typically only £3 per ton.

In the end, Allerton became a fairly unpopular person in Plymouth, but he may have been tied to the colony more than he wished by his wife Fear, the daughter of Elder Brewster; and his sister's family, the Godbertsons. Isaac was taxed in Plymouth in 1633 at the highest rate of anyone, £3 and 11 s, but the following year in 1634 his estate had dropped below that of Edward Winslow, and he was only taxed £1 16 s. Godbert Godbertson died in the autumn of 1633, and Isaac's own wife Fear died in 1634. With no significant family ties left in Plymouth, Allerton seems to have pulled up roots and moved around as his trading schemes demanded. He spent a good part of his time the next few years in Marblehead, a town belonging to the Massachusetts Bay Colony. In February 1634/5, his trading post at Marblehead was destroyed by a fire, and within a year he gave his property there to Moses Maverick, who had married his daughter Remember on 6 May 1635.

Edward Winslow, in a private letter to Gov. John Winthrop of the Massachusetts Bay, dated 1 July 1637, gives his opinion of Allerton: "If such a thing be, I persuade myself it never was without my old neighbor Isaac, whose head is always full of such projects, and hath too great familiarity with our common adversaries: but were he as well known to yours as us, they would rather have kept him here than anyway have encouraged his going over: but what I write I would not have made public; but the truth is he loveth neither you nor us.[75]" Isaac remarried to Marblehead native Joanna Swinnerton around this time.

By 1639, Isaac Allerton is seen trading corn at the New Amsterdam colony in present-day New York, and he appears to have frequented the New Haven colony in Connecticut as well. By 1642, much of the legal wrangling over who owed what for the *White Angel, Friendship,* and other Allerton-related business ventures was concluding, and he was finally able to put that part of his life behind him. The following two years, 1642 and 1643, he made several sales, including a barque and a piece of property, in New Amsterdam.

In 1643, he petitioned the New Haven Colony on behalf of the Dutch to send troops under Captain Underhill to help New Amsterdam fight the Indians there. The New Haven Colony ultimately decided against Allerton's request, "not clearly understanding the rise and cause of the war.[76]" In 1644, Allerton's trading ventures expanded to the New Sweden Colony, where he is seen selling goods at Fort Cristina at various times over the subsequent decade.

Allerton appears to have maintained a dual residence between the English at New Haven, and the Dutch at New Amsterdam. In a letter of attorney dated 13 October 1646, Allerton calls himself "of New Haven." A couple weeks later on 27 October 1646, Allerton allowed his son-in-law Thomas Cushman, husband of daughter Mary, to collect any of his debts within the Plymouth Colony from the estate of John Coombs, who had recently died as a debtor to Allerton. In that record, he calls himself "of New Amsterdam, in the province of the New Netherlands.[77]" Several months later, on March 10, he was assigned a seat at the New Haven meetinghouse for the general court session. Allerton was fined by the New Haven court in 1647 for failing to provide his servant John Bishop with a gun—but the fine was reduced in half on account that Allerton is "much absent" and promptly took care of the situation when he found out about it.[78]

Isaac Allerton died in New Haven in 1659. His will is mostly just a list of the debts that were owed to him, or which he owed. It indicates that Allerton had a very complicated estate, and that he had business engagements all around the New World and Europe. Many of his debts were to Dutch merchants at New Amsterdam, where they were recorded in the books of an Englishman, George Woolsey, who had taken up residence in Holland and later came to New Netherlands about 1643.

Allerton's estate inventory was taken at New Haven on 12 February 1658/9, and includes a house, orchard, barn, and two acres of meadow valued at £75, and wearing clothes valued at nearly £7. For livestock, he only appears to have had two sows and four pigs. Kitchen goods included warming pans, iron pots, frying pan, two old kettles, old skillets, candlesticks, pewter, and a mortar and pestle. Bedroom goods included a chest of drawers, bedstead, featherbed, bolster, pillow, chairs, blankets, a sea chest, curtains and valence for a bed, and carpeting. He also had some spectacles, an old hat and cap, a parcel of old linen thread, brimstone, some sheep's wool, and two bushels of apples.[79]

Many have claimed that Isaac Allerton died in debt, but there is no indication of this whatsoever: an examination of his estate inventory seems to clearly show otherwise. Allerton reports that he is owed more than 3200 guilders and £100, due from various individuals—whereas his own debts he lists at little over 420 guilders and £20, plus about £3 of debts to various people in New Haven. On top of that, he had 1300 guilders worth of book lace, and an estate (house, livestock, household goods) valued at over £118. Isaac Allerton bequeaths "what is overplus I leave to my wife and my son Isaac."

JOHN ALLERTON

John Allerton was presumably a relative of *Mayflower* passenger Isaac Allerton, perhaps a brother. Isaac Allerton also had a sister Sarah living in Leiden; she was the widow of a man named John Vincent, and married Degory Priest on 4 November 1611.

John Allerton is mentioned in only one Leiden record: he buried a child at St. Peter's on 21 May 1616.[80] His place of residence was given as near the *Pieterskerkhof* in Leiden, which was the same place of residence given by Isaac Allerton when he buried a child there about four years later on 5 February 1620.[81] From this burial record, we can deduce that he was married, but no information about his wife, or any other children, has surfaced.

William Bradford contributes most of the other historical facts known about *Mayflower* passenger John Allerton. He wrote "John Allerton . . . was reputed as one of the company, but was to go back (being a seaman) for the help of others behind." So, John Allerton had come on the *Mayflower*, but he was hired as labor to help build up the colony the first year. He was then supposed to return to Leiden to help the other church members prepare for their later voyages to America.

John Allerton was one of the forty-two signers of the Mayflower Compact on 11 November 1620, his signature falling between two other seamen, Richard Gardinar and Thomas English. He was one of the nineteen men who went out on the final expedition set forth from the *Mayflower* anchored at Cape Cod on December 6, to seek out a place to build the colony. The expedition was attacked by Nauset Indians, but everyone escaped unharmed—only to nearly wreck their shallop on Clarke's Island that evening in a storm that tore their mast into three pieces. There, they explored Plymouth Harbor the next few days, and decided it was the best place to build their colony.

Bradford continues on simply to state that John Allerton "died here, before the ship [the *Mayflower*] departed." Elsewhere, he recorded: "John Allerton died in the general sickness." John Allerton, having died the first winter at Plymouth, was never able to fulfill his appointed task of returning to Leiden to assist the others in preparing to come over later.

JOHN BILLINGTON,

HIS WIFE ELLEN, AND THEIR CHILDREN JOHN AND FRANCIS

Whenever you get a large number of families together, there always seems to be one that is a little more profane, a little rougher, and a little more obnoxious and rowdy than the others in the group. For the *Mayflower* passengers and the settlers of early Plymouth Colony, that family was the Billingtons.

Governor William Bradford recorded that the Billington's "came from London," which simply meant that is where they joined up with the *Mayflower*. In 1970, R. N. Whiston noted that Francis Billington, son of John Billington, was named as an heir for Francis Longland on the 1650 Survey of the Manor of Spalding.[82] The property in question was located in Cowbit, Lincolnshire, and Francis Longland was living at the time in Welby, aged seventy. The document states "Francis Billington (as it is informed) was living about a year since in New England aged forty years or thereabouts." This matches perfectly and is almost certainly a reference to the *Mayflower* passenger then living in Plymouth. Presumably, John and Ellen Billington were somehow related to Francis Longland, and possibly to the joint heir, Francis Newton. Unfortunately, extensive research in Lincolnshire probate and parish registers has thus far failed to turn up any additional clues.[83]

John and Ellen Billington came on the *Mayflower* with their two sons John and Francis. William Bradford stated, "I know not by what friends shuffled into their company," indicating even he was not sure exactly how the Billingtons got associated with the *Mayflower*'s voyage. But they did, and they came. Although many have assumed that the Billingtons had a hand in the "mutinous speeches" that forced the drawing up of the Mayflower Compact shortly after the *Mayflower*'s arrival, there is not any historical evidence to substantiate this belief.

It did not take long, however, for the Billington family to find ways to make trouble. On 5 December 1620, while the *Mayflower* was still at anchor off the tip of Cape Cod, the Pilgrims escaped "a great danger by the foolishness of a boy," thirteen-year-old Francis Billington, who:

> [I]n his father's absence, had got gunpowder, and had shot off a piece or two, and made squibs, and there being a fowling piece charged in his father's cabin, shot her off in the cabin, and there being a little barrel of powder half full, scattered in and about the cabin, the fire being within four foot of the bed between the decks, and many flints and iron things about the cabin, and many people about the fire, and yet by God's mercy no harm done.

Hyperactive Francis Billington was up a tree a month later, after the men had finally decided on settling at Plymouth. At the top of the tree that was itself on the top of a high hill, young Francis saw "a great sea," and on January 8 he persuaded one of the master's mates of the *Mayflower*, presumably either John Clark or Robert Coppin, to go explore it with him. After a three-mile hike, they found it was not a great sea, but instead it was two lakes full of fresh water, fish, and fowl. They also stumbled across about eight Indian houses that appeared to have been long abandoned, but it still put them in great fear because the Pilgrims had not yet met with any Indians and were not sure if they were friendly. Realizing they were just one man, one boy, and one gun, they hurried back to the safety of the other colonists. The two ponds, even today, still carry the name "Billington's Sea."

The Billington family made it through the first winter entirely unscathed, something that cannot be said for the majority of families.

In March 1621, John Billington, the father, got himself into trouble and became the first person to commit a crime in New England. He was brought "before the whole company" for refusing to obey military captain Myles Standish's "lawful orders." Instead of obeying, Billington responded with "opprobrious speeches, for which he is adjudged to have his neck and heels tied together." John Billington repented: "but upon humbling himself and craving pardon, and it being the first offense, he is forgiven.[84"]

A few months later, son John Billington, then about fifteen years old, wandered off and got lost in the woods. According to Bradford, he "wandered up and down some five days living on berries and what he could find," until he stumbled across an Indian village at Manomet, about twenty miles south of Plymouth. He was then spirited farther off to the Nauset, out on Cape Cod. After receiving word that he was being held by the Nauset, the Pilgrims sent ten men on a voyage to recover the boy. They departed on June 11, but within a few hours they encountered thunder, lightning, and even saw a water spout. After arriving, the Pilgrims were very cautious and careful, the Nauset being the group of Indians that had initially attacked them while they were first out exploring Cape Cod after arrival. But the Pilgrims and the Nauset managed to exchange gifts and negotiate a peace. They carried John Billington out to the waiting shallop, "behung with beads."

In 1623, Billington received three acres in the division of land. It is not entirely certain why Billington only received three acres—he should have received four: one for himself, one for his wife, and two for his sons John and Francis. It appears that legal custody of John Billington (the son) may have been transferred to Richard Warren, as Richard Warren has an extra, unexplained share, and John Billington the younger was apparently living with Richard Warren at the time of the 1627 division of cattle.

One of the biggest scandals in early Plymouth occurred in 1624, and was instigated by John Lyford, with co-conspirator John Oldham. John Lyford was a reverend and preacher who managed to initially make a good impression on the Plymouth Church; but it was not long before there were strains. Lyford began holding secret church meetings and gaining allies among the disaffected of Plymouth, even going so far as to administer Anglican sacraments. Oldham and Lyford began to write letters of dissent back to England to try to stir up political and business problems for the colony. Suspicious, Governor Bradford had the letters intercepted and secretly transcribed. When the matter finally came to court, John Lyford tried to gain open support from those who had secretly supported him. He named John Billington, among others, as being with him, but when confronted, Billington "denied the things and protested he wronged them," although Billington appears to admit he attended some of the secret meetings. Oldham and Lyford were both convicted and banished from Plymouth, but Billington appears to have escaped censure in the matter.

John Billington was still mad about something the following year. In a letter written by William Bradford to Robert Cushman in June 1625, Bradford wrote "Billington still rails against you, and threatens to arrest you, I know not wherefore; he is a knave, and so will live and die."

In 1627, John, Ellen, and Francis Billington were joined with Stephen Hopkins, and the Snow and Palmer families, sharing a stake in the "black weaning calf" and "the calf of this year to come of the black cow," plus two female goats. John Billington the younger was apparently living with Richard Warren, and received a share consisting of the smooth-horned heifer that came in the ship *Jacob*, along with two female goats. Sometime between the 1627 and 1630, John Billington the younger died, just shy of turning twenty-five years old—the cause of his young death is not known, although his master Richard Warren died in 1628 at a fairly young age as well, so perhaps there was a sickness in the household.

The murderous events of 1630 are what John Billington the elder is most remembered for. William Hubbard, writing in the mid or late 1600s, provides the most detailed account of what happened:

> About September 1630, was one Billington executed at Plymouth for murder. When the world was first peopled, and but one family to do that, there was yet too many to live peaceably together; so when this wilderness began first to be peopled by the English, when there was but one poor town, another Cain was found therein, who maliciously slew his neighbor in the field, as he accidentally met him, as himself was going to shoot deer. The poor fellow perceiving the intent of this Billington, his mortal enemy, sheltered himself behind trees as well as he could for awhile; but the other not being so ill a marksman as to miss his aim, made a shot at him, and struck him on the shoulder, with which he died soon after. The murderer expected that either for want of power to execute for capital offenses, or for want of people to increase the plantation, he should

have his life spared; but justice otherwise determined, and rewarded him, the first murderer of his neighbor there, with the deserved punishment of death, for a warning to others.[85]

William Bradford, governor of Plymouth, gives the incident little more than a passing comment:

> This year John Billington the elder (one that came over with the first) was arraigned; and both by grand, and petty jury found guilty of willful murder; by plain and notorious evidence. And was for the same accordingly executed. This as it was the first execution amongst them, so was it a matter of great sadness unto them; they used all due means about his trial, and took the advice of Mr. Winthrop, and other the ablest gentlemen in the Bay of Massachusetts, that were then newly come over, who concurred with them that he ought to die, and the land to be purged from blood. He and some of his, had been often punished for miscarriages before, being one of the profanest families amongst them; . . . His fact was, that he waylaid a young man, one John Newcomen (about a former quarrel) and shot him with a gun, whereof he died.

Thomas Morton, ever an opponent of Plymouth, had a slightly different perspective on the matter when he wrote about it in 1637, nicknaming Billington "Old Woodman":

> There is a very useful stone in the land [the whetstone], and as yet there is found out but one place where they may be had, in the whole country. Old Woodman (that was chocked at Plymouth after he had played the unhappy marksman when he was pursued by a careless fellow that was new come into the land) they say labored to get a patent of it to himself. He was beloved by many, and had many sons, that had a mind to engross that commodity.[86]

Even after John Billington's execution, the family failed to keep itself out of trouble. Widow Ellen Billington was sued for £100 by John Doane for slander on 7 June 1636. The exact nature of the slander is not recorded, but Ellen was sentenced by the jury to sit in the stocks, be whipped, and pay a fine of £5. Ellen Billington remarried to Gregory Armstrong in September 1638, and died sometime between 1642 and 1650.

Francis Billington married in July 1634 to Christian (Penn) Eaton, the widow and third wife of *Mayflower* passenger Francis Eaton. He appears to have mellowed out after his marriage, though he did get a small fine for smoking on the highway in 1638, and was fined again for an unspecified reason in 1645. Francis and Christian Billington had nine children together from 1635 through 1652, and lived in Plymouth until 1669. The family then moved to Middleboro, where both Francis and Christian died in 1684 of old age, in the care of their son Isaac.

WILLIAM BRADFORD

AND HIS WIFE DOROTHY (MAY)

William Bradford was baptized on 19 March 1589/90 in the small village of Austerfield, co. Yorkshire, England. Bradford's early childhood was marked with repeated tragedy. His father, also named William, was buried when young Bradford was just a year old. His mother remarried to a man named Robert Briggs on 23 September 1593. When he was barely seven years of age, his mother also died, apparently of complications following the birth of William's stepbrother Robert. William's stepfather, Robert Briggs turned William over to his grandfather, John Hanson, to be raised. John was the father of William's mother Alice. But when William was barely twelve, his grandfather died.[87]

Following his grandfather's burial on 27 February 1601/2, twelve-year-old William was turned over to the custody of his uncle, probably his father's brother Robert Bradford. William Bradford's uncle tried to raise and train him in the trade of husbandry, working the farm and fields, but young Bradford was frequently ill and often too weak to be of any use. He began to take a strong interest in reading, and even at this young age his interest in studying the Scriptures was profound. As a young teenager, he began attending the ministry of Richard Clyfton, the rector of the neighboring community

The church of St. Helens, Austerfield, where William Bradford was baptized, as it appeared in the late 1800s.

of Babworth. Richard Clyfton, and John Smyth, leader of the Gainsborough, co. Lincolnshire congregation, both befriended and contributed to the education of young Bradford.

As the reign of Queen Elizabeth came to an end and King James assumed the throne in 1603, persecution against Protestants began to increase, and some of the more radical groups—including Clyfton's and Smyth's—were drawn underground. Though pressured and dissuaded by his uncles and neighbors, Bradford continued his association with the underground congregation, which began secretly meeting at the Scrooby Manor, then under the day-to-day administration of one of the other church members, William Brewster. He also began teaching himself both Latin and Greek, and in later years he would also pick up Dutch and try to learn Hebrew as well.

By the age of eighteen, Bradford and the other church members were under increasing pressure, and some had even been arrested and fined for various offenses. The church made the decision to flee to Holland. During their first attempt in 1607, they were deceived by a ship captain and turned over to authorities in Boston, co. Lincolnshire, where they were imprisoned for about a month. Bradford, then only eighteen, was freed somewhat earlier than the others. The congregation would make another attempt to leave, and ultimately Bradford would make his way to Amsterdam in 1608. Upon arrival, he was turned into Dutch authorities by an officer (for having illegally fled England), but the Dutch magistrates allowed Bradford to remain when they learned his reasons. In Amsterdam, Bradford took a job as an apprentice or servant to a Frenchman who dealt in silks.

After a year in Amsterdam, the church group led by Clyfton, Robinson, and Brewster decided it was best to split from the other group led by Smyth because the latter was turning toward Anabaptism. So, Bradford and the former Scrooby congregation removed to the town of Leiden, Holland.

William Bradford was the only son of his parents; his only sister, Alice, died just before Bradford left for Holland. When Bradford turned twenty-one years of age, he assumed legal control of his "comfortable inheritance." Bradford sold it off and took everything in ready money. A couple years later, on 10 December 1613 (oddly, in Amsterdam), the twenty-three-year-old Bradford married Dorothy May, a sixteen-year-old girl from Wisbeach, co. Cambridge, England.

In establishing his family so early in life, Bradford quickly consumed his estate—a mistake he would regret, but which he would attribute to God's teaching him an early and valuable lesson on living humbly and avoiding vanity.[88] Bradford took a job as a fustian weaver in Leiden to bring in enough to support himself and his wife.

William and Dorothy Bradford had their first son, John, who was probably born about 1617; and in June of that year, William took out a loan for a house on the *Achtergracht* between the *Paradijssteeg* and the *Bouwenlouwensteeg* in Leiden. Very shortly thereafter, the Leiden congregation decided to move forward with a plan to remove to some "uninhabited" section of the Americas—they eventually decided upon Northern Virginia. Bradford began taking an active role in preparations, and became one of the leading members of the Leiden congregation. In April 1619, he sold his house[89]; and a year later, he and wife Dorothy boarded the *Speedwell* for Southampton, and then boarded the *Mayflower* for the voyage to America. They left their three-year-old son John behind, intending to send for him after the colony had been better established.

After the *Mayflower* arrived, he was one of the first men to sign the Mayflower Compact, and he participated in writing some of the earliest journals that were compiled together a couple years later and published by George Morton, a Leiden church member who had remained behind (intending to come on a later ship). From these journals, we learn that William Bradford, then about thirty, was an active participant in all of the early explorations sent out by the Pilgrims to locate a place to establish their colony. When the first men were set out to explore Cape Cod, on 15 November 1620, they were led by Captain Myles Standish, "unto whom was adjoined for counsel and advice, William Bradford, Stephen Hopkins, and Edward Tilley." William Bradford was also one of the eighteen men who were a part of the third and final exploration sent out on December 6. On that voyage, they would circle the entire cape from modern-day Provincetown all the way around and into Plymouth Harbor. Along the way, they dug up some Indian stores of corn which had been buried for the winter (and some Indian graves in the process), and were the next morning attacked by a group of Nauset—though no one was harmed during the attack. The next day, sailing along the coast of the cape, the Pilgrims encountered a strong storm that broke their rudder, and then broke their mast into three pieces. Nearly cast away, they managed to use the oars to direct their course onto an island, which they barely made it to just as night was falling upon them. They kept careful guard all that night through the rain, still rattled by the Indian attack the previous morning. When morning came, they discovered it was a fairly secure island, which they named Clark's Island in honor of the master's mate John Clark, who had managed to get them to the island safely. It was Sunday, so they did not work. On Monday, they resumed their exploration, and found several places they felt were suitable for their plantation.

They returned to the *Mayflower* to consult, and eventually a consensus was reached and they settled at what is now Plymouth. Upon returning, however, Bradford would learn some tragic news: in his absence, his wife Dorothy, "his dearest consort," had accidentally fallen overboard and drowned.[90]

William Bradford apparently suffered greatly during the first winter at Plymouth; on several occasions, being near death. On January 11, "William Bradford being at work, (for it was a fair day) was vehemently taken with a grief and pain, and so shot to his huckle-bone, it was doubted that he would have instantly died; he got cold in the former discoveries, especially the last, and felt some pain in his ankles by times, but he grew a little better towards night and in time through God's mercy in the use of means recovered." As Bradford lay recovering, on January 14, a spark from the fire flew into the thatch of the house that had been serving as a hospital for the sick, and the whole roof went up in flames. "The most loss was Master Carver's and Master Bradford's, who then lay sick in bed, and if they had not risen with good speed, had been blown up with powder: but through God's mercy they had no harm, the house was as full of beds as they could lie one by another, and their muskets charged, but blessed be God there was no harm done."

In April, after the first winter had passed by and the *Mayflower* had departed back for England, Governor John Carver suddenly and unexpectedly died, apparently of sunstroke: "their Governor (Mr. John Carver) came out of the field very sick, it being a hot day, he complained greatly of his head, and lay down, and within a few hours his senses failed, so as he never spoke more till he died, which was within a few days after." The colonists would then elect William Bradford governor, with Isaac Allerton his assistant, because Bradford was "not recovered of his illness, in which he had been near the point of death." Bradford would be reelected governor of Plymouth thirty-one times: every year until the year of his death in 1657, with only five exceptions (1633, 1634, 1636, 1638, and 1644).

As governor, Bradford's biography from this point on is, in a sense, a history of Plymouth. His first year as governor included marrying Edward Winslow to Susanna White. Edward's wife Elizabeth, and Susanna's husband William, had both died the first winter. The Pilgrims believed that marriage was a civil affair, to be handled by the magistrates (i.e., the governor), and not a religious affair to be handled by the church. Bradford then sent out Edward Winslow and Stephen Hopkins to meet with Massasoit, the neighboring sachem, "to bestow upon him some gratuity to bind him the faster to them, as also that hereby they might view the country, and see in what manner he lived, what strength he had about him, and how the ways were to his place." Later that month, young John Billington lost himself in the woods, and survived for five days on berries before he encountered an Indian village at Manomet. He was then transferred to the Nauset, the same Indians that had originally attacked the Pilgrims on their December explorations. Bradford used the opportunity to send an envoy from Plymouth to the Nauset, who successfully recovered the boy, made peace, and repaid the Indians for the corn they had taken from them the first winter. Plymouth also had its first run-in with an unfriendly neighboring sachem called Corbitant, and when rumors came back that he had killed Squanto, the Pilgrims' primary interpreter, Bradford sent out a force of fourteen well-armed men under Myles Standish to determine if Squanto had been killed. If he had been killed, they were authorized by Bradford to "cut off Corbitant's head, but not to hurt any but those that had a hand in it." The men, however, found Squanto alive. And in September, Bradford sent out ten men, with Squanto as guide, to trade with the Massachusett Indians to the north.

About October, they "began now to gather in the small harvest they had." Bradford sent men out fishing for cod and bass, and sent some men out fowling. "[A]nd besides waterfowl, there was great store of wild turkeys, of which they took many." Massasoit and some ninety of his men came to Plymouth, and everyone partook in a three-day harvest festival, feasting and sporting. The Indians brought five deer to the feast, giving one to Bradford.

With the colony all set for the winter and rations stored, Plymouth got a surprise: a ship, the *Fortune*, arrived with thirty-five more men—but no food or supplies. "[T]here was not so much as biscuit cake or any other victuals for them, neither had they any bedding, . . . nor pot, or pan to dress any meat in, nor over-many clothes." Unprepared for the near doubling of the colony's size just as winter was approaching, the colonists went short on food.

Bradford had the *Fortune* loaded with clapboard, and two hogsheads of beaver and otter skins. The freight was estimated to be worth about £500. Unfortunately for the joint-stock company, the *Fortune* was intercepted by a French pirate, who held the ship, crew, and the couple of passengers for several weeks at the castle on the Isle d'Yeu in Poitou, France, confiscating all their goods and sending them home with just the clothes on their backs and some stale biscuits.

The poor financial return caused strife amongst the English investors in the colony, and one of the leading organizers and investors, Thomas Weston, sold out and quit the company, and then turned around and sent out his own group of colonists to establish a competing colony to the north in the Massachusetts Bay, at Wessagussett. His colonists, however, arrived in New England poorly supplied, and they ended up scrounging off Plymouth's meager resources until they were strong enough to go set up their own colony. Bradford took some criticism for helping them out—they were competition, after all—but as Bradford saw it, they were also Englishmen who would have starved and died without their help. The Wessagussett Colony would be nothing but trouble for Plymouth. The poorly organized and poorly governed colonists began stealing from the Indians for their food, sending English-Indian relations down the tube. Plymouth heard all the complaints from the Indians, but could do nothing; and when the Indians in the region had finally gotten fed up enough, they organized a conspiracy, and Bradford felt obligated to protect the English at Wessagussett from Indian attack by sending out Captain Myles Standish and some of his Plymouth men to kill the conspirators. Although generally supported by Massasoit and the neighboring Indian groups, Plymouth's killing of neighboring Indian leaders was a black spot that Bradford would have difficulty erasing.

On 14 August 1623, William Bradford married to the widow Alice (Carpenter) Southworth—it was the fourth marriage at Plymouth. In a letter from September 1623, Plymouth resident Emmanuel Altham wrote:

> Upon the occasion of the Governor's marriage, since I came, Massasoit was sent for to the wedding, where came with him his wife, the queen, although he hath five wives. With him came four other kings and about six score men with their bows and arrows, where when they came to our town, we saluted them with the shooting off of many muskets and training our men. And so all the bows and arrows was brought into the Governor's house, and he brought the Governor three or four bucks and a turkey. And so we had very good pastime in seeing them dance, which is in such manner, with such a noise that you would wonder . . . And now to say somewhat of the great cheer we had at the Governor's marriage. We had about twelve pasty venisons, besides others, pieces of roasted venison and other such good cheer in such quantity that I could wish you some of our share. For here we have the best grapes that ever you saw, and the biggest, and divers sorts of plums and nuts which our business will not suffer us to look for.[91]

During his first decade in office as governor, Bradford had a number of issues he had to deal with. In 1623, Rev. John Lyford arrived and joined the Plymouth church, and became a confidant of Bradford "in their weightiest businesses." But over time, Bradford and others became suspicious of Lyford and another man, John Oldham. When Bradford observed that John Lyford was spending an unusually long time writing letters back to England, he took a trip out to the ship, and intercepted and read the letters. Bradford "found above 20 of Lyford's letters, many of them large, and full of slanders and false accusations," so Bradford made copies of them and held a few of the more incriminating originals, passing along copies and rebuttals to the intended recipients in England. Rather than immediately present the letters, Bradford chose to hold on to them and let the conspiracy fester, to better understand who all was involved and what their intents were. In the end, Oldham and Lyford were taken into custody and banished.

As divisions and disagreements grew between the London investors and the leaders of Plymouth, Bradford helped to organize a group of men in Plymouth and four from London to buy the company from the factious shareholders, a process that began in 1626. In 1628, Bradford began communications with the Dutch, who were then settled at New Amsterdam, in modern-day New York; and that same year, he authorized the expedition to take Thomas Morton into custody. Morton was a notorious troublemaker then residing in the Massachusetts Bay, who was living irreligiously and selling weapons to the Indians.

In 1629, John Endicott and the first settlers of Salem arrived, as did the remaining Leiden church members who had stayed behind in Holland. The coming decade would see an enormous increase in migration to New England, as the Massachusetts Bay Colonists, led by John Winthrop, began arriving. As more and more English settlers arrived, tensions with the Indians were also on the increase. The Pequot and the Narragansett had both begun to threaten the English.

William Bradford presided over his first capital punishment case in 1630, after John Billington had shot and killed John Newcomen, apparently the result of a long-standing dispute. Billington was sentenced to death, and was hanged.

In 1633 and 1634, Bradford was not elected governor. It is unclear whether this was voluntary, but it may well have been the result of a perceived mishandling of Isaac Allerton, whom Bradford had trusted for many years, but whom continually put his own financial advantage over those of the other shareholders, bringing trade goods for himself while giving the company the leftovers and unwanted goods. Edward Winslow was elected governor in 1633, and Thomas Prence in 1634. Those same years, Bradford was taxed £1 16 s, and £1 7 s. Edward Winslow was also elected governor in 1636, after he returned from a successful business voyage the previous year. And in 1638, Thomas Prence was elected governor once more.

Bradford would be elected governor throughout the 1640s, with the exception of 1644 when Edward Winslow was elected. The year 1644 was a tough one for Plymouth, and Governor Winslow authorized

an official investigation into whether or not Plymouth should be moved
to Nauset, farther out on the tip of Cape Cod. Bradford was a strong
critic of this idea. In the end, the town would decide not to move, but
many residents ended up moving there anyway, founding the town of
Eastham, and further depleting Plymouth's resources. Bradford was
reelected in 1645, and would remain governor until the year of his death
in 1657. Throughout Bradford's remaining years, he would struggle to
maintain the town of Plymouth, but lament its condition and
deterioration over time. All the leading residents had, for the most part,
either died or moved to neighboring communities, leaving Plymouth
but a shadow of its former days. About this time, Bradford penned a
poem entitled "A Word to New Plymouth," which begins:

> O poor Plymouth, how dost thou moan,
> Thy children all are from thee gone,
> And left thou art in widow's state,
> Poor, helpless, sad, desolate.
>
> Some thou hast had, it is well known,
> That sought thy good before their own,
> But times are changed; those days are gone,
> And therefore thou art left alone.
>
> To make others rich thyself art poor,
> They are increased out of thy store,
> But growing rich they thee forsake,
> And leave thee poor and desolate.[92]

In his later years, he took on additional responsibilities, acting as
Plymouth's commissioner for the United Colonies—a mutual
gathering of all the New England colonies. The commissioners met
together to discuss and decide upon items of concern to all the
governments of the region. In 1652 and 1656, Bradford was elected
president of the United Colonies.

Beginning in the winter of 1656, William Bradford fell ill, and
through spring his health continued to decline. The day before he
died, Bradford reported that "the God of Heaven so filled his mind
with ineffable consolations." His loss was greatly mourned with "many

deep sighs, as well as loud volleys of shot." Shortly after his death, an unknown person penned the following lines:

> The ninth of May, about nine of the clock,
> A precious one God out of Plymouth took;
> Governor Bradford then expired his breath,
> Was call'd away by force of cruel death.
> A man approv'd in town, in church, in court,
> Who so behav'd himself in godly sort,
> For the full space of thirty-seven years,
> As he was means of turning many fears
> Away from thee, poor Plymouth, where he spent
> The better part of time that God him lent.
> Well skill'd he was in regulating laws,
> So as by law he could defend the cause
> Of poor distressed plaintiff, when he brought
> His case before him, and for help besought.
> Above all other men he loved thos
> Who gospel truths most faithfully unclose,   .
> Who were with grace and learning fully fraught,
> Such as laboriously the gospel taught.
> Sweet Brewster, he is gone some time before;
> Wise Winslow, whose death we lament so sore;
> And faithful Standish, freed from horrid pain,
> To be with Christ, in truth, the greatest gain;
> Now blessed, holy Bradford, a successor
> Of blessed, holy Bradford, the confessor,
> Is gone to place of rest, with many more
> Of precious ones, whom I might name, great store;
> And commendation of each one have given;
> But what needs that? Their names are writ in heaven.

William Bradford had deferred the writing of his will in the hope he could get the help of his friend, Thomas Prence, but "feeling himself very weak and drawing on to the conclusion of his mortal life," he made out a nuncupative will the day of his death.

He stated that his sons John and William already had been given their portion of the lands from his estate, and requested that his son

Joseph be made "in some sort equal to his brethren out of my estate."
He appointed his wife Alice to be his sole executrix, and gave her his
stock in the Kennebec trade; he requested Thomas Prence, Thomas
Willet, and Thomas Southworth to supervise his estate.

Bradford also noted he had "some small books written by my own
hand" including "a little book with a black cover wherein there is a
Word to Plymouth, a Word to Boston, and a Word to New England,
with sundry useful verses." These and several other poems written by
Bradford still exist and have been published.

William Bradford's estate inventory was taken on 22 May 1657.[93]
In the "old parlor," there was a feather bed and bolster, canvas bed
and bolster, two pillows, several white blankets, a green rug and a
white rug, an old pair of say curtains, wainscot bedstead, four leather
chairs, a great leather chair, two wooden chairs, a table and two stools,
a wainscot chest and cupboard, a case with six knives, three matchlock
muskets, a snaphance musket, a birding piece, and a pistol. In the "great
room," he had a number of chairs and a table, sheets and linens, a
fowling piece, a number of cushions, four "fine" shirts and four "other"
shirts, several dozen cotton and linen napkins, various tablecloths,
nearly a hundred pounds of pewter platters, basins, saucers, plates
and other dishes, three chamber pots, a pewter candlestick, four Venice
glasses, and seven earthen dishes. In the kitchen, he had numerous
kettles, pans, skillets, candlesticks, andirons, stewpan, pots, tongs, fire
shovel, iron dripping pans, four dozen trenchers, two jugs, a suit with
silver buttons and a coat, a "sad colored cloth suit," a pair of black
britches, a lead-colored cloth suit, a sad-colored short coat, a light-
colored coat, a green gown, a violet cloak, two pairs of stockings, a
black and a colored hat, a great chair, two stools, a carved chest, and a
table. In the study, he had fourteen pairs of shoes, various fabrics,
including cotton, mohair, and cloth, olive-colored kersey, whitish
kersey, gray kersey, sad-colored kersey, seven small moose skins, a
desk, two cases of empty bottles, and some remnants of cushions.

He also had a large library consisting of about one hundred books.
Many of the books were theological in nature, including works by
Martin Luther, John Calvin, William Perkins, Henry Ainsworth,
Thomas Cartwright, and four books that had been written by the
Pilgrims' pastor, John Robinson. Also in Bradford's library was Jean
Bodin's *Six Books of the Commonwealth*, a book on politics; the

French Academy, a morality textbook; *A General Description of the World*, and Peter Martyr's *Common Places*, both travel and geography books; *Method of Physic*, a medical text; a *History of the Netherlands*; and William Gouge's *Of Domestical Duties*, a book on household government and the roles of husband and wife in the family.

For livestock, Bradford owned about ten sheep, five horses, twenty-six cattle, and ten swine. His house and orchard in Plymouth were valued at £45, and the Kennebec trade stock he left to his wife was valued at £256.

WILLIAM BREWSTER,

HIS WIFE MARY, AND THEIR CHILDREN LOVE AND WRESTLING

William Brewster was born about 1566, somewhere in the vicinity of Scrooby, Nottinghamshire—just a stone's throw from the legendary Sherwood Forest. William's father, also named William Brewster, was appointed the receiver and bailiff of Scrooby Manor by the Archbishop of York, on 4 January 1575, when young Brewster would have been about nine years old.

Scrooby Manor had quite a storied past. It was enumerated in the Doomsday Book in 1086 AD, and King John stayed there in August 1212. King Henry VII's daughter Margaret stayed there in June 1503, on her way to marry King James IV of Scotland. And King Henry VIII stayed there in August 1541 and held there a meeting of the privy council. The manor belonged to the Archbishop of York, who used it as a seat for business and leased it out. As the receiver and bailiff, William Brewster Sr. was the archbishop's legal representative, in charge of the guests and the administration of the manor. For his office, Brewster received a meager salary of a little over £3 per year—but the benefit was the fact that he and his family could take up residence at the enormous, well-kept estate, and play host to the dignitaries who stopped in.[94]

Scrooby Manor then consisted of a large manor house. The estate had its own chapel, bake house, beer-brewing house, a great hall and gallery, a large orchard, a number of houses and horse stables, plenty of livestock, a fish pond, gardens, and grassy fields. The estate was surrounded by a moat on three sides, and the river Ryton on the fourth side. There was a large gate entrance and gatehouse.

At the age of about fourteen, young William Brewster—having lived at Scrooby Manor for about five years—went off to Peterhouse College at Cambridge University, entering there on 3 December 1580.

At Cambridge, William Brewster would have been introduced to the religious ideals that would later influence his direction.[95]

In 1582, while young Brewster was away at college, Queen Elizabeth took an interest in Scrooby Manor—she asked the Archbishop of York, Edwin Sandys, to lease it to her for £40 a year. Edwin Sandys, as much as he loved his queen, could not accept the offer—he calculated his loss on that deal to be about £70,000 "at the very least." Edwin Sandys quickly turned around and leased the estate to his son Samuel, perhaps in an effort to prevent any further inquiries into the availability of the estate.

Back at Cambridge, young Brewster, for whatever reason, did not receive a bachelor's degree. He took on a secretary job under William Davison, and in 1585 accompanied Davison on a diplomatic mission to the Netherlands, which was then at war with Spain. Queen Elizabeth had made the decision to assist the Netherlands, and Davison was sent to negotiate the terms of English aid with the Dutch. He returned to England, where a short time later Queen Elizabeth signed the Treaty of Alliance. That same day, word reached England that the city of Antwerp had fallen to the Spanish. Queen Elizabeth hastened her army and sent Davison back to the Netherlands. Davison, again, brought with him his secretary, William Brewster, who was then just about twenty years of age. In exchange for military services, Davison took custody of two cities, Flushing and Brill, essentially as collateral. Davison symbolically took custody of the keys of Flushing, which on the return trip to England he entrusted to the care of his secretary Brewster—who remembered keeping them under his pillow at night.

The Earl of Leicester was sent to the Netherlands to take command of all military forces in 1586, and there worked closely with Davison. Contrary to Queen Elizabeth's orders, the Earl of Leicester accepted the title of supreme governor general from the Dutch authorities. He sent William Davison back to England to explain. The Dutch had presented Davison with a gold chain to present to Queen Elizabeth, which he also entrusted to the care of young Brewster, who was instructed to wear it as he and Davison proceeded through London to meet with Queen Elizabeth. Davison found the queen in an angry mood, furious at the Earl of Leicester, and she blamed Davison for not opposing and dissuading him. The Earl of Leicester, likewise, became angry at Davison for not persuading the queen hard enough on his behalf.

Somewhat surprisingly, Queen Elizabeth shortly thereafter appointed Davison to the Privy Council, and named him secretary of state. It was a promotion not only for himself, but also his staff—which included William Brewster. But such high positions within a monarchy can be very dangerous, as Davison would soon find out.

Queen Elizabeth's cousin, Mary Queen of Scots, married Henry Stuart in 1565, but later coplotted to have him killed (which was accomplished). However, many of her subjects revolted and she fled to England, where she asked Queen Elizabeth for help. She was jailed instead. From prison, Queen Mary, via smuggled letters, began conspiring to have Queen Elizabeth assassinated. But unbeknownst to Queen Mary, her letters were actually being intercepted and read. The plot discovered, the Privy Council tried her and sentenced her to death. All that was needed was the queen's signature on the execution order. But Queen Elizabeth apparently did not have it in her to execute her cousin. But the public wanted the execution, and the Privy Council wanted it. It was Davison's job to get the queen to concede to the execution. Eventually she did, and Mary was beheaded in 1587. Queen Elizabeth then publicly blamed Davison for carrying out the execution order without further consulting with her—he was imprisoned in the Tower of London, disgraced.

William Brewster, Davison's faithful secretary, was out of a job. He returned to Scrooby Manor about 1588. His father had recently been promoted to postmaster of Scrooby, in addition to being bailiff and receiver; meaning, he was responsible for carrying government mail and dispatches to the neighboring posts. It was probably a busy year for government dispatches—that was the year the Spanish Armada attacked England and was defeated. William's father was aging, so he began handling more and more of the postmaster duties. In June 1590, his father died. William Brewster, now twenty-four years old, went to London to request the position of postmaster be transferred to him. Unfortunately for Brewster, the new postmaster, Sir John Stanhope, had appointed his cousin Samuel Bevercotes to the position before Brewster could secure it for himself. Brewster was desperate for the position, however, and asked William Davison to write a letter on his behalf to the postmaster. With Davison's intercession, Brewster got his job back—a position which paid over £30 per year.[96]

About 1591 or 1592, William Brewster married to a woman named Mary, whose maiden name has not been documented (although plenty of theories have been put into print). Their first child, Jonathan, was born on 19 August 1593. Two other children were born in Scrooby—Patience about 1600, and Fear about 1606.

In March 1603, Queen Elizabeth died. Her successor was James I, the son of Queen Mary of Scots. When King James proceeded from Scotland to London to take the throne, he passed within a few miles of Scrooby, and it is likely that Brewster was present for the procession through Nottinghamshire. The king would later request to buy the manor of Scrooby, but again Sir Edwin Sandys would turn down the offer. In June 1603, Brewster received a pay increase to more than £36 per year.

As King James came to power, he began to reassert the powers of the Church of England, opposing religious reformers such as the Puritans and driving them underground. Richard Clyfton, a preacher at Babworth, a small parish a few miles to the south of Scrooby, had begun giving Puritan sermons, as did John Smyth at a congregation at Gainsborough, ten miles to the east.

About 1606, feeling pressure from the English authorities, Smyth and his congregation left for Amsterdam to seek a safer and more secure place for their church. Clifton and a relatively new pastor, John Robinson, remained in England for the time, but took their new church underground. With William Brewster's help, they began meeting secretly on Sundays at Scrooby Manor.

It was a risky business, and it was not long before the authorities were on to them. In November 1607, church member Gervase Neville was charged with being "one of the sects of Barrowists,

Scrooby Manor, as it appeared in the late 1800s.

or Brownists, holding and maintaining erroneous opinions and doctrine repugnant to the Holy Scriptures and the Word of God," and he was sentenced to the custody of the Castle of York, "not permitting him to have any liberty or conference with any, without special license from three at the least of the said Commissioners." Less than a month later, church member Robert Jackson was served for "disobedience in matters of religion," but he refused to appear in court and was fined £20.[97]

William Brewster, himself, was also discovered. In August 1607, probably feeling some pressure from the authorities, he collected his £73 salary for his past two years as Scrooby postmaster, and then resigned his position, ending his residency at Scrooby and likely ending the church's ability to secretly meet there. Francis Hall, his replacement, was in place by September 30. On 1 December 1607, "Information is given that he [Brewster] is a Brownist or disobedient in manners of religion." Like Jackson, he did not appear when summoned, and was fined £20. When Brewster and Jackson refused to appear, the Court of High Commissions authorized William Blanchard to apprehend them, "but he certifieth that he cannot find them, nor understand where they are." Robert Rochester, another church member, was also on the wanted list.[98]

Remaining in England was no longer an option for the church members. They were being fined, imprisoned, and their estates were being confiscated. The group decided to flee to Holland. On their first attempt to escape, they were lured aboard a ship with promises to be taken to Amsterdam, only to be betrayed to the authorities in Boston, co. Lincolnshire. Ransacked, stripped of their money, books, and goods, they were then imprisoned. Most were freed shortly thereafter, but "seven of the principal were still kept in prison and bound over to the assizes." The records of this do not exist, but presumably William Brewster was among the principals.

Their second escape attempt met with disaster as well. A Dutch ship master offered to provide transportation, but as some of the men were boarding the ship, a great company of officers "both horse and foot, with bills and guns and other weapons" approached. The Dutch ship master panicked and fled the scene, taking some of the men with him but leaving behind the women and children. For the men trapped onboard the ship, their last sight of England consisted of watching their wives and children onshore being rounded up and arrested. After being passed from jurisdiction to jurisdiction, the women and children were eventually released and were able to make it over to their husbands in Amsterdam.

By August 1608, the majority of the congregation had made itself to Amsterdam. However, the new arrivals were not particularly pleased with some of the newly professed religious beliefs of John Smyth, who was turning his Amsterdam congregation more toward Anabaptism. Fearing too close of an association, Pastor John Robinson and William Brewster, in February 1609, led their congregation south to another Dutch city, Leiden. Pastor Richard Clyfton, then an old man, decided his days as preacher were done, and retired in Amsterdam.

During the first few years in Leiden, William Brewster was active in helping the congregation get settled. He took guardianship of a girl, Ann Peck, apparently his niece, on 12 June 1609; and about a week later, on 20 June 1609, he buried an unnamed child (presumably an infant). Five days after that, he signed a receipt for some cloth. In 1610 and 1611, he witnessed the betrothals of church members William Pontus, William Bassett, Randall Thickens, and William Buckram. At some point (it is not clear exactly when), he became the church's elder, the highest position in the Leiden church underneath Pastor John Robinson.

Somewhere around 1616, William Brewster, with assistance from Thomas Brewer, Edward Winslow, and others, established a printing press. Brewster started out printing fairly innocuous books, such as John Dod's *Exposition on the Ten Commandments* translated into Dutch, but over the next two years he became more involved in printing tracts that were illegal in England, which he had smuggled into the country. In July 1619, Brewster's publishing of *Perth Assembly* got him into some hot water. The English ambassador to the Netherlands, Sir Dudley Carleton, undertook an investigation and discovered William Brewster was behind it. But Brewster could not then be found—he was rumored to have returned to London. And those of London had heard he had returned to Leiden. Some thought he spent most of his time in Amsterdam. Others thought he was at Middleburg. Some thought he had gone to live at Leiderdorp. Brewster managed to avoid detection. His copartner, Thomas Brewer, was not so lucky; and in September 1619, he was arrested and placed in the prison of Leiden University. The printing press and types were found and confiscated. Brewster was out of business.

But the printing business was not the only activity Brewster was engaged in. Beginning in 1617, he initiated contact with Sir Edwin Sandys, the son of his old Scrooby landlord, Archbishop of York Edwin Sandys. Sir Edwin Sandys happened to be a leading member of the Virginia Company of London; in 1619, he would become the treasurer. The Leiden congregation wanted to remove to America, and they hoped the Virginia Company would help. Brewster made a couple of trips to London, but much of the business was carried out by church deacons John Carver and Robert Cushman. By 1619, Brewster had to keep a very low profile—he was, after all, wanted by English authorities. Robert Cushman, in a letter sent to the Leiden church, dated 8 May 1619, mentioned that "Mr. B. is not well at this time; whether he will come back to you or go into the north, I yet know not."

Somehow he quietly boarded the *Mayflower*, and arriving in America he was finally outside the reach of English authorities. He brought with him on the ship his wife Mary, and his two youngest sons, Love and Wrestling; also in his custody were Richard and Mary More, young children whose father had disposed of them after a bitter divorce, to prevent them from inheriting any of his estate. Brewster left his eldest son Jonathan and daughters Fear and Patience with the church in Leiden. Jonathan would come a year later on the ship *Fortune* in 1621, and his daughters Patience and Fear would come in 1623 on the ship *Anne*.

Brewster and the church were still somewhat unsure how far England might go in trying to arrest him if they discovered he was at Plymouth, so in the earliest publications and letters from New Plymouth, he is dubbed "Master Williamson" to conceal his identity; he was likewise referred to as Master Williamson in the first probate record signed at Plymouth. But the pseudonym would not last long— apparently, the English lost interest in pursuing him. As early as 1624, Captain John Smith had published Brewster's name in print as being the elder of the church at Plymouth.

William Brewster was one of the first signers of the Mayflower Compact, drawn up immediately after anchoring off Cape Cod on 11 November 1620. He did not participate in any of the early explorations of Plymouth, perhaps due to his age—he was then fifty-four years old—or perhaps due to his status as Church elder.

During the first winter at Plymouth, when more than half the colonists died from scurvy and pneumonia, William Brewster was one of only a few men who actually stayed healthy the whole time. He, along with Captain Standish, helped attend to the needs of the weaker colonists, performing all the "necessary offices . . . which dainty and queasy stomachs cannot endure to hear named."

When the Plymouth colonists had their first meeting with the Indian leader Massasoit in March 1621, William Brewster and Captain Myles Standish were the two men who met him at the brook, and escorted him to the house of Governor Carver. Brewster, as the highest ranking church member at Plymouth, led the Sunday services and attended to the congregation's needs. The Pilgrims kept church and state separate, so while Elder Brewster may have been called upon to provide religious opinions and interpretations to the governors, he was never in a position of political power and was not allowed to hold elective office in Plymouth's government.

From the earliest days, Plymouth had two streets, initially just called "the street" and "the highway." Brewster's house was located on the southeast corner where the street and highway intersected. He received six acres in the 1623 division of land "on the south side of the brook to the baywards." His son Jonathan, a passenger on the *Fortune* in 1621, received an acre "beyond the first brook to the wood westward." And his daughters Patience and Fear received two acres "beyond the brook to Strawberry Hill." Mary Brewster, William's wife, died in April 1627, at the age of about sixty. In the 1627 division of cattle, William Brewster and his children, joined by Henry Samson, Humility Cooper, and the Prence family, received "one of the four heifers came in the *Jacob* called the Blind Heifer and 2 she-goats."

On 10 April 1624, William Brewster's son Jonathan married Lucretia Oldham, sister of John Oldham. Not long after the marriage, John Oldham conspired with Rev. John Lyford in an attempt to overthrow the Plymouth Church (and William Brewster, the elder), hoping to establish a church at Plymouth that was more in line with the Church of England. The attempt failed and led to Oldham and Lyford's banishment from Plymouth Colony. Lucretia Oldham, no doubt, was in an awkward position, with her brother expelled from Plymouth for attempting to disrupt the church that was led by her father-in-law.

Jonathan Brewster's marriage was not the only one in Brewster's family that would cause tension. William Brewster's daughter Fear married long-time church member Isaac Allerton. At the time of their marriage, about 1626, Isaac was assistant governor under William Bradford. Isaac began making trips back and forth to England on company business beginning about 1627, and soon found himself intertwining personal business with company business—to the point that there was a substantial conflict of interest. He even went so far, apparently, as to use his father-in-law Brewster's name to secure personal loans for himself—debts the colony and Brewster would eventually be saddled with when Allerton's schemes failed to return the expected profits. Isaac's detrimental business tactics were overlooked by the leading members of Plymouth for much longer than they would normally have done, because they were afraid to bring up anything that might grieve their beloved reverend elder.

William Brewster lived to a fairly old age for his time, dying on 10 April 1644, just short of eighty years. Bradford noted: "His sickness was not long, and till the last day thereof, he did not wholly keep his bed; his speech continued till somewhat more than half a day, and then failed him, and about 9 or 10 o'clock that evening he died, without any pangs at all; a few hours before, he drew his breath short, and some few minutes before his last, he drew his breath long, as a man fallen into a sound sleep, without any pangs or gaspings, and so sweetly departed this life, unto a better one."

As might be expected from a former book printer and church elder, William Brewster had amassed a very sizeable library—in fact, it was undoubtedly the largest in early New England. According to his estate inventory[99], it included at least sixty-four books written in Latin, mostly religious texts by such men as Calvin, Beza, Cartwright, Erasmus, and Musculus. He had more than four hundred books in English, again primarily theological texts, though he owned plenty of nontheological texts as well. He had Dodoen's *New Herbal*, the works of Seneca, an unusual book entitled *A Thousand Notable Things of Sundry Sorts* (the *Ripley's Believe It or Not* of the seventeenth century), a book on how to use silk worms, a German history, John Smith's *Description of New England*, the *Catalogue of Nobility*, *News from Virginia*, *Sufficiency of English Medicines*, Abbot's *Brief Description of the Whole World*, and Bodin's *Six Books on the Commonwealth* (a book on politics), among others. In 1890, Dr. Henry Dexter attempted to catalog and classify each of the books. He concluded that the library consisted of ninety-eight expository works, sixty-nine practical religious texts, sixty-three doctrinal works, fifty-four miscellaneous texts, thirty-six ecclesiastical works, twenty-four historical works, fourteen poetical works, and six philosophical works.[100] Some were duplicates and some were unidentifiable. More than three-fourths were published before 1620, so it is likely he brought a sizeable number of the books with him on the *Mayflower*.

Outside of books, Brewster's estate inventory included clothing (stockings, waistcoats, including a green one, blue cloth suit, black coat, green drawers, leather drawers, black suit and cloak, doublet, black hat, gloves, red cap, laced cap, quilted cap, and shoes); bedding (feather bed and bolster; sheets, pillows, blankets); a pistol; rugs; curtains and valence; cushions; several chests; a chamber pot; tools (hammer, bellows, tongs); pewter cups and earthen pots; scissors; lamp and candlesticks; "a brass hook to hang a hat upon"; tables and chairs; tobacco, several tobacco cases, and some pipes; sugar; and some silver. His livestock included an old and young pair of oxen, a two-year-old steer, eight cattle, and three pigs.

RICHARD BRITTERIDGE

Richard Britteridge is enumerated on William Bradford's list of *Mayflower* passengers, in a section that indicates he was an adult male, as opposed to an indentured servant or child. The fact he was an adult is further substantiated by the fact he was listed as one of the signers of the Mayflower Compact on 11 November 1620. Bradford simply lists a group of adult men, including Richard Britteridge, followed by the statement "All these died soon after their arrival in the general sickness that befell . . . [they] left no posterity here."

Richard Britteridge's exact death date was 21 December 1620, a date captured by Thomas Prince in his *Chronological History of New England*, published in 1736. One of Prince's sources for his *History* was a "Register of Births and Deaths," in the hand of Governor William Bradford—a register which unfortunately no longer exists, having disappeared around the time of the Revolutionary War.

Richard Britteridge was therefore one of the six colonists who died in December, at the very beginning of the general sickness that would eventually kill more than half the Pilgrims—most of whom died much later, in February and March.

With only a name to work with, it is very difficult to conclusively prove an English origin. However, the name Richard Britteridge is very uncommon. Therefore, it is entirely possible that the Richard Brightridge baptized on 31 December 1581 at Crowhurst, co. Sussex[101], could be the *Mayflower* passenger. No other Richard Britteridge baptisms have been found in England during the appropriate time period. This Richard Brightridge was the son of Anthony Brightridge. The only other apparent sibling of Richard was one John Brightridge, baptized on 22 February 1579, and buried on 27 January 1580 at Crowhurst.

PETER BROWNE

Mayflower passenger Peter Browne was baptized on 26 January 1594/5 in Dorking, Surrey, England—the same hometown as another *Mayflower* family, the Mullinses. My discoveries relating to his English origins were published in July 2004 in *The American Genealogist*[102], and are only summarized here.

Peter Browne was the son of William Browne of Dorking, and had two older siblings, Jane and Thomas, and three younger brothers, Samuel, John, and James. When Peter was just ten years old, his father William died, so the children were likely apprenticed out to relatives, neighbors, or family friends. The three youngest children, Samuel, John, and James, all became weavers, so probably they were apprenticed out to a local weaver.

Mayflower passenger William Mullins was a fairly successful shoe and boot maker in Dorking, and he was one of the Londoners who was involved in supporting and investing in the Pilgrims' joint-stock company. Peter Browne likely learned of the voyage through a connection with the Mullins family. Peter Browne's sister Jane was married to John Hammon in Dorking in 1610. John Hammon's mother Jane appointed William Mullins as the administrator of her estate. And John's sister Susan married Ephraim Bothell, to whom William Mullins sold his house and lands prior to his voyage on the *Mayflower*. So, there indeed are social and family connections between Peter Browne and the Mullins family in Dorking.

The twenty-five-year-old single man Peter Browne, perhaps just emerging from an apprenticeship, boarded the *Mayflower* with the Mullins family, and headed off to the New World. After sighting land and anchoring off the tip of Cape Cod, Peter Browne was one of the men who signed the Mayflower Compact on 11 November 1620.

Toward the end of December 1620, the Pilgrims had finally decided upon where to settle, and in early January they began constructing their settlement. On January 12, Peter Browne, John Goodman, and two other men had gone into the woods about a mile and a half from the plantation, to gather and cut thatch for the houses. After noon, Peter Browne and John Goodman headed further into the woods, while the two other men remained behind to bundle up the thatch. After the men were done tying the thatch, they followed after Browne and Goodman, but were not able to find them anywhere. They returned to the colony to inform the others. Two search parties were sent out that afternoon and evening, but failed to find the two lost men.

As it turned out, Peter Browne and John Goodman had gone to a small lake to eat lunch, when their two dogs, a mastiff and a spaniel, saw and began chasing after a deer. The men ran after the dogs, and soon were disoriented and completely lost. According to the report, "they wandered all that afternoon being wet, and at night it did freeze and snow, they were slenderly appareled and had no weapons but each one his sickle," and they had no food either. As night fell, they thought they heard lions in the forest, so they climbed a tree for shelter—only to find that it was far colder off the ground. So, they huddled around the roots of the tree, ready to climb up at a moment's notice. The next day, after much aimless wandering, they finally got the idea to climb up the highest hill they could find, which having done, they were able to spot the harbor and reorient themselves for the trek home, where they arrived sore, frost-bitten, and famished, but alive.

In a 1620 sketch of the Plymouth house locations, it is apparent that Peter Browne and John Goodman were neighbors, with Peter Browne's house being the closest to the bay on the south side of the street, though the storehouse neighbored him closer yet to the bay. Peter Browne received one acre of land in the 1623 division of land, "on the south side of the brook to the baywards."

Shortly after the division of land, Peter Browne married the widow Martha Ford, who had come as one of the only women onboard the ship *Fortune*, arriving in November 1621. Her husband apparently died on the voyage, or shortly after arrival; Martha herself gave birth the day after arrival. By the 1627 division of cattle, Peter Browne and Martha had a child of their own, Mary, and she was pregnant with another daughter, Priscilla. Also in the household were Peter's stepchildren, John and Martha Ford. In the division of cattle, they were joined by the Fuller and Annable families, and received "a red heifer came of the cow which belongeth to the poor of the colony" and two female goats.

Around 1630, Peter's wife Martha died, and Peter remarried to a woman named Mary, whose maiden name and parentage have not been discovered. With his second wife, he had two more children, Rebecca about 1631, and another child about 1633 whose name is not known and who died before reaching adulthood.

Peter Browne's health appears to have become a problem in late 1632. On January 1 and 2, he was fined by the Plymouth Colony Court for failing to appear at the court session. When he did appear on January 7, he was sued by his neighbor, Dr. Samuel Fuller, for "divers accounts . . . wherein they differ." They were sent to arbitration, which was overseen by Robert Hicks and Francis Cooke; the outcome was not recorded. Peter Browne died later that year, probably in early autumn. His estate inventory was taken on 10 October 1633. His inventory shows a debt to the widow of Dr. Samuel Fuller for one peck of malt and some purgative, and a debt for "letting her man bleed." Purgatives and blood-letting were two of the techniques that seventeenth-century doctors used to rebalance the body's four humors—which they presumed were the cause of most illnesses. Peter's estate also owed Kenelm Winslow twelve shillings for building the coffin.

Peter Browne's estate inventory shows that he owned at his death 130 bushels of corn, six milch goats, eight sheep (five of which were young lambs), ten swine, and one heifer. Among the inventoried items were his fowling piece and twelve ounces of shot, a mortar and pestle, several axes, spades and hoes, a handsaw, chisel, a featherbed, a suit of clothes and a cloak, pillows and blankets, kettles, reap hooks, candlesticks, iron and brass pots and pans, pewter cup, an old chest, Irish stockings, gridiron, two pairs of shoes, a "smoothing iron," a Bible, six table napkins, and a cradle.

Following his death, the widow Mary received custody of her two biological children, but Peter Browne's two daughters by his first marriage, Mary and Priscilla, were apprenticed out to John Doane and William Gilson, respectively, until they turned seventeen years old. When the two girls turned seventeen, they requested the Plymouth Court assign their custody over to their uncle, John Brown, a weaver then living in Duxbury, the town immediately to the north of Plymouth.

WILLIAM BUTTEN

William Butten's voyage on the *Mayflower* must have been a miserable one. He was "a youth," and had come as an indentured servant to Samuel Fuller, a long-time member of the Leiden church and the person appointed to be the doctor for the colonists. The fact he was a young indentured servant would typically indicate that his father had died while he was young, and his mother had been unable to financially care for him.

Butten was presumably sick for a good portion of the two-month voyage on the *Mayflower*, and died on November 6—just three days before Cape Cod was sighted.[103] William Bradford recorded "in all this voyage there died but one of the passengers, which was William Butten, a youth, servant to Samuel Fuller, when they drew near the coast."

Searching for the English origins of William Butten is complicated by the fact he died so young, and so little is known about him to begin with. Since he was the indentured servant of Samuel Fuller, a long-time member of the Leiden congregation, it could be speculated that the Butten family somehow had a connection with the early Separatists. Thus, the William Butten baptized on 13 March 1605 at Worksop, Nottinghamshire, son of John, would seem to be a very real possibility.[104] Worksop, Nottinghamshire, was one of the parishes where the early Separatist church developed, and several Leiden church members had connections there. Not far away is Austerfield, Yorkshire, where William Bradford was born and raised; and in that parish there was also a William Butten baptized on 12 September 1589, but that date is far too early to have been the "youth" that traveled to America.

ROBERT CARTER

Robert Carter was an apprentice or manservant belonging to *Mayflower* passenger William Mullins. Since Robert Carter did not sign the Mayflower Compact in November 1620, he was almost certainly under the age of twenty-one at the time. Since he was a servant to William Mullins of Dorking, Surrey, it would be reasonable to speculate that Carter came from this vicinity as well. Although no conclusive link or identification has yet been made, it is interesting and worthwhile to note that a Thomas Carter married a Jane Bothell in Dorking on 3 April 1648. Jane Bothell was the daughter of Ephraim Bothell, to whom William Mullins sold his house and manor holdings in 1619 before he left to come on the *Mayflower*. Perhaps this Thomas Carter is a relative in some way to the Robert Carter who came on the *Mayflower*.

Robert Carter's master William Mullins died the first winter in Plymouth on 21 February 1620/1. In Mullins's will, he instructs his overseers "to have a special eye to my man Robert which hath not so approved himself as I would he should have done.[105]" Presumably, then, Robert Carter was old enough to have had such a judgment cast upon him; probably an older teenager. The overseers would not need to look after Robert for very long: he died shortly thereafter, another casualty of the first winter.

JOHN CARVER

AND HIS WIFE KATHERINE (WHITE)

The early years of John Carver, the first governor of the Plymouth Colony, are very sketchy at best. Charles Banks, in 1929, suggested he may have been the John Carver, son of Robert, baptized at Doncaster, Yorkshire, England, on 9 September 1565, but this is only a guess.[106] In fact, the name "John Carver" is common enough that there are dozens of other potential candidates, and a birth year of 1565 seems too early for a man who apparently buried an infant child in 1617. The parish of Doncaster is, however, in the same vicinity as Austerfield and the other small parishes that eventually gave rise to the Separatist church that would eventually flee to Holland and then to America.

Jeremy D. Bangs noted in 1996 that John Carver appears to have joined communion with the French Walloon church in Leiden, Holland, on 8 February 1609, with wife Mary de Lannoy of L'Escluse, France.[107] The English separatists were not the only reformed church that was fleeing their home country to take up life in Holland: so were the French Huguenots. Perhaps John Carver's early years in Leiden were more in pattern with that of *Mayflower* passenger Francis Cooke, who also took communion with the French church in Leiden with his French wife Hester Mahieu before they finally established themselves as part of the later-arriving English congregation of Pastor John Robinson. Francis and Hester also spent time at Norwich, co. Norfolk, where there was also a sizeable Huguenot population at the time. John Carver's wife Mary is presumably a relative of Philip de Lannoy, son of Jan de Lannoy and Marie Mahieu. Philip came to Plymouth in 1621 on the ship *Fortune*, a year after the *Mayflower*.

Leiden records indicate that John Carver buried a child on 10 July 1609 at St. Pancras, about five months after taking communion in the French church.[108] Since he was married and had a child in 1609, we can estimate he was probably born sometime before 1584, but that is about the best that can be determined about his age. Sometime shortly thereafter, his wife Mary died.

It was not until John Carver married Katherine White, one of the more prominent women in the English separatist church at Leiden, that he began to come on record as a member of the English congregation located there. John Carver's marriage to Katherine gave him kinship with many of the leaders and prominent members of the Leiden congregation. Katherine was the daughter of Alexander White of Sturton-le-Steeple, Nottinghamshire; her sister Bridget was married to the Leiden congregation's pastor John Robinson. Her other siblings were also married to active Leiden church members: sister Jane was married to Randall Thickens, sister Frances was married to Francis Jessop, and brother Roger White was also a prominent Leiden church member. The exact marriage date of John Carver and Katherine White is not recorded, but Katherine Carver was a witness to the betrothal of Roger Chandler and Isabella Chilton on 22 May 1615 in Leiden, so it was clearly sometime before this point.[109] Shortly thereafter, John Carver makes his first appearance in the records as a member of the Leiden congregation, witnessing the betrothal of Henry Wilson and Elizabeth Nicholas on 13 May 1616. Then, Katherine witnessed the betrothal of Robert Cushman and Mary Singleton on 19 May 1617.[110]

Robert Cushman was a deacon of the church in Leiden, and shortly after his marriage in 1617, he and John Carver were sent to London by the Leiden congregation on an important task: negotiate with the Virginia Company for a grant of land in Virginia under which they could govern themselves under English law, yet be free to follow their religious consciences. One of the first people they contacted was Sir Edwin Sandys, a leading member of the Virginia Company, and an acquaintance of the Leiden congregation's church elder, William Brewster. In order to begin the process, Carver and Cushman put together for the council for Virginia a series of seven articles, signed by all the leading church members, intended to allay the fears and objections of some of the council who opposed officially supporting religious dissidents such as these "Brownists" from Leiden. The articles included statements acknowledging the king as the supreme governor, acknowledging his power to appoint bishops to oversee the churches, and assenting "wholly" to the published "Confession of Faith by the Church of England." Sir Edwin Sandys wrote back to Pastor John Robinson and Elder William Brewster that Carver and Cushman "carried themselves" with "good discretion."

A day after Edwin Sandy's letter, John Carver's wife buried a child, presumably an infant, on 11 November 1617 at St. Pancras in Leiden. [111] Back in England, Carver and Cushman continued their intensive negotiations, and by late 1618 they had finally secured a patent under the name of John Wincop. Though they could never get King James to formally recognize their right to practice their religious beliefs unmolested, at least they did get his private assurance that he would not meddle with them.

With patent in hand, the Leiden congregation's next hurdle was to find some way to pay the enormous costs involved in transporting hundreds of church members to the New World, and supplying them with all their needs. The church was poor enough as it was, with most of its members having taken up low-paying, labor-intensive jobs in Holland's textile industry: weaving, combing wool, making hats, and selling fabrics.

Leiden church member Edward Pickering was from the London area, and in Leiden he was acting as an agent for an English merchant by the name of Thomas Weston. Weston, always on the lookout for some kind of profitable business scheme, decided he could help the would-be Pilgrims. He would organize a group of London merchants into a joint-stock company that would fund the voyage and supply the colonists. Each colonist would be required to buy at least one share in the company—assuring that the colonists had a financial stake in the company. The merchants would also buy shares. The colonists would work for seven years in the employ of the company, trading for furs, and shipping back some of the natural resources of the New World such as lumber and fish. At the end of the seven years, the company would be liquidated, and the profits distributed amongst all the shareholders.

Once again, the Leiden congregation called upon John Carver and Robert Cushman to negotiate the details of the business arrangements with Thomas Weston. By June 1620, John Carver was in charge of purchasing supplies in Southampton for the voyage. Money was extremely tight, and in the end they had to sell off some of their less-critical supply of butter and oil to be able to clear port.

With about 130 passengers combined onboard two ships, the *Mayflower* and the *Speedwell,* the Pilgrims attempted to depart from Southampton on 5 August 1620. They were forced in to Dartmouth on account of the leaking *Speedwell.* The ship was fixed, and they embarked again about August 23, only to be forced back to Plymouth once more on account of the leaky ship.[112] It was eventually decided to leave the *Speedwell* behind, send about twenty passengers home, and combine everyone else together onto just one ship, the *Mayflower.*

John Carver had invested a significant amount of his own personal estate into the voyage and joint-stock company, and as a result was able to transport a significant number of indentured servants that were joined to his family: Desire Minter, a teenage girl from the Leiden congregation whose father had died; two man-servants, John Howland and Roger Wilder; a young eleven-year-old boy, William Latham; another older teenage maidservant named Dorothy; and seven-year-old Jasper More, one of the four More children.

They departed England for the last time on 6 September 1620, and anchored off the tip of Cape Cod on 11 November 1620, following a sixty-six-day voyage. John Carver appears to have been elected governor of the ship for the course of the voyage, his counterpart governor on the *Speedwell,* Christopher Martin, having left a bad impression on most of his subjects. Following the signing of the Mayflower Compact, John Carver was "chosen, or rather confirmed" governor of the new civil body politic that had been created. He was probably the author of the compact itself, and was also its first signer.

The *Mayflower* passengers, now anchored off Cape Cod, set out several expeditions to search out a place where they could build their colony. Carver, as governor, apparently did not go on the first two expeditions in November, but on December 6, he was among eighteen men who volunteered to undertake the third and final exploration to seek out a place to settle. They set forth, "but it was very cold, for the water froze on our clothes, and made them many times like coats of iron." Along the way they saw some Indians carving up a large fish on shore, but there was no chance to meet with them. They found what appeared to be a burial ground, and dug up a few graves, hoping to find Indian corn buried there—they had found Indian corn buried on an earlier expedition and were hopeful to find some more. They made a small rendezvous near modern-day Eastham, and spent the night.

In the early morning, as they were getting ready for their predawn breakfast, they were attacked by the Nauset Indians. The Nauset had brutally killed a French crew in 1617, in retaliation for wrongs done by Englishman Thomas Hunt in 1614 when he kidnapped twenty-four natives and sold them into slavery in Malaga, Spain—they thought the Pilgrims had come to avenge the deaths of the Frenchmen. The Indians did not understand the difference between Englishman and Frenchman, any more than the English understood the difference between the various native groups. The fact the Pilgrims dug up a few graves and stole some of the Indian corn that had been buried in the ground to preserve it for next year's planting time, certainly did not help their cause in establishing peaceful relations. Nobody was injured in the skirmish, however, and the Pilgrims continued on around the cape, leaving behind the angry Nauset and traveling into Plymouth Harbor and spending the next night on Clark's Island, as well as the following day, which was the Sabbath (they did not perform any work on Sunday to honor the Sabbath). After a brief look around Plymouth Harbor, they decided it was good enough—winter was coming on fast, supplies were getting low, and they had seen no better option. They returned to the *Mayflower* with the good news: after a month and a half of exploring, they had finally found a place to build their colony.

John Carver would be highly criticized by the merchants back in London for having wasted so much time discussing and consulting. The Pilgrims did not start bringing their supplies ashore and building the first structures until the very end of December—it had taken them two months just to orient themselves and decide where to settle.

They were off to a bad start, and it would only get worse. As the men struggled to build the colony in the rain and snow, the women, children, elderly, and sick remained in the squalid quarters of the *Mayflower* anchored offshore. Illness began to take a heavy toll. On January 6, Christopher Martin, treasurer of the colonists and sometime despised governor of the *Speedwell*, lay sick in his bed on the *Mayflower*. John Carver was called aboard the next morning, and they discussed his accounts. Christopher Martin died on January 8.[113] John

Carver himself was sick in bed on the night of January 13, onshore inside a small storage house that had been constructed, when a spark from the fire suddenly caught the roof on fire: "the most loss was Master Carver's and William Bradford's, who then lay sick in bed, and if they had not risen with good speed, had been blown up with [gun] powder: but through God's mercy they had no harm." By mid-February, the situation had become even more grave; on some days, as many as two or three people were dying. February 21 was just such a day: William White, William Mullins, and two others died.[114] John Carver, along with *Mayflower* ship's surgeon Giles Heale and *Mayflower* master Christopher Jones, drew up and signed the last will and testament of William Mullins.

With half the colonists sick or dead, with all the winter weather that hampered construction, with the accidental fires—what more could possibly go wrong? On February 16, some tools mysteriously disappeared from the woods; and the next day, some Indians stood on a hill overlooking the new settlement, waving and making signals. When the Pilgrims sent some armed men to investigate, they heard "a great noise of many others," but the Indians went into hiding and could not be located.

On March 7, on a day that was "cold, but fair," John Carver and five other men went to the "Great Ponds" just west of their new town, and discovered the area to be "beaten and haunted by deer," and saw good fishing areas and many wildfowl.

By mid-March, the colonists were finally starting to recover their health, but not before half of them had died. Governor John Carver remained reluctant to send away the *Mayflower*; he felt the colonists needed the added security of a ship that could return them home, at least until their health was more assured, and their safety from the Indians more secure. But the *Mayflower*'s presence was not free of charge: they were paying the ship, the crew, and the master by the day; and each day was costing the already cash-strapped joint-stock company more and more money.

On March 16, the Pilgrims were caught off guard as an Indian named Samoset walked right into their colony and welcomed the Pilgrims in broken English. The Pilgrims sat him down and gave him some "strong water" (he had asked for beer, but their supply of beer had long since run out), some biscuit, butter, cheese, pudding, and piece of mallard. He informed the Pilgrims that he was just visiting the area from Mohegan, and that he had learned English from the English ships that fished off the coast there. He told the Pilgrims that the area they had chosen to settle had been abandoned by the Patuxet people after they had been wiped out by a substantial plague, and that their nearest neighbors were led by an Indian named Massasoit. He also informed the Pilgrims that there was another native, named Tisquantum (or "Squanto") who could speak even better English. And he informed them that they were attacked on Cape Cod because the Nauset were angry at the Englishman Thomas Hunt, who had kidnapped twenty-four of their people. Samoset stayed in the house of Stephen Hopkins that night, and the next day he was sent away with a knife, bracelet, and ring, with promises to bring some of Massasoit's men to trade furs.

When Samoset returned with some men to trade, it was the Sabbath, and the Pilgrims refused to trade with them but only sent them away with some small trinkets. By Wednesday, some Indians stood upon a nearby hill, and made threatening gestures, as they "rubbed and whetted their arrows." When pursued, they ran away.

Finally, on March 22, the Pilgrims first met Tisquantum, who acted as a translator for Governor John Carver. The Wampanoag leader Massasoit and his brother Quadequina both paid visits to Governor Carver that day, and they hammered out a peace treaty and mutual protection alliance. The next day, March 23, John Carver was reelected governor of Plymouth, "a man well approved amongst us.[115]"

A tenuous peace with the Indians now established, and the sickness of the first winter apparently ended, John Carver finally saw fit to send the *Mayflower* back home to England. The *Mayflower* departed Plymouth Colony on April 5, and arrived back home on May 6—making the crossing home in nearly half the time.[116] The London merchants would be in for a disappointment: the ship was empty. Where were the furs, where was the lumber, where were the fish? How could the company survive and resupply the colonists if they did not get any profits back from the New World? In large part, they blamed the Pilgrims' leaders, and foremost John Carver. The ship *Fortune* would arrive at Plymouth the following November, with more men for the colony to support and feed that winter, but without any significant resupply of food, supplies, or trading goods.

Also in the ship *Fortune* were a series of letters from angry and frustrated London investors directed at John Carver. He would never see them. Just a week or two after sending away the *Mayflower*, he unexpectedly died.

> In this month of April whilst they were busy about their seed, their Governor (Mr. John Carver) came out of the field very sick, it being a hot day, he complained greatly of his head, and lay down, and within a few hours his senses failed, so as he never spoke more till he died, which was within a few days after: whose death was much lamented, and caused great heaviness amongst them, as there was cause. He was buried in the best manner they could, with some volleys of shot by all that bore arms.

Nathaniel Morton, writing in 1669, added:

> This worthy gentleman was one of singular piety, and rare for humility, as appeared by his great condescendancy, when as this poor people were in great sickness and weakness, he shunned not to do very mean services for them, yea the meanest of them. He bare a share likewise of their labor in his own person, accordingly as their extreme necessity required; who being one also of a considerable estate, spent the main part of it in this enterprise, and from first to last approved himself not only as their agent in the first transacting of things, but also all along to the period of his life, to be a pious, faithful, and very beneficial instrument, and now is reaping the fruit of his labor with the Lord. His wife, who was also a gracious woman, lived not six weeks after him; she being overcome with excessive grief for the loss of so gracious an husband, likewise died.[117]

JAMES CHILTON

AND HIS WIFE, AND DAUGHTER MARY

James Chilton was born about 1556, in Canterbury, Kent, England.[118] He was the son of Lyonel Chilton, and is mentioned in the February 1582 will of his father. Lyonel, in turn, is mentioned in the 1549 will of his father, Richard Chilton, all of Canterbury.[119] James Chilton became a freeman in Canterbury in 1583, and the following year he made an appearance at the Canterbury Quarter Sessions, where he is referred to as a tailor.[120] He married about 1586 or shortly before (based on the baptism date of his first child). The name of his wife has not been discovered. John Hunt suggested his wife was his stepsister, Susanna Furner[121], but more recent research has dispelled this possibility.[122] However, there has been a tradition that James's wife was named Susanna, apparently dating back as far as 1840 in Nahum Mitchell's *History of Bridgewater*, but no primary source has been found to document this. [123]

The parish registers of Canterbury, and later Sandwich, record the baptisms and burials of James Chilton's children. His first two children, Isabella and Jane, were baptized in 1587 and 1589 at St. Paul's, Canterbury. His next five children, Joel, Mary, Elizabeth, James, and Ingle, are enumerated in the parish registers of St. Martin's, Canterbury. On 25 July 1598, James Chilton, tailor, acted as a surety to Richard Allen of St. Paul's, Canterbury, at the West Kent Quarter Sessions Court. [124] About 1600, the Chilton family left Canterbury and took up residence in Sandwich, co. Kent, where daughter Christina was baptized in 1601, son James in 1603, and daughter Mary on 31 May 1607.[125]

Just a couple years after the baptism of Mary, their last child, Mrs. Chilton managed to get herself into trouble with the church authorities.

On 8 May 1609, the "wife of James Chilton," along with Moses Fletcher and several others, were accused of "privately burying a child of Andrew Sharp of St. Mary's parish . . . which they secretly conveyed to the earth without any notice given to me or my clerk . . . which act some of them seem now since to dissent by calling into question the lawfulness of the king's constitutions in this and other behalfs, affirming these things to be popish ceremonies and of no other force."[126] Mrs. Chilton, Thomas Bartlett, and Moses Fletcher were excommunicated from the church on 12 June 1609, which was publicly announced on 1 July 1609.

The family disappears from the records for a time following the excommunication, but appears next in Leiden, Holland, where on 21 July 1615 their eldest daughter Isabella married to Roger Chandler.[127]

James Chilton appears for the first time himself in a Leiden record on 30 April 1619, when he made a statement to the Leiden Remonstrant. He deposed that two days previous, on April 28, he was at a courtyard at Langebrug, when a group of about twenty boys began shouting anti-Arminian slurs, and throwing stones. One stone hit James in the head, injuring him seriously enough that he had to seek the services of town surgeon Jacob Hay. The incident was witnessed by his twenty-two-year old daughter Ingle.[128] Ironically, the Pilgrims' church in Leiden was opposed to Arminianism, so in a sense James was hit by "friendly fire."

James Chilton, his wife, and youngest daughter Mary all came on the *Mayflower*. By the time of the *Mayflower*'s voyage in 1620, James was about sixty-four years old, making him the oldest *Mayflower* passenger; his daughter Mary was about thirteen. Daughters Isabella and Ingle were left behind in Leiden. The whereabouts of his other children remain undiscovered, but several died in infancy.

On 11 November 1620, James Chilton signed the Mayflower Compact. He died less than a month later, on December 8, onboard the *Mayflower* still anchored in what is now Provincetown Harbor. The exploration parties sent out by the Pilgrims would not locate the place they wanted to settle—Plymouth—for another couple weeks. It is not clear when Mrs. Chilton died, but she was also a casualty of the "First Winter," orphaning young daughter Mary. William Bradford recorded of the Chiltons: "James Chilton, and his wife also, died in the first infection."

An ancient tradition, dating to the early eighteenth century, relates that Mary Chilton was the first female to step ashore at Plymouth, upon Plymouth Rock

Plymouth rock, which by tradition was first stepped upon by Mary Chilton, became the stepping stone used by the passengers to come ashore. The rock was cracked in half in 1774 when Plymouth townspeople attempted to move it; the larger half was put on display and the smaller half left in the ground. The date "1620" was carved into it in 1880 when the two pieces were reunited.

Young Mary was probably assigned to the household of Myles Standish, and in the 1623 division of land at Plymouth, sixteen-year-old Mary Chilton received three acres of land situated between John Alden and Myles Standish on the north side of town. By the 22 May 1627 division of cattle at Plymouth, she was married to John Winslow, a younger brother of *Mayflower* passenger Edward Winslow. As they had no children yet, and given her fairly young age—only about twenty—they were probably married earlier that year. John had himself come on the ship *Fortune* to Plymouth in November 1621. John and Mary (Chilton) Winslow were joined in the division of cattle with the Shaw, Adams, Bassett, and Sprague families, and their group's share consisted of the "lesser of the black cows came in the *Anne*, which they must keep with the biggest of the 2 steers." The lot also included two female goats.

John and Mary Winslow continued their lives together in Plymouth for about thirty-five years. Mary had ten children beginning about 1628, with first son John, and continuing with Susanna (c1630), Mary (c1632), Edward (c1636), Sarah (c1639), Isaac (c1641), Joseph (c1643), Samuel (c1646), a child whose name is not known and who died young (c1650), and Benjamin (born 12 August 1653).

Mary's husband John Winslow was taxed eighteen shillings in both the 1633 and 1634 taxes at Plymouth, and is found in the Plymouth section of the 1643 census of men able to bear arms for the colony. During the early 1650s, John held several positions with the Plymouth Court, including deputy, but generally kept himself out of public service, showing more interest in the private sector where he was a fairly successful merchant.

About 1655, Mary and husband John moved to Boston, so that he could continue advancing his trade as a merchant. Over the years, John acquired stakes in two small trading vessels, the *Speedwell* and the *John's Adventure*, and over the course of several decades built up a sizeable estate as a merchant trader.

In John's will of 1673, he gives a large amount of cash to his wife, £400, in addition to their house and household goods. He also mentions "my will is that my Negro girl Jane (after she hath served twenty years from the date hereof) shall be free, and that she shall serve my wife during her live and after my wife's decease she shall be disposed of according to the discretion of my overseers." He gives significant sums of money to his children, grandchildren, brothers, and even gives £5 to a niece and a local widow. And in a somewhat unusual clause, he requests that the remainder of his estate be equally divided amongst his children unless "any extraordinary providence befall them by way of any eminent loss," in which case the overseers of his will were to distribute the money as charity necessitated.

Mary herself died about five years later, in 1679, at Boston, and she left behind a will, dated 31 July 1676, in which "principally I commend my soul into the hands of Almighty God my Creator hoping to receive full pardon and remission of all my sins; and salvation through the alone merits of Jesus Christ my redeemer."

Mary's husband John had willed her the house and lands she lived on "during the term of her natural life," and then it was to pass to eldest son John. But Mary did own all her household goods, along with whatever she may have bought with the £400 she received from her husband. She gave her "great square table" to son John; her best gown and petticoat and silver beer bowl to daughter Sarah; a great silver tankard to grandson William Paine. To daughter Susanna she gave a large cupboard, bedstead, bed, the furniture in the chamber "where I now lie," a small silver tankard, six silver spoons, a case of bottles, and all her remaining wearing apparel. She gave to her grandchild Anna Gray a trunk of linen, and a bedstead, bolster and pillows in "the chamber over the hall," and £10 cash. To granddaughter Mary (of her son Edward) she willed "my largest silver cup with two handles" and to Sarah daughter of Edward she willed "my lesser silver cup with two handles." To Edward's children she willed also six silver spoons. To grandchild Parnell Winslow she gave £5, as she did also for grandchild Chilton Latham. To grandchild Mary Pollard she gave forty shillings, and to granddaughter Mercy Harris she gave "my white rug." To grandchild Susanna Latham she gave "my petticoat with the silk lace," and to "Mary Winslow daughter of my son Joseph" she gave £20. Lastly, she gave £5 to Mr. Thomas Thatcher, pastor of the Third Church of Boston. Everything else was to be equally divided between her children. The inventory of her estate was taken on 29 July 1679, and totaled just over £212.

RICHARD CLARKE

Richard Clarke came on the *Mayflower* as an adult male. William Bradford, in his *Mayflower* passenger list, simply relates that Richard Clarke was one of those who "died soon after their arrival in the general sickness that befell." Aside from his enumeration in Bradford's passenger list, and his signing of the Mayflower Compact on 11 November 1620, and the fact he died the first winter, nothing is known about this passenger. The name "Richard Clarke" is so common in England that it would be next to impossible to ever identify him. He is listed in a section of Bradford's passenger list that suggests he was not a member of the Leiden congregation.

FRANCIS COOKE

AND SON JOHN

Francis Cooke's exact origins have not been discovered. Based on several lines of evidence, his birth year can be pinned to around 1583, which would have made him about thirty-seven years old at the time of the *Mayflower*'s voyage.[129]

He first appears in the historical record on 25 April 1603 in Leiden, Holland, where he was a witness to the betrothal of Raphael Roelandt.[130] Francis Cooke was in Leiden six years prior to the arrival of Pastor John Robinson's congregation, but his reasons for being there are not known. It was there at the French Walloon Church in Leiden, on 30 June 1603, that he was betrothed to Hester Mahieu. Hester was a French Protestant, or Walloon, whose family had fled from the vicinity of Lille, France, to England, where Hester was born sometime during the late 1580s; then, about 1590, the family moved to Leiden. Hester was officially admitted to the Walloon church in Leiden on 1 June 1603, a month before her betrothal to Francis. A year or two later, Francis and Hester had their first child, Jane, probably named after Hester's mother.

Mary Mahieu, probably a sister of Hester, married Jan de Lannoy in Leiden. Francis Cooke witnessed the baptism of their child, Philip de Lannoy, on 6 November 1603 in Leiden. Philip "Delano" would later join up with the English Separatist church, and would come to Plymouth in 1621 on the ship *Fortune*.

In August 1606, Francis and Hester left Leiden and went to Norwich, co. Norfolk, England. This might very well be where Francis Cooke originated, but nothing conclusive has been found in Norwich records, though there are several men of that name living there throughout the sixteenth century. The Cookes did not remain in Norwich for long, however. Their son John was baptized at the Walloon Church in Leiden between January and March 1607, and the couple was received back into communion in Leiden on 1 January 1608. Later that year, on May 20, Francis and Hester buried a child, name not recorded, at the Pieterskirk. A year later, in February 1609, the English Separatist church led by Pastor John Robinson arrived in Leiden. The Cookes did not immediately become members. Their daughter Elizabeth was baptized on 26 December 1611 at the Walloon church. But sometime shortly thereafter, they appear to have joined up with the Leiden congregation. Hester's sister Francoise married Daniel Cricket, a woolcomber from Sandwich, England, on 10 June 1611 in Leiden. Daniel was likely a member of Robinson's congregation. Since the Leiden congregation also consisted of a number of Separatists who had fled from Norwich, it is possible Francis and Hester may have had some contacts with some of the members of the English church.

Francis and Hester's next children, Jacob, Hester, and Mary, are not found in the baptism records of the Walloon church, suggesting that the couple had probably joined to the English congregation sometime shortly after 1611.

When the English Separatist church in Leiden, led by Pastor John Robinson, decided to remove to America, Francis Cooke decided it was best to bring just himself and his eldest son, thirteen-year-old John, opting to leave his wife and younger children behind in Leiden until the colony was better established and more secure.

Upon arrival at Cape Cod, Francis Cooke was one of those who signed the Mayflower Compact on 11 November 1620. He is not mentioned in any of the accounts of the explorations of Cape Cod and Plymouth that took place in November and December. But on Friday, February 16, someone who was out hunting for geese spied about twelve Indians walking toward Plymouth. He returned quickly to the town and gave the alarm. It was the first sighting of Indians near Plymouth since the Pilgrims had started building their colony back in late December. Francis Cooke and Captain Myles Standish had been out working in the woods when the alarm was given, so they left their tools and returned home quickly.

Men working with tools in an orchard. Woodcut from Gervase Markham's *A New Orchard* (London, 1631).

After a while, when there appeared to be no danger and no more Indians were seen, Cooke and Standish went back to retrieve their tools, only to find them missing. They would not get their tools back until late March, when the Indians Samoset and Tisquantum ("Squanto") eventually helped broker a peace treaty between the Pilgrims and the neighboring Wampanoag led by Massasoit.

Francis Cooke's house plot assigned in 1620 was located on the west side of the highway, on the south side of the street, between the houses of Isaac Allerton and Edward Winslow. His wife and children came to him in July 1623 aboard the ship *Anne*. In the division of land in 1623, he received two acres, one for himself and one for son John "on the south side of the brook to the baywards," while also receiving four acres "beyond the brook to Strawberry Hill" for his wife and children who came on the *Anne*. In the 1627 division of cattle at Plymouth, he is named, along with his wife and children John, Jacob, Jane, Hester, and Mary. Their share in the division consisted of "the

least of the 4 black heifers [that] came in the *Jacob*, and two she goats."
Included in their family were nephew Philip Delano; another Leidenite,
Dutchman Moses Simonson ("Simmons"); and several single men,
including Experience Mitchell, John Faunce, and Phineas and Joshua
Pratt. Very shortly after the division of cattle, Francis's eldest child,
daughter Jane, would marry Experience Mitchell.

On 3 January 1627/8, Francis Cooke was one of the six men named
to lay out the boundaries for the twenty-acre land grants that would
be made to everyone who came as a planter under the employ of the
joint-stock company: a duty for which he was to receive a peck of
corn for every share of land he surveyed and laid out.[131]

Francis Cooke would live the last forty-three years of his life at
Plymouth. Throughout his fifties and sixties, Francis held a number
of public-service positions, but never had any significant forays into
government or politics. In 1633 and 1634, he was taxed eighteen shillings
and nine shillings respectively, indicating he and his family were on the
lower end of the wealth spectrum in early Plymouth, but certainly self-
sufficient. In early 1633, he was called upon by the court to help arbitrate
a financial dispute between Peter Brown and Dr. Samuel Fuller.[132]

He was regularly employed as a surveyor by the Plymouth Court.
In 1634, he was one of seven men from Plymouth appointed to lay
out the highways.[133] In 1637, Francis Cooke was again appointed, with
eleven others, to "lay forth such highways about the towns of
Plymouth, Duxbury, and the Eel River equally and justly, without
respect of persons, and according as they shall be directed by
information of others, and as God should direct them in their discretion
for the general good of the colony, and with as little prejudice to any
man's particular as may be, and to mark the trees upon the said way,
and so it to remain a way forever.[134]" Francis Cooke and the others
performed their duty, and reported back to the Plymouth Court two
months later. In May 1640, Francis Cooke and son John Cooke were
among the seven men appointed to "view the meadows about Edward
Doty's, and to compute the number of acres, and make report thereof
to the next court.[135]" Later, in October of the same year, Francis Cooke
was appointed to "range the bounds of the land betwixt Mr. Thomas
Prence and Clement Briggs at Jones River.[136]" In 1640/1, he was one of
twelve men appointed by the court to lay out some additional
highways, and to more formally survey and mark the bounds of certain

land plots in the town of Plain Dealing.[137] The next year, he was appointed to survey the highway for Jones River, and was designated one of four surveyors for Plymouth.[138] He held the position of surveyor of highways again in 1645.[139]

Even when Francis Cooke was nearly seventy years old, he was still participating in highway surveys. In June 1650, he and twelve others reported to the Plymouth Court "we have found out and marked a new way from Jones River to the Massachusetts Path through John Rogers his ground, and are all agreed the said way by us marked out to be the most convenient and least prejudicial.[140]" And if that were not enough, at nearly seventy-seven years old, he was called upon once more by the Plymouth Court to be an arbitrator in a land boundary dispute between Thomas Pope and William Shurtliff in August 1659.[141]

Surveying and laying out highways appears to have been a special interest or skill of Francis Cooke, but he did perform a few other civil-service duties as well. He was on several petty and grand juries, for example. In 1638, he was on the jury that found Edward Shaw guilty of felony theft for stealing fifteen shillings from William Corvannell. The jury's sentence for Edward Shaw: a severe whipping, and then to be burned on the shoulder with a hot iron. Mark Mendlove, an accomplice, was also sentenced to a whipping. Three civil lawsuits were also heard by this jury, but in all cases the defendants were exonerated, and the plaintiffs were required to pay damages and court costs. He also served on the juries hearing civil cases at the September and December 1639, March 1640, June and September 1642, and March 1643 court sessions. Most of the civil cases revolved around generic "action of trespass," while others were related to debts or charges of slander.

Being on the grand jury was perhaps a little more action filled: that was the "grand inquest" jury who decided which people would get charged with crimes, both misdemeanors and felonies, at the next court session. Francis Cooke was on four grand juries: 1638, 1640, 1642, and 1643. At the 1638 grand jury, for example, Francis Cooke and John Cooke, along with twenty other jurors, decided the following individuals should be tried at the court: Webb Adey for working in his garden on the Lord's Day and for "disorderly living in idleness and nastiness"; John Holmes and Giles Rickard for keeping their swine un-ringed; *Mayflower* passenger William Latham for "entertaining of John Phillips into his house contrary to the act of the court"; *Mayflower* passenger Stephen Hopkins for selling beer and wine for twice as much as it was worth; and William Reynolds for drunkenness.[142]

Perhaps the most gruesome duty performed by Francis Cooke as a part of his public service was being on a coroner's jury, sworn in by Governor Bradford on 22 July 1648. It was this coroner jury's duty to "make inquiry of the death of the child of Alice Bishop, the wife of Richard Bishop." The coroner's jury, which also included John Cooke, made the following report:

> We declare, that coming into the house of the said Richard Bishop, we saw at the foot of a ladder which leadeth into an upper chamber, much blood; and going up all of us into the chamber, we found a woman child, of about four years of age, lying in her shift upon her left cheek, with her throat cut with divers gashes crossways, the wind pipe cut and struck into the throat downward, and a bloody knife lying by the side of the child, and with the said knife all of us judge, and the said Alice hath confessed to five of us at one time, that she murdered the child with the said knife.[143]

The seventeen members of the grand jury agreed that she should be put on trial for murder at the next session of the Plymouth Court. There, in early October 1648, Alice was charged with "felonious murder by her committed, upon Martha Clark, her own child, the fruit of her own body," and was tried by a jury of twelve. She was found guilty, "so she had the sentence of death pronounced against her . . . to be hanged by the neck until her body is dead, which accordingly was executed.[144]"

In 1651, William Bradford wrote that Francis Cooke was "a very old man, and hath seen his children's children have children." A decade after that was written, Francis Cooke began to think about his own mortality. He made out his will on 7 December 1659, calling himself "at present weak and infirm in body." Francis Cooke's will was plain and simple, and fairly unusual for the time: he simply gave everything to "Hester my dear and loving wife."

He still had more than three years left in him, though. In 1662, he was among those granted permission by the Plymouth Court to seek out some additional land, in recognition of being one of the first comers.

Francis Cooke died in the spring of 1663, and an inventory of his estate was taken on 1 May 1663. His entire estate, excluding land and house, amounted to just over £86. In Francis Cooke's kitchen, there was an iron skillet, pot hooks, pewter basin, porrigers, spoons, pewter candleholder, trenchers (plates), mortar and pestle, wooden dishes, brass kettle, wooden pails, warming pan and frying pan, knives, one great chair and three small chairs, a gridiron, fire shovel, and tongs, pot hangers, a table, and earthen pots, among other things. In perhaps a utility room of some kind, he had scissors, a cheese press, two old firkins and some soap, two old baskets and yarn, sieves, and a sifting trough. In some bedrooms he had featherbeds and bolsters, a pound of candles, a cushion, several pairs of sheets, two chests and three boxes, bolsters, pillows, and two old curtains and valence. For clothing he had two hats, a long coat, two short coats, an old coat, two pairs of britches, one pair of drawers, gloves, shoes, four shirts, and eight pairs of stockings. For livestock, he had two mares and a yearling mare, two cows and a calf, a two-year-old and a yearling heifer, and four pigs.

From his estate inventory, it would appear that Francis Cooke was more heavily involved with sheep and wool than many of his fellow Plymouth residents. He had sixteen sheep and five lambs, a "woolen wheele & scales," three pairs of sheep sheers, and twenty pounds of wool.

Francis Cooke's eldest son John came on the *Mayflower* at the age of about thirteen, and was married in Plymouth on 28 March 1634 to Sarah Warren. Sarah had come to Plymouth on the ship *Anne* in 1623, at the age of about ten, with her mother Elizabeth and three sisters. Her father, Richard, had come on the *Mayflower*, but had died in 1628. In 1636, John took on a sixteen-year-old apprentice, Samuel Eaton, who had traveled on the *Mayflower* himself as a "sucking child." Like his father, John Cooke was on several minor committees, and was on several juries. Unfortunately, another man named John Cooke arrived and took up residence in Plymouth in 1633, making it difficult to distinguish the two in many records.

John and Sarah Cooke had five children of record born in Plymouth, namely Sarah (born about 1635), Elizabeth (born about 1640), Hester (born 16 August 1650), Mary (born about 1652), and Mercy (born 25 July 1657). John was probably still in Plymouth in 1659, when he is named as an executor in father Francis Cooke's will, and perhaps even in 1663, when the will was executed. In October 1665, he may have been the John Cooke who, with brother-in-law Nathaniel, was appointed to "treat with Philip the Sagamore about the sale of such lands as are to be sold by him, and to purchase them in the behalf of the country." Philip the Sagamore, sometimes called Metacom, was the son or grandson of Massasoit, and leader of the Wampanoag Indians. He would later be dubbed "King Philip" during the Wampanoag's war he led against the English in 1676. But at that time, John Cooke and Nathaniel Warren simply met with him to discuss buying additional lands for the colony—the Wampanoag and English were still eleven years away from their war.

By 5 June 1667, John Cooke had moved to the town of Dartmouth; on that date, the Plymouth Court noted that "John Cooke was appointed by the Court to solemnize marriage in the town of Dartmouth, and to give oath to witness for the grand inquest and for the trial of causes.[145]" In July, his position was reconfirmed, with additional powers to issue arrest warrants, give subpoenas, and bind people over for trial. John Cooke apparently abused his powers slightly, as he was sued on 2 March 1668/9 by John Smith and others for summoning them twice to appear in court as delinquents without proving any just complaint against them, to their defamation and great expense and trouble. They sued John Cooke for £100, but the court only awarded them fifty shillings. In 1672, John Cooke swapped some lands with brother Jacob Cooke, giving up his lands at Rocky Nook in Plymouth and receiving additional acreage in Dartmouth. John Cooke deeded land throughout the 1670s to his children and their spouses in Dartmouth.

John Cooke made out his will on 9 November 1694, and died the following year on 23 November 1695. His will was presented to the court on 16 April 1696. His estate inventory was taken on 7 December 1696, and was valued at about £300, of which £200 was his house and lands. His livestock amounted to £20, and he had more than £25 in silver money. Other items listed in his estate were his wearing apparel, bed and bedding, cloth remnants, pewter and tin vessels, a warming pan, two Bibles and six other books, iron pots, skillets and kettles, linen, yarn, six spoons, two chains and plow irons, a gun, a sword, powder and bullets, two chests, a table, five bushels of corn, and "lumber of all sorts."

HUMILITY COOPER

Humility Cooper was one of the youngest *Mayflower* passengers. She came in the custody of her aunt and uncle, Edward and Ann (Cooper) Tilley of Henlow, Bedfordshire, England. Her father was apparently Robert Cooper, who is found living in Leiden.

According to William Bradford, writing in 1651, "Edward Tilley, and his wife both died soon after their arrival; and the girl Humility their cousin [niece] was sent for into England, and there died."

Robert Leigh Ward located what appears to be her baptism on 17 March 1638/9, at Holy Trinity in the Minorities, London.[146] The baptism record states she was then nineteen years old. Assuming this is the *Mayflower* passenger, it would make young Humility just one year old at the time of the voyage.

John Crackston

And His Son John

John Crackston first appears in Leiden records on 16 June 1616, when he, along with Moses Fletcher, was witness to the betrothal of Zachariah Barrow. The next year, in Leiden, he was the groom's witness for the betrothal of Henry Collet to Alice Thomas on 19 May 1617.[147]

John Crackston's daughter Anna married in Leiden to Thomas Smith on 12 December 1618, a marriage that John Crackston also witnessed. His daughter Anna is called a spinster from Colchester, co. Essex. Searches in Colchester records, however, have turned up fairly empty. Robert S. Wakefield found a couple of Crackston records in Colchester, namely a lay subsidy roll for 1523 naming a John Crackston, and the baptism of a Margaret Crackston, daughter of William at St. Botolphs, Colchester on 6 April 1569.[148]

However, just about eight miles north of Colchester, Essex, is the parish of Stratford St. Mary, Suffolk. There, on 9 May 1594, a John Crackston married to Catherine Bates.[149] The Crackston surname is extremely rare in England, so this record is almost certainly that of the *Mayflower* passenger; the timing matches very well with having a daughter Anna marrying in 1618. Catherine Bates, the wife of John Crackston, was baptized at Stratford St. Mary, Suffolk on 5 October 1567, the daughter of Thomas and Agnes Bates.

John Crackston and his son John both came on the *Mayflower* to Plymouth in 1620. The elder John signed the Mayflower Compact on 11 November 1620, but younger John apparently was not yet twenty-one years of age.

William Bradford, in his passenger list of the *Mayflower*, recorded "John Crackston died in the first mortality," but the exact date of his death the first winter is not known. His son John survived the first winter, and is named in the 1623 division of land, where he received his plot "on the north side of the town next adjoining to their gardens which came in the *Fortune*," situated between that of John Goodman and John Alden. He is also named in the 22 May 1627 division of cattle, where he is listed in the household of Isaac Allerton, whose lot included "the Great Black cow came in the Anne to which they must keep the lesser of the two steers, and two she goats."

John Crackston the younger died shortly after the division of cattle in Plymouth, perhaps the next winter. William Bradford recalled that he died about five or six years after his father, "having lost himself in the woods, his feet became frozen, which put him into a fever, of which he died."

Edward Doty

Edward Doty came on the *Mayflower* as a servant to Stephen Hopkins. Since he signed the Mayflower Compact, he was likely over the age of twenty-one, yet as a servant he must have been under twenty-five. This places his birth at approximately between the years 1595 and 1599. Doty's English origins have not been determined, but there is a promising Doty family in East Halton, Lincolnshire.[150]

Edward Doty is one of those *Mayflower* passengers for whom a definite personality can be assigned. He had a quick temper that often got the better of him, and he was very shrewd in his business dealings to the point of being fraudulent in some cases. Unlike other Plymouth Colony troublemakers who would eventually end up leaving the colony, Doty stayed put his entire life.

After arriving on the *Mayflower* and signing the Mayflower Compact, he went with his master Stephen Hopkins on some of the early explorations sent out by the Pilgrims to locate a place to build their colony.

Doty's first run-in with the law came very shortly after the Pilgrims had begun constructing their town. Thomas Prince, making notes in the early eighteenth century from a now-lost manuscript of William Bradford, records[151]:

> June 18. The second offense is the first duel fought in New England, upon a challenge of single combat with sword and dagger between Edward Doty and Edward Leister, servants to Mr. Hopkins; both being wounded, the one in the hand, the other in the thigh, they are adjusted by the whole company to have their head and feet tied together, and so to lie for twenty-four hours,

without meat or drink, which is begun to be inflicted, but within an hour, because of their great pains, at their own and their master's humble request, upon promise of better carriage, they are released by the governor.

It would not be Doty's last fight; the Plymouth Court would become a familiar place for Edward. The Plymouth Court records do not exist prior to 1632, so we lose about ten years of Doty's court activities. What follows is a chronological summary of Doty's numerous lawsuits during the course of his life at Plymouth[152]:

2 January 1632/3: Joseph Rogers complained that Edward Doty failed to deliver six pigs that were due him. The court ordered Doty pay four bushels of corn to Joseph.

3 January 1632/3: William Bennett claimed that Doty dealt fraudulently with him, for selling a flitch of bacon for three pounds of beaver; but after seeing the bacon, it was judged to be only worth half that value. The court ordered Robert Hicks and Francis Eaton to arbitrate how much Doty owed to Bennett as a result. Bennett also claimed Doty had not yet paid him for some boards he had sold. The court ordered Doty to pay the debt in as much bacon as ordered by arbitrators Hicks and Eaton.

1 April 1633: William Bennett sued Edward Doty for slander, accusing "the said Edward to have called him a rogue." The court record continues, "which being proved by divers testimonies, the jury, Joshua Pratt being foreman, found the defendant guilty, and amerced him in fifty shillings fine, whereof thirty to go to the plaintiff." Edward was given eight months to make payment.

2 January 1633/4: John Smith, an apprentice of Edward Doty, sued to be freed from his ten-year term on the grounds Edward was not giving him anything in return for his labor. The court, "finding the said Edward had disbursed but little," ordered that Edward pay John Smith double apparel, and shortened John's term from ten to five years.

26 March 1633/4: Edward Doty and Josias Cooke were fined six shillings and eight pence by the court for fighting with each other. "And whereas the said Edward drew blood from the said Josias, the said Edward was awarded to give him 3s 4d for the same," which was to be paid within one month.

28 March 1634: Edward Doty sued Francis Sprague for twenty shillings. After hearing the case, the court awarded Edward just six shillings and six pence, plus half a peck of malt.

5 October 1636: Edward Doty and Joseph Beedle sued and countersued each other, "their matters being raw and imperfect." They were referred to arbitration.

7 March 1636/7: George Clarke sued Edward Doty for £12, for "a deceitful bargain made with him for a lot of land." The court ordered that Edward should either repay George Clarke the £8 he had paid thus far on the deal and cancel the bargain, or else accept just £4 more for payment and sign over the property.

2 October 1637: George Clarke sued Edward Doty for £20, for "denying him liberty to hold land for the term he had taken it for." The jury awarded him ten shillings for damages. George Clarke also sued Edward Doty for £5 for assaulting him; the jury awarded him twelve pennies, plus court costs.

2 January 1637/8: Edward Doty was fined ten shillings by the court for assaulting George Clarke (this was the criminal fine for the assault, his civil lawsuit resulted in only twelve pennies damages). That same day, Edward Doty sued John Holmes for "an action of trespass," to the damages of £40. The jury found for John Holmes, and fined Edward Doty five shillings for not proving "he sustained any damage thereby."

25 October 1638: Richard Derby sued Edward Doty for £14. Court records do not indicate what happened with this complaint. It probably related to a £150 land sale that Doty made to Richard Derby on 12 July 1637.

5 November 1638: Edward Doty acknowledged that he owed £40 to the king. The cause for the fine or debt is not stated, but Samuel Gorton also acknowledged the same debt. Samuel Gorton would leave Plymouth and become a thorn in the side of every colony wherein he settled. Doty paid off half the £40 the next year, and slowly made payments on it over the subsequent decade.

3 March 1638/9: John Shaw sued Edward Doty for £10 for an unspecified "trespass." The jury agreed with Shaw, but only awarded him £3 15s, plus court costs.

1 September 1640: The widow Bridget Fuller sued Edward Doty for £30, in a generic "trespass" case that appears to have involved

wintering of cattle. The jury found for Bridget, but awarded her only £3 10s damages plus court costs.

7 December 1641: Edward Doty sues James Luxford for £7 damages, the result of the case is not seen in the records.

1 February 1641/2: Edward Doty and John Jenny came to court over differing accounts. The court ordered John Jenny to take possession of Edward Doty's money currently in the possession of Thurston Clarke, and then to pay Doty five and a half bushels of corn, plus three pennies. The court also ordered George Clarke to pay Edward Doty four bushels of corn. In addition, the court warned Edward Doty that he should build a keep for his cattle, or else be liable for any damage they do to other men's corn.

6 March 1642/3: Edward Doty was ordered to pay five bushels of corn to Mr. Hanbury.

2 January 1643/4: Edward Doty was sued by Manasseh Kempton, and was ordered by the court to pay him five bushels of corn, plus court costs.

7 December 1647: Samuel Cutbert sued Edward Doty for "taking away some wood of his land." The court ordered Doty to pay seven shillings damages.

6 March 1649: Edward Doty sued John Shaw, Jr. for £10. The jury awarded Doty five shillings, and ordered John Shaw to "make good the iron work unto the plaintiff."

7 May 1650: Edward Doty sued James Shaw and John Shaw, Jr., and won thirty-five shillings damages plus court costs.

7 August 1650: Edward Doty was sued by Edward Gray and Samuel Cutbert for "damage done by the calves and other cattle of the said Edward Doty's in the corn of the said Edward Gray and Samuel Cutbert." The court ordered him to pay them each a bushel of corn.

7 October 1651: Edward Doty was sued by John Holmes for assault. John Holmes asked for £10 damages, but got just one shilling and court costs instead.

Despite his regular appearance in Plymouth court, Doty was never subjected to any criminal punishment beyond modest fines, so although he occasionally got into fights and many people sued him for fraudulent trades and sales of goods, the matters were in almost all cases civil affairs and did not involve activities deemed criminal. Aside from his duel in 1621, he altogether avoided any kind of physical punishment, such as whippings, brandings, banishment, and the stocks that were used as punishment for more criminal acts such as theft, serious assaults, or adultery. He carried on a regular life in Plymouth; he was a freeman with a vote at the town meetings, he paid his taxes, and he accepted the outcome of all court cases and paid all his debts. And all the while, he was raising a sizeable family. The court periodically made land grants to him, just as it did for other residents, and he participated in all the additional land benefits of being classified a "first comer."

Edward Doty married Faith Clarke on 6 January 1634/5. According to William Bradford, Faith was Doty's second wife, but he had no children by his first wife, and she must have died fairly young. Nothing has been discovered about Doty's first wife, not even her name. Faith was the daughter of Thurston and Faith Clarke. Since several of Doty's lawsuits involved Thurston and George Clarke, it would appear some of his legal disputes and fights were probably domestic squabbles. Edward and Faith Doty had nine children. Eldest son Edward was born about 1637, John about 1640, Thomas about 1642, Samuel about 1643, Desire about 1645, Elizabeth about 1647, Isaac on 8 February 1648/9, Joseph on 30 April 1651, and Mary about 1653. Edward Doty died on 23 August 1655 in Plymouth.

Edward Doty did not participate in any government or political activity beyond his attending the town meetings and court sessions, as was required of any freeman. He was never on a grand or petty jury, nor did he ever hold any political office. He was never appointed to any committees, highway surveyor teams, or anything of that nature. The only instance of any service he seems to have provided is from a town meeting held on 10 February 1643, when he was assigned, along with George Clark, John Shaw, Francis Billington, and a couple others, to build a wolf trap at Plain Dealing.[153]

Edward Doty made out his will on 20 May 1655, calling himself "sicke and yet by the mercye of God in perfect memory." He gave his land at "Coaksett" to his sons, with eldest Edward to get a double portion. He gave his house, meadows, and lands, "together with all Chattles and moveables," in Plymouth to his wife, minus his outstanding debts. His will was witnessed by John Howland, John Cooke (brother of the Josias Cooke that Doty had a fight with in 1634), James Hurst, and William Hoskins. Doty signed the will with a mark, as he did also his property deeds, indicating he never learned how to write. The will was presented to the court on 5 March 1655/6, and an estate inventory was also presented, dated 5 November 1655. At the time of his death, Doty's estate totaled £137 19s 6d, with just £6 2d of debt.[154]

The house and lands in Plymouth he willed to his wife were valued at £25, with the adjoining meadows valued at £10. The land at Coaksett given to his sons was valued at £20. He also owned a yoke of oxen valued at £12, with other livestock, including a cow, a two-year-old steer, a heifer, two calves, two "fat swine," and four yearling swine. He owned a lot of farming equipment and tools, including a cart and wheels, iron plow, yokes, axes, hoes, pitchforks, hay knife, cow bells, and hook and sickle. He had thirty-seven bushels of rye, ten and a half bushels of peas, six bushels of wheat, eighty bushels of Indian corn, and twelve loads of hay. For his kitchen, he had six pewter dishes and a candlestick, two iron pots, numerous earthen pots and pans, four wooden trays and a wooden bowl and straining dish, and a table. He had two chairs and a cradle, two chests, "a great wheel and a little wheel and a pair of cards" (for wool), a bed and coverings, linen, five barrels of tar, a cow hide, and a matchlock musket.[155]

FRANCIS EATON,

HIS WIFE SARAH, AND SON SAMUEL

Francis Eaton was baptized on 11 September 1596 at St. Thomas in Bristol, co. Gloucester, England, the son of John and Dorothy (Smith) Eaton. Francis had younger siblings born shortly after him, namely Jane in 1598/9, Samuel in 1600, and Welthian in 1602, but all his brothers and sisters died in March 1603—presumably a devastating illness that spread through the family.[156]

By the age of nineteen, Francis Eaton had become a house carpenter, and was living in a tenement described as "a garden ground, with a lodge in the same, in the parish of St. Phillip's," in Bristol.[157] Francis is not found named in any Bristol records after 1615. William Bradford lists Francis Eaton in a section of his passenger list that would seem to suggest he was one of the members of the Leiden congregation—so, it is possible he moved from Bristol to Leiden sometime shortly thereafter.

Probably around 1618 or 1619, Francis Eaton married a woman named Sarah. The marriage record has not been found, so her maiden name is not known. They had a son Samuel in 1620, and with wife Sarah, they all came on the *Mayflower*. William Bradford wrote that Samuel "came over a sucking child." After arrival, Francis Eaton was one of the men who signed the Mayflower Compact.

Francis's wife Sarah died the first winter, leaving him to raise young Samuel himself. But he quickly remarried, about 1621 or 1622, to Dorothy, a young woman who had come on the *Mayflower* as a maidservant to John Carver. In 1626, perhaps through Isaac Allerton who had returned to England that year, Francis and Dorothy Eaton arranged to apprentice John Morgan, son of Edward Morgan of Bristol, for a period of seven years, to learn the trade of carpentry; but it would seem that John Morgan never made the voyage (or perhaps died on the voyage over), and Dorothy had died in the meantime as well.[158] Francis remarried again, this time to Christiana Penn, who had come to Plymouth on the ship *Anne* in 1623.

Francis and Christian Eaton soon began to build a family of their own. Their first daughter, Rachel, was born perhaps in late 1626, and son Benjamin was born in March 1628. They also had another child in 1630, who Bradford referred to as "an idiot" (i.e., mentally retarded). In the 1623 division of land, Francis was assigned four acres of land on "the north side of the town next adjoining to their gardens which came in the *Fortune*." His four acres were: one for himself, one in right of his first wife Sarah, one for son Samuel, and one for his second wife Dorothy. In the 1627 division of cattle, Francis and Christian Eaton, with Samuel and Rachel, received shares in "an heifer of the last year called the White-bellied Heifer and two she goats."

In 1631, Francis Eaton began selling off a number of his landholdings, indicating some financial difficulties. Francis sold four acres of land north of town "between the land of Capt. Myles Standish on the south side and one acre due unto Henry Sampson on the north side." On 25 June 1631, he sold it for "the second cow calf shall fall unto the said Edward [Winslow] . . . the said Edward to deliver the same at the age of six months and if it miscarry before then at 3 percent till payment be made." Then, on December 30, Francis Eaton sold twenty acres of land "at the place commonly called Nothingelse" to William Brewster, for the price of £21 12s, and he sold another ten-acre parcel to Brewster in the same area for £10. About a week later, on 8 January 1631/2, he sold his dwelling house to Kenelm and Josiah Winslow.

In 1633, Francis Eaton was taxed nine shillings, the lowest tax rate, indicating a very low estate. Francis died in the autumn of 1633, one of the casualties of an epidemic that spread through Plymouth Colony that year. On 25 November 1633, the Plymouth Court noted: "[W]hereas Francis Eaton, carpenter, late of Plymouth, deceased, died indebted far more than the estate . . . would make good, insomuch as Christian, his late wife, durst not administer, it was ordered, that Mr. Thomas Prence and Mr. John Doane, in the behalf of the Court, should enter upon the estate, according to the inventory brought in upon oath the day of this present, that the creditors might have so far as the estate will make good, and the widow be freed and acquitted from any claim or demand of all or any his creditors whatsoever."

The estate inventory of Francis Eaton, drawn up the same day by James Hurst, Francis Cooke, and Phineas Pratt, shows just how financially strained Francis actually was. His only two possessions of any notable value were one cow, valued at £20, and one calf valued at £10. He had two young hogs valued at £1, and about £8 of household goods, including a coat, black suit of clothes, two hats, two doublets, four platters, three saucers and a cup, a cheese press, a chest, a table, one chair, one bed, and a frying pan. He had some carpentry tools of minimal value, including a couple saws, a hammer, some gouges, a chisel, a "broken holdfast and a bench hook," three augers, a bevel square, an iron square, six planes, a number of adzes, and some boards. He also had some fishing equipment, and a gun with a shot purse.

Francis had already sold off all his lands and house. In total, his livestock, household goods and carpentry tools amounted to about £65. But he owed debts to John Barnes; Francis Billington, "for work"; Richard Sparrow, "for work in the weir and his grain"; Abraham Shurt, Mr. Hicks, William Latham, Thomas Prence, and Kenelm Winslow, who paid Eaton £5 for work that was never done; Mr. Fogge; Mrs. Fuller, "for physic"; Samuel Eddy; Addy Webb, "for 12 days work about him in sickness"; Will Wilkes, "for a kilderkin of butter"; Mr. Pierce; William Bradford; Mr. Hatherley; Mr. Isaac Allerton, who Francis owed £105; Thomas Prence, "for 19 days work"; John Doane; John Shaw; Mr. Smith; Thomas Cushman; and "his maidservant." In all, more than £168 of debt.

Young Samuel Eaton, who had come on the *Mayflower* as a "sucking child," when he was sixteen years old, apprenticed himself "by the consent and approbation of Christian, his mother-in-law," to John Cooke, who himself had come on the *Mayflower* at the age of twelve. The apprenticeship was to last seven years, beginning in October 1636. At the end of the apprenticeship, Samuel was to receive two suits of clothing (one for everyday wear, and one for the Sabbath), along with twelve bushels of Indian corn and one year-old heifer. [159]

Samuel Eaton moved north to Duxbury before 1646, and first married a woman named Elizabeth, who died sometime between 1652 and 1661. He married second to Martha Billington on 10 January 1660/1 in Plymouth. His second wife, Martha, was the daughter of Samuel's stepmother Christian, by her subsequent marriage to Francis Billington. They continued to reside in Duxbury for a few years, but moved to Middleboro by 1670. He died in Middleboro about 1684.

Thomas English

According to William Bradford, Thomas English was hired to be the master of the shallop that the Pilgrims would use in America for transportation and trade along the coastline. Due to the commonness of his name, and the fact that very little is known about him, attempts to identify him more conclusively are next to impossible. It has been speculated that he may be the same man as the Thomas England who witnessed the betrothal of Jacob McConkey of Scotland to Bletgen Peters in Leiden on 31 May 1613. His name is always immediately preceded or followed by the name of John Allerton in every contemporary account that mentions his name, which might suggest he was also from Leiden, as was Allerton.

Following the arrival of the *Mayflower*, the passengers set out three different expeditions to explore Cape Cod to seek a place to settle. Before they set ashore, they signed the Mayflower Compact on 11 November 1620, and Thomas English signed just prior to John Allerton. On December 6, the third expedition was sent out, and among the explorers were Thomas English and John Allerton, who presumably were acting in their capacity as seamen, helping to sail the shallop.

According to Bradford, Thomas English and John Allerton "died here, before the ship departed," referring to the *Mayflower*, which departed for England in April 1621.

MOSES FLETCHER

Moses Fletcher was born about 1564, probably in or around Sandwich, co. Kent, England, where he married Mary Evans on 30 October 1589. His parish church in Sandwich, St. Peters, was where his ten children were all baptized or buried.[160]

Moses Fletcher was a participant in the early Separatist movement, and by 1609 he found himself in trouble with the church authorities. On 24 or 25 April 1609, he attended the burial of a child of Andrew Sharpe—an illegal burial that was performed outside of the Church auspices. According to the church records, Fletcher and the others were "calling into question the lawfulness of the king's constitutions in this and other behalfs, affirming these thing[s] to be popishly ceremonious and of no other force." The Separatists felt the Anglican burial rituals were popish, and idolatrous. On 12 June 1609, Moses Fletcher, along with the wife of James Chilton, and several others, were excommunicated from the church for this illegal act.[161]

Moses Fletcher was excommunicated again for burying his own daughter Judith on 6 November 1609, which burial, according to church records, occurred "in the sermon time very disorderly and unseemly." His final excommunication from the church was announced publicly on 11 February 1609/10. It appears Moses left Sandwich with the Chiltons and perhaps others, and made their way to Leiden, where they joined up with the Separatist church that had just recently been founded there.

Sometime either just before or just after his removal, his wife Mary died, and Moses remarried in Leiden on 21 December 1613 to Sarah, widow of William Denby. The marriage record calls Moses a blacksmith. In 1616, Moses witnessed the betrothal of Zachariah Barrow to Joan Barrow. In 1618, Moses's eldest son John married in Leiden to Josina

Sacharias, a Dutch woman. Two other children, Priscilla and Elizabeth, are also known to have married in Leiden later.[162]

Moses Fletcher came to Plymouth by himself on the *Mayflower* in 1620—it is unclear whether his wife Sarah had died by that time, or if he initially left her behind with his children. He signed the Mayflower Compact in November 1620, but died sometime the first winter at Plymouth.

EDWARD FULLER,

HIS WIFE, AND SON SAMUEL

Edward Fuller was baptized on 4 September 1575 at Redenhall, Norfolk, England, the son of a butcher, Robert Fuller.[163] Very little is actually known about Edward; additional details on the Redenhall Fullers can be found in the next biography on his more well-known brother Samuel, who also came on the *Mayflower*. Edward is named in his father's will dated 19 May 1614, where he is bequeathed £20 and his father's tenement (after the death of his stepmother Frances). Edward went to Leiden shortly thereafter, where he gets but one incidental mention in a Leiden record—just enough to prove he was living there, at least.[164]

The name of Edward Fuller's wife is not known. He and his wife had only two known children of record, Matthew (born about 1605) and Samuel (born about 1608). James Savage, in his *Genealogical Dictionary of the First Settlers of New England* (1854) gave the name of Edward's wife as Ann, but there is no historical evidence to support this, and he may well have just been mistaken on this count. William Bradford, in his passenger list, simply enumerated "Edward Fuller and his wife, and Samuel their son"; and later, noted "Edward Fuller and his wife died soon after they came ashore, but their son Samuel is living and married and hath four children or more."

Edward Fuller signed the Mayflower Compact on 11 November 1620, but as Bradford noted, he and his wife died soon after they came ashore.

Their orphaned son, Samuel, then about twelve years old, was placed in the custody of his uncle, Dr. Samuel Fuller. Samuel Fuller "Juneor" received three acres in the 1623 division of land at Plymouth, on the "south side of the brook to the woodward." And in the 1627 division of cattle, he, with uncle Samuel, received a share in the "red heifer [that] came of the cow which belongeth to the poor of the colony."

Samuel became a freeman in Plymouth in 1634 and moved to Scituate a year later, marrying Jane Lothrop there on 8 April 1635. In 1641, he moved his family to Barnstable. In all, he and wife Jane had nine children of record, though several died young. He died on 31 October 1683 in Barnstable.

Samuel Fuller

Samuel Fuller was baptized on 20 January 1580/1, at Redenhall, co. Norfolk, England, the son of Robert Fuller, butcher, and probably his first wife Sarah Dunkhorn, who was buried there on 1 July 1584.[165] He moved to Leiden by 1611, where on 7 October 1611 he witnessed the betrothal of Degory Priest to Sarah (Allerton) Vincent.[166] Although this is the first record of him in Leiden, his sister Ann witnessed the betrothal of William Pontus on 13 November 1610, so Samuel was probably in town by this time as well.[167] In 1614, Samuel is mentioned in his father Robert's will, although he was only bequeathed £10, less inheritance than even his sisters, suggesting perhaps his father was not particularly happy with him.

Samuel Fuller appears quite regularly in Leiden records, and was apparently one of the more active members of the church congregation, where he was a deacon. He witnessed the betrothal of William White—apparently not the *Mayflower* passenger of the same name—to his sister Ann on 27 January 1612.[168] On 15 March 1613, he himself was betrothed to Agnes Carpenter, daughter of Alexander Carpenter. They were married on 24 April 1613.[169] The marriage record indicates that Samuel had been married previously to Alice Glasscock, who had died; but no record of this marriage has been found in either England or Leiden.

On 7 May 1613, Samuel Fuller witnessed the betrothal of Alice Carpenter, his sister-in-law, to Edward Southworth.[170] Alice would later be widowed and would marry Governor William Bradford in 1623. On 16 May 1614, Samuel witnessed the betrothal of Samuel Terry, who was a French Huguenot from Caen, Normandy, France, that had joined up with the Pilgrims' Leiden congregation.[171]

Samuel's wife Agnes would apparently have complications with her first pregnancy. She gave birth to a child who was buried shortly thereafter on 29 June 1615 at St. Peter's, Leiden. She herself died a few days later and was buried on 3 July 1615.[172] In October of that year, he witnessed the marriage of Edmond Jessup; the record states that Samuel was then living in the *Groenepoort* over against the clock tower.[173] Samuel remarried a couple of years later to Bridget Lee, on 27 May 1617.[174] Samuel continued to witness a number of betrothals, including Samuel Butler's on 7 August 1615 and John "Codmoer" (Goodman?) on 16 September 1619.[175]

As a deacon for the Plymouth church, Samuel was involved in the church's decision to remove to Northern Virginia. On 10 June 1620, Samuel Fuller, along with Edward Winslow, William Bradford, and Isaac Allerton, wrote a letter to agents in England who were organizing the voyage (John Carver and Robert Cushman) to complain about the last-minute changes that were being made to the terms and conditions of the voyage. They felt it was unreasonable that the London merchants would get to keep half of the housing and lands when the company was liquidated; they thought the lands and houses should belong to the settlers! And they complained that the change in the terms to allow only one day per week off from labor, instead of the previously agreed upon two days, would be a hardship to everyone—since their day off would be Sunday, and in order to honor the Sabbath they could not work on Sunday for their personal benefit.

In the end, nobody would agree on the terms and conditions, and the passengers departed without having finalized the agreement. Samuel Fuller taught himself medicine, perhaps in preparation for the voyage and knowing the Pilgrims would not have any doctors of their own. Deacon and doctor Samuel Fuller left behind his wife Bridget and their young one-year-old daughter Bridget in Leiden, and brought only a servant, a youth named William Butten. Despite being a servant to the doctor, young William Button would end up being the only *Mayflower* passenger to die during the voyage, dying just three days before land was sighted.

On 11 November 1620, Samuel Fuller was one of the signers of the Mayflower Compact, which was signed as the *Mayflower* was at anchor off the tip of Cape Cod, in what is now Provincetown Harbor.

After Plymouth had become better established, Samuel's wife Bridget came on the ship *Anne* in 1623. Samuel received his two acres in the 1623 division of land "on the south side of the brook to the baywards," and wife Bridget received her share "in with a corner by the pond." In 1626, Samuel Fuller was one of the men, along with Bradford, Brewster, Winslow, Standish, Allerton, and others, who purchased the joint-stock company from the colonists as a whole. In the 1627 division of cattle, Samuel and Bridget Fuller are listed as heading the eighth company, which received for its lot "a red heifer came of the cow which belongeth to the poor of the colony . . . also two she goats."

In 1629, John Endicott led a group of settlers who arrived and founded the town of Salem. But many arrived sick, and the colonists were also in need of some advice on how to organize their church, so Plymouth sent their deacon and doctor, Samuel Fuller. John Endicott, in a letter to William Bradford dated 11 May 1629, wrote "I acknowledge myself much bound to you, for your kind love and care, in sending Mr. Fuller amongst us, and rejoice much that I am by him satisfied, touching your judgments, of the outward form of God's worship." The colonists would choose Mr. Skelton their pastor, and Mr. Higginson their teacher.

Dr. Fuller would perform similar duties the following year for the colonists that settled at Charlestown. In a letter he wrote to Governor William Bradford on 28 June 1630, Samuel Fuller reported: "The gentlemen here lately come over . . . are resolved to sit down at the head of Charles River, and they of Mattapan propose to go and plant with them. I have been at Mattapan, at the request of Mr. [John] Warham, and let some twenty of these people blood.[176]"

Doctors during this time period believed that most medical problems were caused by an imbalance of the four "humors," namely blood, yellow bile, black bile, and phlegm. And the way to cure a disease was to determine which humor was out of balance, and then attempt to adjust it, either by laxative, inducing vomiting, or most commonly— draining off "excess" blood.

In another letter written by Samuel Fuller, dated 2 August 1630, he reported: "The sad news here is, that many are sick, and many are dead; the Lord in mercy look upon them! . . . Mrs. Coddington is dead."

Thomas Morton, a troublemaker with no love for the Plymouth colonists or their church leaders, wrote his own less-than-praising analysis of Samuel Fuller, in his 1637 book, *New English Canaan*:

> The Church of Plymouth, having due regard to the weale public, and the Brethren, ... and knowing that they would be busily employed to make provision for the cure of souls, and therefore might neglect the body for that time: did hold themselves to be in duty bound, to make search for a fitting man that might be able, (if so need required) to take the charge upon him in that place of employment: and therefore called a council of the whole Synagogue: amongst which company they choose out a man, that long time had been nursed up in the tender bosom of the church: one that had special gifts: he could write and read, ... they style him doctor and forth they send him to gain employment and opinions. He was born at Wrington in the county of Somerset [*sic*, that is where his wife was from], where he was bred a butcher. He wears a long beard, and a garment like the Greek that begged in Paul's Church. This new-made doctor comes to Salem to congratulate: where he finds some are newly come from the sea, and ill at ease.
>
> He takes the patient and the urinal: views the state there: finds the *Crasis Syptomes*, and the *attomi natantes*: and tells the patient that his disease was wind, which he had taken by gaping, feasting, overboard at sea, but he would quickly ease him of that grief, and quite expel the wind. And this he did perform, with his gifts he had: and then he handled the patient so handsomely, that he eased him of all the wind, he had in an instant .... [i.e., killed him].
>
> How he went to work with his gifts is a question: yet he did a great cure for Captain Littleworth [Morton's nickname for John Endicott], he cured him of a disease called a wife ...

By this means he was allowed 4p. a month, and the surgeon's chest, and made physician general of Salem: where he exercised his gifts so well, that of full 42 that there he took to cure, there is not one has more cause to complain, or say black's his eye. [i.e., they are all dead].

But in mine opinion, he deserves to be set upon a palfrey, and led up and down in triumph through New Canaan, with a collar of Jurdans about his neck, as was one of like desert in Richard the Second's time through the streets of London, that men might know where to find a quacksalver.

Samuel Fuller was taxed eighteen shillings in Plymouth in 1633. But that summer, Dr. Fuller himself fell ill with a sickness that spread through Plymouth that autumn. As Nathaniel Morton (no relation to Thomas Morton) noted in his 1669 *New England's Memorial*:

> This year [1633] it pleased God to visit Plymouth with an infectious fever, of which many fell very sick, and upwards of twenty died, men, women, and children, and sundry of them were of their ancient friends; amongst the rest, Mr. Samuel Fuller then died, after he had much helped others, and was a comfort to them; he was their surgeon and physician, and did much good in his place, being not only useful in his faculty, but otherwise, as he was a godly man, and served Christ in the office of a deacon in the church for many years, and forward to do good in his place, and was much missed after God removed him out of this world.

Samuel Fuller made out his will on 30 July 1633, calling himself "sick and weak." His will was proved 28 October 1633, and his estate inventory was presented to the court the following January 2. In his will, he bequeathed the education of his children to brother Will Wright, excepting daughter Mercy who was to remain with goodwife Wallen; and requested that Mrs. Hicks be their teacher. But if his wife Bridget recovered from her illness, then she was to have control of the children's education.

Samuel Fuller seems to have taken in quite a few additional children. He was caring for Sarah Converse, who he also turned over to brother-in-law William Wright, or to Thomas Prence if William did not want her, to "perform the duty of a step father . . . and bring her up in the fear of God as their own, which was a charge laid upon me per her sick father when he freely bestowed her upon me." Another girl, Elizabeth Cowles, from Charlestown, was to "be conveniently appareled and returned to her father or mother." Young George Foster was to be likewise returned to his mother at Sagos. Thomas Symons and Robert Cowles were servants, and their contracts were to be transferred to William Wright. As an addendum to the will, Samuel noted that "whereas the widow Ring committed the oversight of her son Andrew to me at her death, my will is that Mr. Thomas Prence, one of my overseers, take the charge of him and see that he be brought up in the fear of the Lord . . ."

Samuel gave most of his estate and lands to his son Samuel, then still a toddler, and also notes that Samuel his kinsman (i.e., Samuel, son of Edward Fuller) was also living with him.

He bequeathed to his sister-in-law Alice Bradford "twelve shillings to buy her a pair of gloves." He also gave gloves to John Winthrop, governor of Massachusetts, and gave more gloves to John Jenny and John Winslow. He adds, "whatsoever is due unto me from Capt. Standish I give unto his children," and similarly he gives a small debt due from John Endicott to John's children. He gave Mrs. Hicks twenty shillings, and gave Elder William Brewster "my best hat and band which I have never wore."

Samuel Fuller's estate inventory included a number of books, including several Bibles, several religious works (including the ever-popular *Exposition of the Ten Commandments* by John Dod), and several medical texts, including Lupton's *Thousand Notable Things of Sundry Sorts*, and miscellaneous "Physic [medical] books" valued at £1. Given the value of the other books in his estate, he probably had about ten or twenty medical texts. Also amongst his other household goods are found two beakers, a dozen alchemy spoons, and a surgeon's chest with the things belonging to it. For livestock, Samuel Fuller had more than most anyone at Plymouth during this time period: an ass, three milch cows and two steer calves, six ewe goats, two wethers and two lambs, six barrow hogs, six sows, two young sows, and sixteen weaning pigs. He also had two houses, one "in the town" and one "country house."

RICHARD GARDINER

Richard Gardinar was possibly the man baptized on 12 February 1582 at Harwich, Essex, England, the son of John and Lucy (Russell) Gardinar.[177] Lucy Russell was a step-aunt of the *Mayflower*'s master, Christopher Jones, and presumably was also a relative of the *Mayflower*'s cooper, John Alden.

Richard Gardinar is rarely mentioned in the historical record. William Bradford, writing about 1651, reported that "Richard Gardinar, became a seaman, and died in England, or at sea." Since John and Lucy Gardinar were from a maritime family, the statement that he later became a seaman tends to support his Harwich identification.

Richard Gardinar is recorded as having signed the Mayflower Compact on 11 November 1620. In the 1623 division of land at Plymouth, he received one acre "on the south side of the brook to the baywards."

That year, the London investors sent to Plymouth a new forty-four-ton ship, the *Little James*, which they had outfitted for fishing and trading for the colony's use and profit. Unfortunately, problems with the *Little James* began almost immediately. During a storm at sea, she was knocked around and blown off course, causing her to arrive later than expected. Worse yet, the crew of the *Little James* claimed they had been told they were going on a privateering voyage, and so agreed to go on the voyage without a wage—they would all split a share of the profits. But when a French ship was spotted, the master John Bridge passed up the pirating opportunity, and aroused a near mutiny among the angry crew, who now realized they were simply being used as unpaid labor. After arrival, the men refused to work, until Governor Bradford altered their contract and agreed to pay them wages. Bradford then sent the ship out on a trading voyage to the Narragansett, but because of the lack of trade goods, they only returned with a small amount of corn and beaver. On her return, she was struck by a storm, and the crew cut off her mast to prevent themselves from being driven aground by the strong winds.[178]

In March 1624, with new mast and rigging installed, the *Little James*, with Richard Gardinar onboard perhaps acting as a crew member, was sent to Damariscove on a fishing voyage. But shortly after arrival, it was again hit by a strong storm, and driven against some rocks "which beat such a hole in her bilge as a horse and cart might have gone in." Two men, including the ship's master John Bridge, were drowned, and all the provisions were lost. The ship was eventually patched up and refloated, and sailed back to England later that year.

Emmanual Altham, another man who was onboard, wrote a letter about the incident to James Shirley in London. In his letter of May 1624, he writes[179]:

> And he [Bradford] hath sent me word that he will provide me a sufficient man for master, notwithstanding Richard Gardinar hath earnestly requested it, claiming it as his due by place, but some say not by sufficiency. I will say no more concerning him because I know you shall understand it by others; only thus much I must needs say: that so far as he could, he was willing to help us with the ship. And now he takes it somewhat unkindly that, seeing the Company have sent our ship's company assurance for their wage, that he is not intimated therein. So much for that, which is to be left to your and the Company's wisdom.

Apparently, Richard Gardinar put in a lot of work as a seaman and helped out as much as he could with the ship, and as a result he felt that he should receive a wage for his services, even though he was one of the colonists, not an official member of the ship's hired crew.

Richard Gardinar is mentioned in no more American records following the shipwreck of the *Little James*. William Bradford reported in 1651 that "Richard Gardinar became a seaman and died in England or at sea." The exact time that Richard Gardinar left Plymouth is not found, but since he was not named in the 22 May 1627 division of cattle he must have returned prior to that date. He may very well have returned to England on the *Little James* in late 1624.

JOHN GOODMAN

John Goodman's English origin remains elusive. There is a Leiden marriage record of a "Jan Codmoer" of England, widower of "Marytgen Backers," marrying to Sarah Hooper, on 5 October 1619, with witnesses Samuel Fuller, Anna (Fuller) White, and Rosamond Jepson, all members of the Leiden congregation.[180] It has been suggested that this could possibly be John Goodman, the *Mayflower* passenger. If that is the case, then researchers might want to investigate the marriage of John Goodman to Mary Barker on 26 October 1604 in Everdon, co. Northampton.[181] It appears that John Goodman was a member of the Leiden congregation, as Bradford lists his name in the section of his passenger list that includes all the other Leiden congregation members.

After the *Mayflower*'s arrival, John Goodman was one of the signers of the Mayflower Compact, signing between the names of fellow Leiden church members Moses Fletcher and Degory Priest.

John Goodman is not mentioned again in the historical record until 12 January 1620/1, when that morning he and Peter Brown, and two others, went to cut some thatch in the nearby woods. The story of the event was recorded by one of the *Mayflower* passengers:

> John Goodman and Peter Brown, having cut thatch all the forenoon, went to a further place, and willed the other two, to bind up that which was cut and to follow them; so they did, being about a mile and a half from our plantation: but when the two came after, they could not find them, nor hear anything of them at all, though they hallowed and shouted as loud as they could, so they returned to the company and

told them of it: whereupon Master Leaver and three or four more went to seek them, but could hear nothing of them.

These two that were missed, at dinner time took their meat in their hands, and would go walk and refresh themselves, so going a little off they find a lake of water, and having a great mastiff bitch with them and a spaniel; by the water side they found a great deer, the dogs chased him, and they followed so far as they lost themselves, and could not find the way back. They wandered all that afternoon being wet, and at night it did freeze and snow, they were slenderly appareled and had no weapons but each one his sickle, nor any victuals. They ranged up and down and could find none of the savages' habitations; when it drew to night they were much perplexed, for they could find neither harbor nor meat, but in frost and snow, were forced to make the earth their bed, and the element their covering. And another thing did very much terrify them, they heard as they thought two lions roaring exceedingly for a long time together, and a third, that they thought was very near them, so not knowing what to do, they resolved to climb up into a tree as their safest refuge, though that would prove an intolerable cold lodging; so they stood at the tree's root, that when the lions came they might take their opportunity of climbing up. The bitch they were fain to hold by the neck, for she would have been gone to the lion; but it pleased God so to dispose, that the wild beasts came not: so they walked up and down under the tree all night. It was an extreme cold night, so soon as it was light they traveled again, . . . In the afternoon, it pleased God from an high hill they discovered the two isles in the bay, and so that night got to the plantation, being ready to faint with travel and want of victuals, and almost famished with cold. John Goodman was fain to have his shoes cut off his feet, they were so swelled with cold, and it was a long while after ere he was able to go.

An English spaniel "water dog," as depicted in a woodcut from Gervase Markham's *Whole Art of Fowling* (London, 1621).

But Goodman's adventures were not yet over. A week later, on January 19, John Goodman decided he needed to exercise his lame feet, so he took the little spaniel with him for a walk in the evening. What happened this time was again recorded by a *Mayflower* passenger:

> This day in the evening, John Goodman went abroad to use his lame feet, that were pitifully ill with the cold he had got, having a little spaniel with him. A little way from the plantation, two great wolves ran after the dog, and the dog ran to him and betwixt his legs for succor. He had nothing in his hand but took up a stick, and threw at one of them and hit him, and they presently both ran away, but came again. He got a pale board in his hand, and they sat both on their tails, grinning at him a good while, and went their way and left him.

William Bradford, writing in 1651, states that John Goodman "died soon after arrival . . . in the general sickness that befell." However, he appears to have been mistaken on this count. John Goodman was alive (but perhaps not well) on 19 January 1620/1 when he met the wolves on his walk. His early house plot in 1620 was situated south of the street and east of the highway, between the houses of William Brewster and Peter Browne. He even received a share in the 1623 division of land, though some have suggested this may have been simply land held in trust for an heir to his estate. Whatever the case, John Goodman had died by the 1627 division of cattle.

WILLIAM HOLBECK

William Holbeck came as an indentured servant with the family of William White. Because he did not sign the Mayflower Compact, we can presume he was under the age of twenty-one, probably a teenager. It would be reasonable to speculate that he originated from the same region in England as his master's family; but unfortunately, the English origins of William White have not been found yet either.

The surname of Holbeck is not particularly common, and the name William Holbeck is found most frequently during the early seventeenth century in the neighboring parishes of Shustoke and Fillongley, Warwickshire, and also in Gainsborogh, Lincolnshire.

William Bradford simply reports that "Mr. White and his two servants died soon after their landing" the first winter at Plymouth.

JOHN HOOKE

John Hooke was born about 1607 in Norwich, co. Norfolk, England, making him about thirteen years old at the time of his voyage on the *Mayflower*. His parents John and Alice (Thompson) Hooke were married on 9 August 1605 at St. Peter Mancroft, Norwich, co. Norfolk.[182] At some point, the Hooke family moved from Norwich to take up residence with the Separatist church in Leiden led by Pastor John Robinson—who incidentally was a pastor for a time in Norwich.

John Hooke's father John died in Leiden, and his mother Alice remarried to Leiden Church member Henry Gallant. On 8 January 1619, Henry and Alice apprenticed out the twelve-year-old John Hooke to Isaac Allerton of Leiden, tailor, with the term to begin on February 2. The apprenticeship was contracted to last for a period of twelve years, during which time Allerton was required to teach John how to read and write; provide food, clothing, and shelter; and to educate him in religion and the fear of God.[183]

When Isaac Allerton came on the *Mayflower* with his pregnant wife Mary, and three young children, he also brought along his servant John Hooke. Isaac's wife Mary and his servant John Hooke both died the first winter at Plymouth.

STEPHEN HOPKINS,

HIS WIFE ELIZABETH, AND CHILDREN CONSTANCE, GILES, DAMARIS, AND OCEANUS

Although several of the *Mayflower* crewmembers had been to North America on previous voyages, Stephen Hopkins was the only passenger who had been there before. He was baptized on 30 April 1581, at Upper Clatford, Hampshire, the son of John and Elizabeth (Williams) Hopkins.[184] Not much is known about his early life in Hampshire, but his family appears to have removed to Winchester, Hampshire, by 1586. His father died there about 1593, and by 1604 he had moved to Hursley, Hampshire, and was married to a woman named Mary. She gave birth to their first child, Elizabeth, baptized in Hursley on 13 March 1603/4. Daughter Constance was baptized there on 11 May 1606, and son Giles was baptized on 30 January 1607/8.[185]

Stephen Hopkins was fined on 19 May 1608 at the Merdon manorial court, but for what reason is not recorded. Perhaps it was a fine for not attending the court session, a commonly assessed fine. In any case, Stephen Hopkins was preparing for something very new and unusual. He was hired by a minister, Rev. Richard Buck, to be his clerk, and to read the Psalms and Chapters at Sunday services for the Virginia Company. He took the job as minister's clerk, and left behind his wife and three young children, departing Plymouth, England on 2 June 1609, headed for Jamestown, Virginia.

The Jamestown Colony had only been established for a couple of years, and it was struggling with famine, Indian attacks, laziness, and mismanagement. So, the Virginia Company sent out seven ships and two small pinnaces, with a new governor, Sir Thomas Gates, knight, to restore the colony's supplies, provide a new labor pool, and establish new leadership. The seven ships remained together for more than a month until they encountered a storm on 24 July 1609 and got separated.

Stephen Hopkins was on the three-hundred-ton *Sea Venture*, which was carrying about 140 men, plus about ten women. Also onboard the *Sea Venture* were Sir Thomas Gates, the governor; Sir George Summers, admiral of the fleet; and Christopher Newport, captain of the *Sea Venture*, who had also been the captain of the ship that had brought the very first English settlers to Virginia several years prior.[186]

Toward the evening of Monday, July 24, the skies darkened, and the winds began whistling through the rigging. On July 25, the situation for the passengers and crew got worse: they discovered the cargo hold had sprung a leak, and was already under five feet of water. The 140 men began a desperate effort to continuously run the bilge pumps, and bail water with buckets. The men ran shifts: one hour pumping or hauling water, followed by one hour of sleep. Despite their tireless efforts, they made no progress—in fact, the waters kept getting higher and higher. The storm raged on, worse than any storm anyone had ever seen. When they tried to raise a small sail to help steer their course, the men holding the whipstaff were thrown around and nearly killed. The waves were so huge that some broke completely over the ship, filling it up with still more water. Twenty-four hours passed, then thirty-six hours, then forty-eight hours, yet there was still no relief. With the cargo hold flooded, there was no access to food or water. With the constant drenching from the ocean, most of the men decided to strip off all their clothes and work naked because it was just too cumbersome to drag around waterlogged clothing. The women and few children huddled below deck, screaming and crying, while the sailors were yelling and running; and the passengers (including the governor and all the gentlemen) were frantically keeping up their laborious one-hour on, one-hour off shifts.

By Friday, everyone was ready to give up. Their bodies were ready to collapse. Cold, wet, hungry, thirsty—many wished to die rather than to continue trying to save themselves. Most everyone onboard agreed that if the storm did not end by that evening, they would just give themselves up to the sea. But just as all hope seemed lost, the storm calmed slightly, and then Sir George Summers called out "Land!"—something that nobody had expected.

The ship was sinking from the leak, so coming to anchor was not an option. The captain and crew pressed sails full ahead, and ran the ship aground as close as they could to the shore, running aground about three quarters of a mile off shore. That evening, the passengers, crew, and cargo were ferried ashore by the ship's longboat—not a single life was lost. But just as the miracle of their survival was sinking in, so was the realization of their new predicament. They were shipwrecked in the Bermudas, the "Isle of Devils," so feared by seamen that they were avoided at all costs. The islands were thought to be haunted by evil spirits and devils, and not fit for human habitation.

The castaways, including Stephen Hopkins, would quickly discover that the Isle of Devils did not live up to its reputation—in fact, the island was so full of resources that the 150 people had little problem sustaining themselves, despite having lost almost all of their food and drink. The weather was temperate, so the colonists were never too cold; and it rained frequently, so there was no shortage of fresh water. The palm trees were full of fruit, and berries were easily gathered. The islands were a year-round nesting ground for many different species of sea birds, so eggs were easily gathered; and the colonists soon discovered they could capture the nesting birds on moonless nights. The bays were full of fish and shellfish, and they had managed to salvage some of their fishing equipment and nets. There were huge sea turtles, just one of which could feed many men, and they laid thousands of eggs as well—more easy pickings. If that were not enough, they found that the islands were full of wild hogs—descendants of previous Spanish shipwrecks.

About a month after landing, the castaways had built up their ship's longboat, outfitting it with a sail and a deck, and sent eight men out on a voyage to reach Jamestown, Virginia, to get help. They were to return at the next new moon, and those on Bermuda would light fires at the highest point on the island to guide in the rescue ships. Led by Henry Raven, the master's mate on the *Sea Venture*, the men embarked on August 28, but were forced back two days later. On September 1, they managed to get off for good. Two new moons passed; the men were never heard from again.

But the same day that Henry Raven departed, Sir Thomas Gates and Sir George Summers began to encounter discontent. Work had just begun on the construction of a small pinnace, in case Henry Raven should not return, and the governor required everyone to contribute to the labor of building it. But the Bermudas had proven to be paradise—food, water, shelter, and temperate climate. Everyone knew that Jamestown was a struggling colony, short of food, in constant danger from the Indians, and in need of large amounts of labor. Why should they be forced to labor so hard to escape paradise just so they could end up in a vulnerable and famished labor camp? On September 1, six men were found to be conspiring against the governor, refusing to perform any labor that would lead to their escape from the island. The governor sentenced them to banishment on a remote island. After several months of realizing they might be stuck there forever, the men begged and pleaded for the end of their banishment, and were eventually allowed to return.

In late November, as it became clear that Henry Raven would not return, Sir George Summers requested that he be allowed to start construction of a second, smaller pinnace—the one under construction not being big enough to get everyone off the island. He took twenty men and a couple carpenters, and went to a neighboring island. Stephen Hopkins remained with Sir Thomas Gates's group. But by January, Stephen himself had become dissatisfied. As minister's clerk, he held some weight when it came to scriptural interpretation, and he began to express his views, making both legal and scriptural arguments that the governor did not actually have authority over them since they were in Bermuda, not Virginia. On January 24, Stephen Hopkins was apprehended and charged with mutiny. He was brought before the entire company in manacles and asked to answer the charges presented. Stephen pleaded simplicity, and profusely apologized, but in the end was found guilty of mutiny and was sentenced to death. One of the passengers, William Strachey, reported what happened next:

> But so penitent he was, and made so much moan, alleging the ruin of his wife and children in this his trespass, as it wrought in the hearts of all the better sort of the Company, who therefore with humble entreaties, and earnest supplications, went unto our Governor, whom they besought (as likewise did Captain Newport, and myself) and never left him until we had got his pardon.

Stephen Hopkins narrowly escaped his death sentence. He had learned his lesson, and appears to have carefully avoided any future controversy. In February, a young girl was born, and was baptized on 11 February 1610. Her name was Bermuda Rolfe, daughter of John Rolfe. John Rolfe's wife would die later, and he would eventually remarry to Pocahontas. By late March, there was yet another conspiracy; this time, led by a man named Henry Paine. He was found guilty and executed.

By the end of April 1610, after nine months, the two pinnaces, named the *Deliverance* and the *Patience*, were ready to set sail. All was gotten ready, and the ships departed on May 10, and sighted Virginia eleven days later. What they found in Virginia was much worse than even the conspirators and mutineers had feared: the Jamestown colonists were starving to death. It was so dangerous to venture into the woods just outside of the fort walls that many had taken to tearing down the houses of the deceased to use as firewood. There were no crops planted, no trade with the Indians, and no fish in the bay. Taking stock of the situation, Governor Gates determined there was about sixteen days' worth of food left, and then the colonists would have nothing. The decision was made to abandon Jamestown and head north to Newfoundland, where they hoped to catch some fishing vessels with enough food to get them back to England before they starved.

After having packed everything up, they departed. But just as they were about to leave the harbor, an English ship arrived with new supplies, new laborers, and a new governor, Lord de la Warr. The colonists reluctantly returned, and reestablished their fort.

Stephen Hopkins remained in Jamestown for several years. Back in England, stories and accounts of the harrowing shipwreck in the Bermudas and the mutinies and dangers of the enchanted islands captured the imagination of the country. William Shakespeare penned his play "The Tempest," which was first presented in November 1611. In the play, a group of passengers encounter a mighty storm and are shipwrecked in the haunted Bermuda islands; a subplot includes a mutinous butler named Stephano. Stephen Hopkins had unknowingly gotten himself written into a Shakespearean play!

Back home, his wife Mary sustained herself, apparently, as a shopkeeper, and presumably got some of Stephen's wages as well to support her three young children. But Mary unexpectedly died in

May 1613, leaving her three young children orphaned. In September 1614, a letter arrived in Jamestown, requiring "Eliezer" Hopkins to be sent home by the next ship. This may be a mistake for "Stephen," or perhaps it is just a coincidence. But Stephen Hopkins did return to England sometime shortly thereafter to take custody of his orphaned children. He took up residence in London, and there on 19 February 1617/8 at St. Mary Matfelon, Whitechapel, he married Elizabeth Fisher. They had a young daughter, Damaris, born about a year later.

Despite having seen all the horrors and hardships in Bermuda and Virginia, Stephen apparently had a strong desire to return. So, when he learned of the Pilgrims' planned voyage to Northern Virginia to establish a colony, he bought in. This time, he was not going alone: he paid to bring his wife Elizabeth (then heavily pregnant), and his children Constance, Giles, and Damaris. His eldest daughter Elizabeth had apparently died before this time. He also brought with him two servants, both probably in their early twenties, Edward Doty and Edward Leister.

So there he was, Stephen Hopkins. He had been shipwrecked in Bermuda, sentenced to death but escaped on a last-minute pardon, then went to Virginia, where he witnessed the disintegration and reestablishment of the colony. He remained there for several years, and undoubtedly had contact with Pocahontas, who married one of his fellow castaways, John Rolfe. Now he was back in England, ready to make the voyage to America again, this time on the *Mayflower*. If anyone had stories to tell during the tediously long *Mayflower* voyage, Stephen Hopkins had them! And if the *Mayflower* passengers thought their storms were bad, Stephen could have told them what a really bad storm was like! What were the Indians like? Stephen could answer that too. During the long exile in Bermuda, two children had been born: one was a girl named Bermuda, and one was a boy named Bermudas. During the voyage of the *Mayflower*, Stephen's wife Elizabeth gave birth to a son, which they named Oceanus.

When the *Mayflower* arrived off the coast of Cape Cod, Stephen Hopkins was a member of most or all of the early exploratory parties. On one of those explorations, the Pilgrims encountered a strange device made by the Indians, which Stephen explained was a snare to catch deer. William Bradford, not hearing the explanation, walked right into it and was caught by the leg. The Pilgrims leveraged Stephen's knowledge of the Indians: when the Pilgrims were first meeting the Indians, they were lodged in Stephen's house; and Stephen went on the early diplomatic visits to Massasoit and his brother Quadequina.

In the 1623 division of land at Plymouth, Stephen Hopkins received six acres of land "on the south side of the brook to the woodward," and an additional note states that the Indian Hobomok's land lie in between that of John Howland and Stephen Hopkins. Hobomok, like the more famous Squanto, assisted the Plymouth Colony and acted in a sense like an ambassador for Massasoit to the Pilgrims. In the 1627 division of cattle, Stephen and his wife Elizabeth headed the seventh lot, receiving "a black weaning calf to which was added the calf of this year to come of the black cow," plus two female goats. Included in the cattle lot were children Giles, Caleb, and Deborah Hopkins, daughter Constance and her husband Nicholas Snow, as well as the Palmer and Billington families.

In the 1633 and 1634 Plymouth Colony tax, Stephen was taxed a relatively high amount of £1 7s and £1 10s, respectively, indicating he was one of the wealthier men in the Colony. He was an assistant to the Plymouth governor from at least 1633, continuing through 1636. In 1637, he volunteered for service in the Pequot War, but the war was over before Plymouth managed to get its troops organized.

About 1637, Stephen began getting into occasional trouble with Plymouth authorities as he apparently resumed his business of shop keeping and dealing in alcoholic drinks. On 2 October 1637, he was presented by the Grand Inquest for "suffering men to drink in his house upon the Lord's Day, before the meeting be ended, and also upon the Lord's day, both before and after the meeting, servants and others to drink more than for ordinary refreshing," and also for "suffering servants and others to sit drinking in his house (contrary to the orders of this court) and to play at shuffleboard and such like misdemeanors," for which he was fined forty shillings. In January 1638, William Reynolds was presented for "being drunk at Mr. Hopkins his house, that he lay under the table, vomiting in a beastly manner," but Stephen was acquitted of the charge of "suffering excessive drinking in his house, as old Palmer, James Cole and William Reynolds." The next year, at the court session of 5 June 1638, he was presented for selling beer for two pence a quart when it was not even worth one pence per quart, and for "selling wine at such excessive rates, to the oppressing and impoverishing of the colony." At the September court session, he was presented three additional charges of selling "wine, beer, strong waters, and nutmeg at excessive rates," and for all five instances he was fined £5. And on 3 December 1639, the court investigated Stephen Hopkins for "selling a looking glass for 16d, the like whereof was bought in the Bay for 9d," but the case was delayed for "further information."

In 1638, Stephen Hopkins had some trouble with one of his maidservants, Dorothy Temple. During her service, she had become impregnated by a man named Arthur Peach. Before anyone had become aware of the pregnancy, Arthur Peach murdered an Indian, and was then executed by the Plymouth court. The Plymouth Court ordered that the baby was Stephen's responsibility: either he would pay for the care and upbringing of the baby, or the court would do it and charge him for it. Stephen completely refused to accept Dorothy back as a servant, and so was found in contempt of court and was "committed to ward for his contempt to the Court, and shall so remain committed until he shall either receive his servant Dorothy Temple, or else provide for her elsewhere at his own charge during the term she hath yet to serve him." Four days later, to get out of prison, Stephen sold his servant Dorothy and the baby to John Holmes of Plymouth for £3 to fill out the remainder of her two-year contract.[187]

On 17 July 1637, Stephen Hopkins sold his house and lands at Broken Wharf toward the Eel River. On 7 August 1638 he was granted liberty to erect a house at Mattachiest and cut hay there to winter his cattle, "provided that it be not to withdraw him from the town of Plymouth." Then, on 30 November 1638, he sold his six acres of land south of Town Brook—presumably the ones he received in the 1623 division of land—to Josias Cooke. On 1 June 1640, he was granted twelve acres of meadow, and on 8 June 1642 he bought a house and fourteen acres of land in Yarmouth and at Stony Cove.

Stephen was not enumerated in the 1643 list of men able to bear arms, because he was older than sixty years (the list was of men aged sixteen to sixty). He died the following year, making out his will on 6 June 1644. In his will, he asks to be buried next to his deceased wife, Elizabeth. He gives his "great bull" to son Giles; twenty shillings to his grandson Giles (son of his son Stephen); he gives his mare to his daughter Constance Snow. Daughter Deborah received a broad-horned black cow and her calf, and half a share in a cow called "Motley." To daughter Damaris, he bequeathed a cow called Damaris's Heifer, and a white-faced calf and the other half of the share in Motley. To daughter Ruth he gave a cow called Red Cow and her calf, and a bull. And to daughter Elizabeth, he gave a cow called "Smythkins" and her calf, and half of the "curled cow" with Ruth. He gave all the moveable household goods to be equally divided amongst his four daughters. He made his son Caleb the executor of the estate, and gave him title to his house and lands and a pair of oxen.

Aside from his cattle and lands, Stephen's estate inventory indicates he had two pigs, poultry, and a large amount of household goods ranging from kitchen items to bedding, chests, ironsmith tools, and "weights and scales" from his shop-keeping business.

John Howland

John Howland was born about 1599[188] to Henry and Margaret Howland of Fenstanton, co. Huntingdon, England. Howland's parentage has been generally identified by the will of his brother Humphrey Howland, citizen and draper of London, which mentions Arthur, John, and Henry Howland, and a debt to a "Mr. Ricks" in New England.[189] The Howland family appears to have had ties to the Randall Thickens, one of the Leiden Church members who owned land in Stepney, co. Middlesex.[190] Randall Thickens and John Carver were brother-in-laws.

John Howland came on the *Mayflower* as a manservant to John Carver, one of the leading members of the Leiden congregation—Carver was a church deacon, and would be elected the first governor of Plymouth.

The voyage on the *Mayflower* for John Howland was rather eventful indeed, and nearly cost him his life. William Bradford recorded the incident:

> In sundry of these storms, the winds were so fierce and the seas so high, as they could not bear a knot of sail, but were forced to hull for divers days together. And in one of them, as they thus lay at hull in a mighty storm, a lusty young man called John Howland, coming upon some occasion above the gratings was with a seele of the ship, thrown into the sea; but it pleased God that he caught hold of the topsail halyards which hung overboard and ran out at length. Yet he held his hold (though he was sundry fathoms under water) till he was hauled up by the same rope to the brim of the water,

and then with a boat hook and other means got into the ship again and his life saved. And though he was something ill with it, yet he lived many years after and became a profitable member both in church and commonwealth.

Though he narrowly survived and was somewhat sick, Howland did sign the Mayflower Compact on 11 November 1620, and then participated in the third major exploration of Cape Cod that began on 6 December 1620. It was the exploration that would eventually lead to the discovery of Plymouth Bay, where the passengers would decide to settle. The third exploration was quite eventful. The explorers were attacked by Nauset Indians on one of the mornings, but everyone escaped unharmed; later that same day, the shallop that everyone was in nearly wrecked upon Clark's Island after the mast and rudder both broke during a storm.

John Howland's master, John Carver, died in April 1621, apparently of sunstroke; and Carver's wife Katherine died about six weeks later, supposedly of a broken heart. Howland's term of service must have been near completion anyway, because sometime shortly before the division of land in 1623 he married fellow *Mayflower* passenger Elizabeth Tilley, daughter of John and Joan (Hurst) Tilley. John Howland received four shares in the division (one for himself, one for his wife Elizabeth, and two for Elizabeth's parents), his lot being located "on the south side of the brook to the woodward." Their first daughter, Desire, was born about 1624—some have speculated that she was named after *Mayflower* passenger Desire Minter, who was probably about the same age as Elizabeth, and who with John Howland was a fellow servant of John Carver. The Howlands' second child, John, was born about 1626.

In 1626, as the joint-stock company that funded the Plymouth Colony was in financial straits, John Howland was one of the primary men, along with Bradford, Brewster, Standish, Alden, and Allerton, who bought out the existing shareholders and took control of the company and its trading rights. Exactly how John Howland, who only a few years before was a manservant, happened to come into enough money to participate in the buyout of the company is unclear— perhaps it came from his wife's parents' estate, they having both died the first winter at Plymouth. Whatever the case, Howland was now one of the leading members of the Plymouth Colony.

In the 1627 division of cattle, he and wife Elizabeth headed the fourth lot, which received "one of the 4 heifers came in the *Jacob* called Raghorn." Unlike the other shares, they were the only lot that did not include two female goats—perhaps Raghorn was an extraordinary heifer, or else they may have drawn one of the shorter straws. That same year, John acted as one of the surveyors for the 1627 division of land, in which each of the residents received twenty acres. In 1629, daughter Hope was born, and Howland gets mentioned as one of the purchasers in the Bradford Patent of 1629/30.

Howland was taxed a modest eighteen shillings in the 1633 Plymouth tax, indicating he was not among the wealthiest of citizens; but by 1634, his tax had increased substantially to £1 4s, indicating he was beginning to bring in more. Daughter Elizabeth was born in 1631, and daughter Lydia in 1633. He was elected assistant to the Plymouth governor in 1632/3, 1633/4, and 1634/5, again indicative of his rising status within the Plymouth Colony.

However, in April 1634, an event happened that appears to have affected Howland's life significantly. He was appointed head of Plymouth's trading post on the Kennebec River. A group of men from Piscataway, a settlement to the north of Plymouth, had taken a small pinnace up the Kennebec River to trade with the Indians, intercepting trade before it came downriver to Plymouth's trading post. The joint-stock company purchased by Howland and the other leading members of Plymouth had been granted exclusive trading rights on the Kennebec, and were also granted the right to defend their territory against illegal incursions; and these men from Piscataway, led by John Hocking, were intruding. John Howland approached in a small bark, and informed Hocking and the others that they should pull up anchor and depart. Hocking refused, and with "foul speeches," insisted Howland should take the matter up with the men of Piscataway, who had sent him out. Howland persisted, and made it known that Hocking and his men would not be allowed to stay.

Unable to get Hocking to leave voluntarily, Howland sent three men to cut his anchor cables—so that the current would take him out to sea. They managed to cut one of them, but they were unable to cut the other cable before the current pushed them away. They returned a short time later with another man, Moses Talbot, hoping that with four men they would have more strength against the current. What happened next is described in a deposition in the Plymouth Colony records[191]:

> Mr. Howland seeing they could not well bring the canoe to the other cable called them aboard and bade Moses Talbot go with them, who accordingly went very readily and brought the canoe to Hocking's cable; he being upon the deck came with a carbine and a pistol in his hand and presently presented his piece at Thomas Savory but the canoe with the tide was put near the bow of the bark which Hocking seeing presently put his piece almost to Moses Talbot's head, which Mr. Howland seeing called to him desiring him not to shoot his man but take himself for his mark saying his men did but that which he commanded them and therefore desired him not to hurt any of them; if any wrong was done it was himself that did it and therefore called again to him to take him for his mark saying he stood very fair; but Hocking would not hear nor look towards our bark but presently shooteth Moses in the head, and presently took up his pistol in his hand but the Lord stayed him from doing any further hurt by a shot from our bark; himself was presently struck dead being shot near the same place in the head where he had murderously shot Moses.

Governor John Winthrop, in a letter dated 22 May 1634, added that "Hocking shot one of them in the canoe dead, upon which one of the Plymouth men out of their pinnace shot at Hocking and killed him upon the place, whereupon another of Hocking's company coming up upon the deck one of the Plymouth men asked Howland if he should kill him also, but he forbade him saying he feared there had been too many killed already."

The incident would cause quite a controversy. The Massachusetts Bay Colony tended to sympathize with the men of Piscataway, feeling that Howland let the situation escalate to bloodshed over something as insignificant as a trading dispute. Others, especially in the Plymouth Colony, felt that Howland adequately attempted a peaceful solution, that Plymouth had full and legal authority to protect and defend its exclusive trading rights to the Kennebec, and that Hocking was the only one at fault—violent and profane to the very end.

Support from the leading members of Plymouth aside, there seems to be a profound change in Howland's activities in Plymouth. He bowed out of public service for more than six years, taking no further positions, elected or appointed, within the Plymouth government. In 1637 he was granted forty acres on Island Creek Pond, and in 1638 he was granted an island called Spectacle in Green's Harbor.[192]

His public service slowly resumed in the 1640s, as he took the position of deputy for the Plymouth Court in 1641; it was a position he would take in many subsequent years, including 1645, and from 1647-1656, and again in 1658, 1661, 1663, 1666, and 1667. In 1642, he was granted six acres of land at North Meadow by the Jones River, and in 1643 he is enumerated on the census list of men able to bear arms in the town of Plymouth. In 1659, he was appointed by the Plymouth Court to a committee on the fur trade.[193]

He and wife Elizabeth continued to raise their large and growing family, having Hannah about 1637, Joseph about 1640, Jabez about 1644, Ruth about 1646, and Isaac about 1649. All ten of John and Elizabeth Howland's children survived to adulthood and married—a highly unusual circumstance. As a result, John Howland likely has more descendants living today than any other *Mayflower* passenger. Franklin D. Roosevelt, George H.W. Bush and George W. Bush, actors Alec and Stephen Baldwin, Humphrey Bogart, Mormon Church founder Joseph Smith, and poet Ralph Waldo Emerson are among those who count John and Elizabeth Howland among their ancestors.

Howland lived out his last years at his house in Rocky Nook, near Kingston. He made out his will on 29 May 1672, and he died on 23 February 1672/3. His will was proved on 6 March 1672/3.[194] In it, he bequeathed to his eldest son John his one hundred acres of land lying on the eastern side of the Tuanton River. To son Jabez he willed his land south of Mill Brook in Plymouth. To son Isaac he willed his land in Middleboro, and six acres of land at the Winnatucsett River in Plymouth. And to his wife Elizabeth, he willed his dwelling house at Rocky Nook, and all remaining lands in Plymouth. Son Joseph was to receive the Rocky Nook property after the decease of Elizabeth. He then gave each of his daughters twenty shillings, and he gave his granddaughter Elizabeth (daughter of his son John) twenty shillings as well.

John Howland's estate inventory was made on 3 March 1673/4. The estate inventory is interesting because it inventories items on a room-by-room basis. The "outward or fire room" included a musket, long gun, cutlass, belt, chimney iron, pot hangers, frying pan, fire shovel, various woodworking tools, cow bells, old chain, sheep sheers, knives and scissors, pots and kettles, candlesticks, several books, and "3 beer vessels."

In the "inward room or bedchamber" was his wearing apparel, including three hats, a "homespun suit and waistcoat," coats, stockings, a Holland shirt and Holland caps, jacket and mittens, silk neck cloths, a pair of boots and two pairs of shoes, plus some unsewn fabric, including serge, kersey, flax, cotton, four dozen buttons, and "homemade cloth." Also in the inward room were his bed and table linens, chair and pots, wineglasses, spectacles, feather bed and bolster, five pillows and five blankets, a parcel of powder, shot, and bullets, and an ink horn.

In the "upper room or chamber," he had another feather bed and bolster, a wool bed, a parcel of sheep's wool, about fifteen pounds of feathers, twenty bushels of Indian corn, four bushels of malt, four bushels of rye, six bushels of wheat, three pecks of peas, two flitches of bacon, half a barrel of beef, fifteen pounds of tallow and candles, thirty-four pounds of butter and lard, fourteen pounds of sugar, six pounds of tobacco, one peck of beans, and a grindstone.

In the fields, he had two mares, one colt, four oxen, four cows, four heifers, two steers, two yearling calves, thirteen swine, and forty-five sheep. He also had a canoe.

Elizabeth Tilley survived her husband, and eventually moved in with son Jabez in her later years, until about 1680. She died on 21 December 1687

The Jabez Howland house in Plymouth, built in 1667 and currently owned by the Pilgrim John Howland Society. Elizabeth (Tilley) Howland lived here for a time after her husband's death, until about 1680.

in Swansea, Massachusetts. She made out her own will, dated 17 December 1686, bequeathing her estate to her various children. She gave daughter Lydia her book, *Observations Divine and Moral*, which had been written by the Pilgrims' pastor in Leiden, John Robinson.

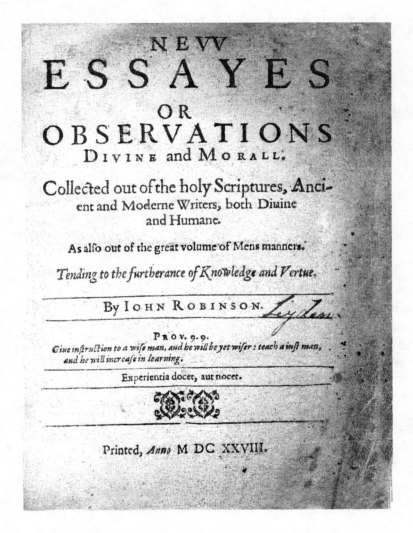

Title page of pastor John Robinson's book, *Observations Divine and Moral*. This was one of the most popular books in early Plymouth. Elizabeth (Tilley) Howland cherished her copy enough to include it in her will.

JOHN LANGMORE

Almost nothing is known about *Mayflower* passenger John Langmore. He came as a servant to Christopher Martin, the treasurer of the joint-stock company. Christopher Martin was originally from Great Burstead, co. Essex, so it seems possible the Langmore family could also be from there. However, there do not appear to be any Langmore families in co. Essex. Since Christopher Martin was purchasing supplies for the *Mayflower* in Southampton prior to the voyage, the John Longmire mentioned in a Southampton will dated 14 August 1616 might be of interest. There are Langmore/Longmire families in Claverly and Alveley, Shropshire and Upper Arley, co. Wocester, as well.

John Langmore did not sign the Mayflower Compact, so was probably a teenager. He died the first winter, as did everyone else in his household, including his master Christopher Martin, Christopher's wife Mary, and their stepson Solomon Prower.

WILLIAM LATHAM

William Latham was just about eleven years old when he came on the *Mayflower* as a servant in the household of Governor John Carver. The William Latham baptized on 4 February 1608/9 at Eccleston by Chorley, Lancashire, England, might be the passenger. *Mayflower* passenger and militia captain Myles Standish hailed from this region as well.

When John Carver and his wife Katherine died in April and May 1621, respectively, the young William Latham was transferred into another household—probably to Governor William Bradford. In the 1627 division of cattle, Latham is included in the Bradford household, receiving a share in the "heifer of the last year which was of the great white-back cow that was brought over in the *Anne*, with two she-goats."

William Latham became free of his apprenticeship by the early 1630s, and was taxed nine shillings in both 1633 and 1634—the lowest tax bracket.[195] In November 1633, the estate inventory of Francis Eaton indicated he had a debt to William Latham of £1 8s.[196] On 1 July 1633, Myles Standish was assigned to mow the land owned by Edward Bumpass and William Latham. Bumpass sold his property to John Washburn in March 1634/5, a transaction that was witnessed by William Latham. Standish was appointed to mow the hay ground at the end of Washburn and Latham's land in March 1635/6.[197]

Beginning about 1638, William Latham, now of Duxbury, appears to have become a little more troublesome to Plymouth authorities. On 5 June 1638, he was presented for the "entertaining of John Phillips into his house contrary to the act of the Court." Duxbury resident Jonathan Brewster was the witness to the infraction. Latham was fined forty shillings. Nonetheless, William Latham and John Phillips shared in the raising of a crop of Indian corn, which was later sold to William Reynolds on 6 July 1638. On November 5, Latham was bonded for £20, on the condition that he "personally appear at the next general court . . . to answer to all such matters as on his Majesty's behalf shall be objected against him concerning his drunkenness at Plymouth and Duxbury." At the court session of 4 December 1638, he acknowledged a £40 bond for his "good behavior toward our sovereign Lord the King, and all his lay people." He was fined for his "misdemeanor in lavish and slanderous speeches" and fined forty shillings—which he paid on 6 January 1638/9.[198]

The next year, on 26 December 1639, he sold his house, twenty acres of land, and one acre of meadow in Duxbury to Ralph Partridge for a little more than £26, and moved to the town of Marblehead, a town belonging to the Massachusetts Bay Colony.[199] In 1641, he made a deposition with attorney Thomas Letchford in a case involving John Moses and Thomas Keyser, in which he gave his age as thirty-two.[200] While in the Massachusetts Bay, he married a young 18-year old woman named Mary. Shortly after the marriage, Mary got herself into some trouble with Bay Colony authorities, so by 1643 the couple had moved back to Marshfield, in the Plymouth Colony, where Latham appeared on the 1643 list of men able to bear arms in the Plymouth Colony.[201]

In February 1643/4, the Massachusetts Bay Colony issued an arrest warrant for William Latham's wife Mary. She was wanted by Bay Colony authorities because of "divers and sundry complaints . . . by godly and credible persons . . . for adultery committed upon the body of Mary by one James Brittaine of Weymouth.[202]" Mary was apprehended and examined by Plymouth Colony Governor Edward Winslow before being extradited to the Massachusetts Bay Colony.

John Winthrop recorded an interesting commentary on the matter:

> At this court of assistants one James Britton, a man ill affected both to our church discipline and civil government, and one Mary Latham, a proper young woman about 18 years of age, whose father was a godly man and had brought her up well, were condemned to die for adultery . . . This woman, being rejected by a young man whom she had an affection unto, vowed she would marry the next that came to her, and

accordingly, against her friends' minds, she matched with an ancient man [i.e., William Latham] who had neither honesty nor ability, and one whom she had no affection unto. Whereupon, soon after she was married, several young men solicited her chastity, and drawing her into bad company, and giving her wine and other gifts, easily prevailed with her, and among others this Britton. But God smiting him with a deadly palsy and a fearful horror of conscience, he could not keep secret.

James Brittaine deposed that "by the seaside near his own house he did what he could to commit adultery with Mary the wife of Mr. Latham but he was not then himself, having been drinking all the night till midnight at his own house." James Brittaine and Mary Latham were convicted of adultery and executed by hanging on 21 March 1644/5.

After the execution of his adulterous wife, William Latham continued to live a short time in the Plymouth Colony. On 28 October 1645, William Latham and Roger Cooke sued John and Ann Barker "for the said Ann's burning of their house accidentally." The jury could not reach a verdict, however, so he and Roger only came away with a token gift of twenty shillings from John Barker "towards their losses."

Shortly after his house burned down, William Latham decided to head back to England, where he then became associated with an expedition to place a colony in the Bahamas. Led by Captain William Sayle and a Captain Butler, the colonists arrived in the Bahamas sometime around 1647 or 1648. Captain Butler subsequently led a mutiny, forcing Captain Sayle and the majority of the colonists to head for another island, where they shipwrecked. Everyone, except one person, made it ashore alive—but most of the provisions were lost, so they had to survive on the limited supply of fruits and animals found on the island. In their new colony, named Eleuthera, many starved to death and died before a resupply was obtained. William Latham was among those who died of starvation.

EDWARD LEISTER

William Bradford reported that Edward Leister came on the *Mayflower* as a servant within the Hopkins family. Stephen Hopkins was originally from Hursley, Hampshire, but moved to the outskirts of London sometime around 1617. It seems reasonable, therefore, that Leister could have come from the vicinity of London.

Edward Leister was the very last signer of the Mayflower Compact, leading some to speculate that he may have been one of the men who were making the "mutinous speeches" that forced the leaders to draw up the compact in the first place. Since Leister signed the document, we can assume he was over the age of twenty-one.

Only one noteworthy event associated with Leister was ever recorded in the historical record, and that was his duel with Edward Doty their first summer at Plymouth[203]:

> June 18 [1621]. The second offense is the first duel fought in New England, upon a challenge of single combat with sword and dagger between Edward Doty and Edward Leister, servants of Mr. Hopkins; both being wounded, the one in the hand, the other in the thigh, they are adjudged by the whole company to have their head and feet tied together, and so to lie for twenty-four hours, without meat or drink, which is begun to be inflicted, but within an hour, because of their great pains, at their own and their master's humble request, upon promise of better carriage, they are released by the governor.

Edward Leister received an acre of land next to his master Stephen Hopkins and fellow servant Edward Doty in the 1623 division of land at Plymouth. The land was "on the south side of the brook to the woodward."

Since Leister appears to have still been a servant of Stephen Hopkins when the 1623 division of land was recorded, he was almost certainly under the age of twenty-five. Combined with the fact he was over twenty-one at the signing of the Mayflower Compact, we can fairly reasonably pin his year of birth at approximately 1598 or 1599. Given that date range and the likelihood he was from the vicinity of London, one reasonable candidate is the Edward Leister baptized on 8 March 1597/8 at St. Michael Wood Street, London, the son of George Leister.

William Bradford reported: "Leister, after he was at liberty went to Virginia, and there died." No record of Leister in Virginia has been noted. Leister is not enumerated in the 1627 division of cattle at Plymouth.

EDMUND MARGESSON

Edmund Margesson is one of the *Mayflower* passengers who died sometime the first winter at Plymouth. William Bradford simply noted that he "died soon after their arrival in the general sickness that befell." Margesson signed the Mayflower Compact, which indicates that he was over twenty-one years of age; he is also listed in a section of Bradford's passenger list that suggests he was not a servant or apprentice, but rather a free adult. No other historical records have been found that relate to him.

The only county in England where the name Edmund Margesson is known to be found is Norfolk. The only potential candidate baptism that I have seen is the Edmund Margetson baptized on 23 November 1586 in Swannington, co. Norfolk, England, about ten miles west of Norwich. An Edward Margetson was also married on 29 April 1610 in North Walsham, co. Norfolk, north of Norwich. Other Edmund Margetsons appear during this time period in Gimingham and Trimingham, both also in Norfolk. Unfortunately, many seventeenth-century parish registers for Norfolk have not yet been indexed, so there may be many other candidates yet unnoticed.

CHRISTOPHER MARTIN

AND HIS WIFE MARY (PROWER)

Christopher Martin first appears in the historical record on 26 February 1607 in Great Burstead, Billericay, Essex, England, when he married a widow, Mary Prower.[204] He was a merchant by trade, although he had not been through the required seven-year apprenticeship. As such, he was sued as the Quarter Sessions court, shortly after his marriage, by another merchant, George Hilles, for unlawful trading.[205] The resolution of the suit is not seen, but Christopher Martin certainly continued to build his estate over the subsequent years. Christopher and Mary Martin had their only known child together, Nathaniel, baptized on 26 February 1609 in Great Burstead. Mary had also brought to the family one child from her previous marriage, Solomon Prower. That same year, Christopher Martin was one of two men with property holdings that were appointed to attend the archdeacon's visitation of that year.

Chistopher Martin was appointed a churchwarden at Great Burstead in 1611, a position that was not necessarily voluntary. The subsequent Easter, 1612, Christopher had his first run-in with church authorities, refusing to kneel at the Easter service and refusing to take Holy Communion.[206] The Puritans did not accept these superstitious ceremonies of the Anglican Church, so his refusal to partake in the ceremonies is a clear indication of his early Puritan views. The incident apparently did not diminish his standing in the community to any significant degree as a month later the Manorial Court admitted him as a landholder of three different properties in Great Burstead.

On 15 January 1616/7, the records of the Virginia Company of London indicate that Christopher Martin paid £25 for the transportation of two people to Virginia with Ralph Hamor.[207] Exactly who Christopher Martin paid for to go to Virginia is not apparent, although it is somewhat interesting to note that Martin was not present at the 1618 and 1619 manorial court—he was perhaps away in London on business.

He was definitely back in Billericay in 1620, if he had ever left at all. He was in trouble with the church again, this time for the behavior of his son and stepson. The Anglican Church had a confirmation ritual where the vicar asked a child, "Who gave you your name?" To which they were supposed to answer, per the *Book of Common Prayer*, "My godfathers and godmothers in baptism." Young Nathaniel Martin answered the vicar "crossly" by saying, "My father gave me my name, who should have else?" And Solomon Prower answered, "I do not know, my father is dead and I do not know who my godfather was." The vicar reported that Solomon then refused to answer any more questions "unless I would ask him some questions in some other catechism." Christopher Martin was then himself cited for refusing to turn over his accounts when he was the churchwarden.[208]

While all this was happening, Christopher Martin was making plans to take his family to America. He purchased four shares in the Virginia Company from George Percy, which was enough to bring himself and three others with him on the *Mayflower*—presumably his wife, son Nathaniel, and stepson Solomon. Why son Nathaniel ended up not coming is unknown; perhaps he died shortly before the voyage. Christopher sold off his land holdings, one of them on 22 June 1617 and the last one on 8 June 1620.[209] Because of his decent estate, his interest in taking his family to Virginia, and his problems with the Anglican Church, he joined up with the London merchants that were helping to sponsor the Pilgrim's Leiden congregation's voyage and settlement.

The Leiden congregation, realizing they were going to be taking on various passengers from England who were not members of their church, decided it would be wise to appoint one of the "Londoners" to join with church members John Carver and Robert Cushman. They would assist in purchasing the goods and supplies for the *Mayflower*'s voyage and for the colony's sustenance for the first year. Christopher Martin got the job; the Leiden congregation would later regret it.

With the power to purchase goods, Christopher Martin began purchasing supplies without consulting anyone or taking any advice on what to get or what were fair prices. When money ran short just before everyone was ready to set sail for America, he was questioned about his accounts and flew into a rage because of the Leiden church's suspicions of him. He refused to show anyone his accounts.

Despite the spat with the Leiden leaders, he was appointed the governor of the passengers that were to travel to America on the *Speedwell.* Robert Cushman, one of the passengers on the *Speedwell,* wrote about Christopher Martin in a letter to a friend in London:

> Near £700 hath been bestowed at Hampton, upon what I know not, Mr. Martin saith he neither can, nor will give any account of it; and if he be called upon for accounts, he crieth out of unthankfulness for his pains and care, that we are suspicious of him, and flings away, and will end nothing. Also he so insulteth over our poor people, with such scorn and contempt as if they were not good enough to wipe his shoes. It would break your heart to see his dealing, and the mourning of our people, they complain to me, and alas I can do nothing for them; if I speak to him, he flies in my face, as mutinous and saith no complaints shall be heard, or received but by himself, and saith they are froward and waspish discontented people, and I do ill to hear them. There are others that would lose all they have put in, or make satisfaction for what they have had, that they might depart, but he will not hear them, nor suffer them to go ashore lest they should run away. The sailors also are so offended at his ignorant boldness, in meddling and controlling, in things he knows not what belongs to; as that some threaten to mischief him, others say they will leave the ship, and go their way; but at the best this cometh of it, that he makes himself a scorn and laughing stock unto them.

Luckily for some of the passengers, the *Speedwell* proved unfit to make the voyage, and they got their chance to either quit the voyage or transfer over to the *Mayflower* that was governed by a much more amicable John Carver.

When the *Mayflower* finally arrived after a two-month voyage, she anchored off the tip of Cape Cod, and a controversy erupted about whether or not they should continue on to Virginia or stay put where they were. To quell any possibility of a split amongst the colonists, they signed the Mayflower Compact, agreeing to form a civil body politic. Christopher Martin was a signer, but stepson Solomon was not yet old enough to sign.

Solomon Prower died on December 24, right as the Pilgrims were first beginning to explore Plymouth Harbor. Christopher Martin, himself, was not far behind; he was so sick that on January 6 Governor John Carver came from the shore back onboard the ship (where the women, children, and sick were living while the houses were being constructed). The two discussed various accounts and business. Christopher Martin died the next day. His wife Mary also died the first winter, although the date of her death is not known.

DESIRE MINTER

Desire Minter was the daughter of William and Sarah (Willet) Minter, who came to Leiden, Holland, from the vicinity of Norwich, Norfolk. William Minter first appears in Leiden records on 3 May 1613, when he became a citizen. The following year, on 10 September 1614, he bought a house from William Jepson on *Groenhasegracht* in Leiden, for 850 guilders.[210] His wife Sarah became the midwife for the Leiden Church, and also was a witness to four betrothals between 1615 and 1617.

William Minter died at some point in late 1617 or early 1618; his widowed wife Sarah was then betrothed to Roger Simmons in Leiden on 14 July 1618, with John Carver acting as one of the witnesses. A little less than four years later, on 10 May 1622, Thomas Brewer acknowledged in a contract that he owed 1900 guilders, plus 120 guilders per year interest, for raising the daughter of William and Sarah Minter.[211] Presumably, when Sarah Minter was widowed, her daughter Desire became a maidservant for Thomas Brewer. But Thomas Brewer ended up having his own problems: he was caught and arrested by the university at the request of the English ambassador to the Netherlands and charged with printing illegal pamphlets. William Brewster was also sought, but could never be found. At some point, Thomas Brewer must have turned the care of Desire over to John Carver, who then brought her with him on the *Mayflower*.

Desire Minter's exact age is unknown, but she was under twenty-one years of age when the 1622 document was drawn up. According to William Bradford, "Desire Minter returned to her friend and proved not very well and died in England." Desire Minter appears to have returned to England prior to the division of land in 1623. Of the roughly one hundred *Mayflower* passengers, Desire Minter was one of the only ones who returned to Europe within a few years of the colony's founding—Humility Cooper may have been another. It is uncertain who in England she returned to. If she returned to Thomas Brewer, then she may have ended up in co. Kent.[212] Brewer, however, was arrested in 1626 for religious dissention, and spent the next fourteen years in prison.

THE MORE CHILDREN:

ELLEN, JASPER, RICHARD, AND MARY

Onboard the *Mayflower* were four young children: Ellen More, aged eight; Jasper More, aged seven; Richard More, aged six; and Mary More, aged four. These children had been distributed amongst the leading members of the Leiden congregation: Ellen was placed in the family of Edward Winslow, Jasper was placed in the family of John Carver, and Richard and Mary were placed with William Brewster.

If there were any gossipers on the *Mayflower*, the subject of the More children would have been great fodder. The complicated story[213] begins back around the beginning of the sixteenth century, when one William More of Larden, in co. Shopshire, England, had two sons: Edward, the eldest, who inherited the Larden estate; and Thomas, a younger son, who went off to London and was appointed an officer of the court of King Henry VIII. When King Henry VIII dissolved the monasteries, Thomas received a lease of part of the abbey of Medmenham, in co. Buckingham. Thomas More's grandson, Richard, would sell off his Medmenham estate and return to co. Shropshire, taking up residence at nearby Linley.

Meanwhile, Jasper, the grandson of Edward, had inherited the Larden estate. Jasper More had two sons that had already died, when his last surviving son, Richard, was killed in a duel in 1608. The only heir to the Larden estate was his twenty-two-year-old unmarried daughter Katherine. Jasper's second cousin Richard had built up a sizeable estate at Linley, and had married Sarah Harris, the daughter of a wealthy wool merchant of Shewsbury.

The More family was concerned that when Katherine would marry, a large chunk of the family estate would fall out of the hands of the family. A scheme was hatched between Richard and Jasper More: if

Samuel More (who was about to turn sixteen years old) were to marry Katherine, the lands would stay within the family, and the estates of the two branches of the More family would be reunited.

On 18 October 1610, Richard and Jasper More reached an agreement. Richard would pay Jasper £600 in a marriage settlement, and Jasper would then agree to provide room and board to the young couple, or £40 per year in lieu of room and board. The deal was sealed. Samuel, about seventeen years old, was married to Katherine, about twenty-five years old, on 4 February 1610/1.

Katherine was not particularly pleased at being sold off to a young boy. She had already established a "friendship" with a tenant that had been living and farming on her father's property for many years—Jacob Blakeway, son of Edward Blakeway. Unlike her seventeen-year-old boy-husband, Jacob Blakeway was about twenty-seven years old.

The parish registers of Shipton, co. Shropshire, England, record the baptisms of the children of Samuel and Katherine More: Ellenor, baptized 24 May 1612; Jasper, baptized 8 August 1613; Richard, baptized 13 November 1614; and Mary, baptized 16 April 1616. But as young Samuel began to come of age, something was becoming more and more apparent to him. Four days after the baptism of daughter Mary, he suddenly cut his four children off from their right to inherit the Larden estate, and his father Richard likewise made similar moves to protect Linley. Samuel More, now twenty-one years of age, had come to the realization that these were not his children after all; in fact, most of them appeared to resemble Jacob Blakeway.

Less than two months later, Katherine filed for an annulment of her marriage, claiming that she had been previously married in the eyes of God (a common-law marriage) to Jacob Blakeway prior to her marriage to Samuel More. Unable to provide two witnesses, however, she lost her case and was fined £20. The next month, Samuel commenced his own legal attack, taking Katherine and Jacob to the Court of High Commissions. Jacob Blakeway managed to obtain a pardon from the king, however, so the case was dropped.

Emboldened by his legal success, Jacob began openly visiting Katherine, and stayed within Samuel More's own estate. His wife was likewise becoming more insolent and incorrigible, a "wicked woman." In March 1619, Samuel More sued Jacob Blakeway for £10 for treading on and damaging his grass. And with a criminal charge pending, he could then sue Jacob for civil damages. Samuel sued for an enormous amount, £1000. The case went to trial, and the jury awarded him £400 in damages. That was not nearly what Samuel had sued for, but it was enough to completely bankrupt Jacob Blakeway. An appeal to the King's Bench failed. Without enough money to pay, Jacob had two options: go to debtor's prison or flee. He chose the latter, and was never seen again; he may have fled to Ireland.

Having disposed of Jacob Blakeway, Samuel turned his attention back to his wife, seeking a separation from her; but she wanted to fight it, perhaps because the terms were not in her favor. Samuel was granted a judicial annulment in early 1619 by the Court of Audience, but Katherine appealed to the High Court of Delegates. At last, on 8 July 1620, her appeal was dismissed. The separation was official. She had no estate, no legal ability to remarry, and she lost custody of her children to their apparent nonbiological father who had already revoked the children's inheritance.

Now it was time to dispose of his children. He had already revoked their inheritance. But concerned about the "blots and blemishes" that would fall upon the bastardized children, which he referred to as the "spurious brood," he arranged to have them shipped off to Virginia. The next ship scheduled to leave for Virginia was the *Mayflower*. The children were brought to London by one of Samuel's father's servants, Philemon Powell, and then were handed over to Robert Cushman and Thomas Weston. The children lived in Thomas Weston's house for a short time before boarding the *Mayflower* and being distributed amongst the leading Pilgrim families. Samuel More purchased the children each a double share, plus an additional £20 investment. The Plymouth Company was contractually obligated to provide each child fifty acres of land after seven years.

Unfortunately for the More children, the stresses of abandonment must have taken their toll. Jasper was one of the first passengers to die after the *Mayflower*'s arrival; he died on December 6. Ellen and Mary More both died sometime the first winter on unrecorded dates as well. Only Richard More survived the first winter, and eventually to adulthood.

Richard More was still living in the Brewster family in 1627, when he received a share in the division of cattle. On 20 October 1636, he married Christian, daughter of Thomas Hunter, at Plymouth. In 1637,

Richard sold all of his property at Duxbury, and moved shortly thereafter to Salem, where he joined the church there on 27 February 1642/3. He would keep his primary residence in Salem for the remainder of his life, but his occupation as a mariner kept him abroad frequently.

On 23 October 1645, a Richard More of Salem in New England married to Elizabeth Woolno at St. Dunstans, Stepney, co. Middlesex. Since Richard was still married to Christian (who died in Salem on 18 March 1676), this seems to suggest Richard More was secretly engaging in bigamy. The other possible explanation is that there was another Richard More in Salem, though the Salem records do not seem to indicate any other man of the same name.

Richard More, mariner, appears in Salem records on various occasions. Richard was sued on 25 January 1641/2 for killing a pig belonging to John Stacy. He was commissioned by the court to examine the bark *Hopewell* in 1661 to see if it was indeed insufficient for a Newfoundland voyage. Richard More made numerous voyages throughout his career, including to Nova Scotia, Virginia, the Carolinas, and Maryland.

Richard and Christian More had seven children, but only three are known to have survived to adulthood and married. Somewhat ironically, his eldest son was named after his "father," Samuel. It is quite possible that Richard More was never made aware of the circumstances of his forced departure to Virginia. His wife Christian died on 18 March 1676 at Salem, and less than two years later Richard More (then aged sixty-four) married to widow Jane Crumpton. Jane's husband had been killed at Muddy Brook Bridge during King Philip's War in 1675. Jane died on 8 October 1686, at the age of fifty-five. Richard More remained living in Salem, dying sometime between 19 March 1693/4 and 20 April 1696—long enough to have witnessed the infamous Salem witchcraft trials of 1692.

WILLIAM MULLINS,

HIS WIFE ALICE, AND THEIR CHILDREN PRISCILLA AND JOSEPH

William Mullins was born about 1572 in Dorking, co. Surrey, England, most likely the son of John and Joan (Bridger) Mullins of that parish. William's father died in February 1583/4, and his mother Joane remarried on 1 November 1585 to Vincent Benham.

William Mullins is first named in a Dorking record on 4 October 1595, when he was fined two pence, apparently for not attending the manorial court session of that year.[214] He was recorded in that record as living in the Chippingborough neighborhood of Dorking. William Mullins then disappears from Dorking records until 1604. I have theorized that he left Dorking about this time, moving to Stoke near Guildford, co. Surrey, where a man of that name appears on a 1596 muster list. On 11 December 1598, an Elizabeth, daughter of William Mullins, was baptized at Holy Trinity, Guildford, co. Surrey, which I believe may be a daughter of the *Mayflower* passenger. Elizabeth apparently died young. It is unclear who William Mullins had married. When he came on the *Mayflower*, his wife was Alice; but she could have been a second wife. Several theories have been published on the identity of his wife or wives, but nothing is at all conclusive.[215]

William reappears in Dorking on 5 October 1604, when he was elected tithingman for the Eastborough neighborhood. The tithingman was the head of a frankpledge, a group of about ten families that were collectively bonded to the king for their good behavior. When a member of the frankpledge was fined or punished, the entire frankpledge was held responsible, which is apparently what happened on 19 September 1605, when William Mullins was summoned and his frankpledge fined 3s 7d for an unspecified transgression.

On 30 March 1612, William Mullins witnessed the will of a neighbor, John Wood; and on 20 December 1612 he was named an overseer of the will of Jane Hammon. In that record, his occupation is mentioned for the first time: shoemaker. Eight days later, he purchased a tenement on West Street in Dorking: a house which still exists today, and is an occasional tourist stop.

Charles Banks noted that there was a William Mullins who was called before the Privy Council in August 1616, and held for a period of time for an unrecorded reason. He speculates that perhaps William Mullins was involved in some kind of religious controversy that might hint at why he decided to join with the Pilgrims on their voyage to America.[216]

In May 1619, William Mullins sold his Dorking manor holding to Ephraim Bothell, apparently in preparation for his voyage on the *Mayflower*. He had apparently made a decent living as a shoemaker because he made one of the larger investments in the Pilgrims' joint-stock company.

When the Pilgrims organized their company, they drew up an agreement containing the conditions on which the passengers would embark—the costs, the amount of land they would receive, how the stock would be liquidated and divided amongst the investors, even which days of the week the Pilgrims would have to work for the benefit of the company. At the last minute, even as the *Mayflower* was being readied to sail, some of the London businessmen decided they wanted to change the agreement or they were pulling out their money. In a letter written by many of the Pilgrims to these investors, they mentioned that many of the passengers had already invested in the company based on the previous terms, and therefore it was unfair to change them. They pointed out that Robert Cushman had delivered William Mullins a copy of the terms, upon which Mullins paid in. The Pilgrims and London investors parted ways without coming to an agreement on the terms by which they would work—the beginning of the rift that would pull apart the company in later years.

William Mullins, then nearing fifty years of age, brought on the *Mayflower* his wife Alice, his daughter Priscilla (probably about seventeen years old), and his son Joseph (probably about fifteen years old). He left behind in Dorking his two eldest children, Sarah and William. He signed the Mayflower Compact on 11 November 1620.

William, Alice, and Joseph Mullins would all die the first winter at Plymouth, as did their servant Robert Carter, orphaning daughter Priscilla in the New World. William himself was apparently the first to die, on 21 February 1620/1. He made out a nuncupative will on his deathbed, which was sailed back on the *Mayflower* to England in April—the only known will of a passenger that died the first winter. In the will, he mentions that "Goodman Wood" was holding £40 belonging to him. Presumably Goodman Wood was one of the members of the Wood family in Dorking that were neighbors and closely associated with the Mullins family there. Of that £40, William gave ten to his wife, ten to his son Joseph, ten to daughter Priscilla, and ten to his eldest son William back in Dorking. He gave his son William all his stocks and bonds, except £10, which he was to give to sister Sarah. For general goods and supplies that William Mullins brought with him to America, he gave half to his wife Alice, and half to be equally divided between Priscilla and Joseph. He also says he had twenty-one dozen pairs of shoes and thirteen pairs of boots, which he offered to sell to the New Plymouth Company for £40, payable over seven years. He gave his nine shares in the joint-stock company as follows: two to his wife, two to Joseph, two to Priscilla, and one he gave back to the company. He also stipulated that if son William came to Plymouth, he would get to inherit any of his land holdings there. The will—the original, which still survives—was witnessed by Plymouth's first governor John Carver, the *Mayflower*'s master Christopher Jones, and the *Mayflower*'s surgeon Giles Heale.

Daughter Priscilla, the lone survivor of the family in America, married to the *Mayflower*'s cooper, John Alden, in 1622 or 1623.

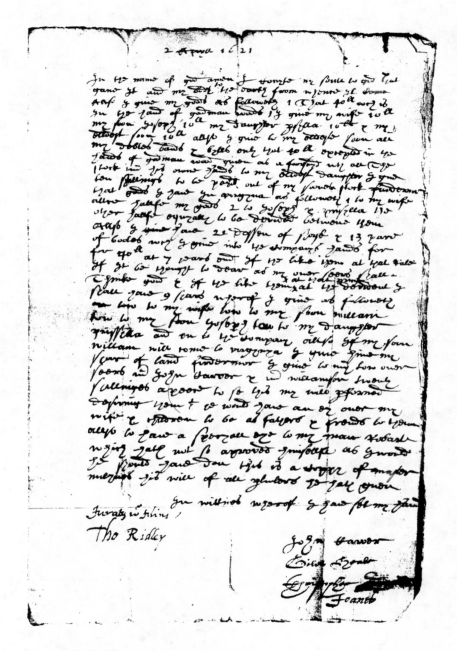

The original will of William Mullins. The will was written onboard the *Mayflower* in February 1621, and signed by Gov. John Carver, *Mayflower* master Christopher Jones, and *Mayflower* surgeon Giles Heale.

DEGORY PRIEST

The English origins of Degory Priest remain unknown. John G. Hunt noted that there was a baptism for a Degory Priest in Hartland, Devonshire, in 1582.[217] However, Devonshire is an unusual place to find an early Leiden Separatist, and the baptism date does not match well with Degory's approximate birth year of 1579, which is based on a couple of Leiden depositions in which he stated his age. I think it is more probable Degory's true origins will be found elsewhere in England.

The first record of the *Mayflower* passenger Degory Priest occurs in Leiden on 7 October 1611, when he was betrothed to the widow Sarah Vincent, who incidentally was the sister of *Mayflower* passenger Isaac Allerton. The couple was married on 4 November 1611, the same date as Isaac Allerton's marriage to Mary Norris.[218]

Degory was relatively active in Leiden compared to many of the other settlers, and appears named in a number of records. On 16 November 1615, he became a citizen of Leiden, with guarantors Isaac Allerton and Roger Wilson. Leiden records indicate Degory was a hatter by trade.

On 29 June 1617, Degory Priest requested that Arthur Stantin and Nicholas Claverly, both tobacco-pipe makers, sign an affidavit stating that when they visited John Cripps on 17 June 1617, they heard Cripps say that Degory had not hit him but only "touched his jabot." A jabot was an ornamental frill on the front of a shirt. Apparently Degory had a confrontation with John Cripps, and wanted this affidavit to help document his innocence.[219] The following day, Degory requested another affidavit, this time indicating that John Cripps, card maker, had been rumored to have committed adultery with Elizabeth, wife of John Mos, a woolcomber in Leiden.[220]

On 18 January 1618, tailor Isaac Allerton signed a statement regarding the estimated value of a crimson coat, and the statement was witnessed by Degory Priest.[221] On 3 May 1619, Richard Tyrill signed a statement stating that Nicholas Claverly had nothing to do with the murder of Tyrill's brother John—and this affidavit was also witnessed by Degory Priest.[222]

Nicholas Claverly, a tobacco-pipe maker, arrived in Leiden about 1615, and had moved into the house belonging to Degory Priest, and was still living there in 1619 when Samuel Lee and Degory Priest, both hatters, signed a certificate of good behavior on his behalf, dated 9 April 1619. In the statement, Degory gave his age as forty years, indicating he was born about 1579.[223]

Degory Priest came by himself on the *Mayflower*, leaving behind his wife Sarah and their two daughters Mary (born about 1612) and Sarah (born about 1614), intending to send for them once the colony was better established. He signed the Mayflower Compact on 11 November 1620. He did not live long after, however: he died early the first winter, on 1 January 1620/1.

Back in Leiden, his wife remarried to Godbert Godbertson, another hat maker, on 13 November 1621. Godbert and Sarah, and her children Mary and Sarah Priest, came to Plymouth on the ship *Anne* in 1623, and were assigned land in the 1623 division of land at Plymouth. Degory's daughters Mary and Sarah both survived to adulthood, married, and had children. Mary married about 1630 to Phineas Pratt, and had eight children. The family moved to Charlestown about 1646. Sarah married about 1631 to John Coombs, and had two children. For unknown reasons, perhaps due to the death of her husband, Sarah went to England about 1645, leaving two children, John and Francis, in the custody of William Spooner. She apparently never returned—perhaps she died in England or on the voyage; Spooner offered to maintain the children.[224]

SOLOMON PROWER

Solomon Prower was a teenage boy when he came on the *Mayflower* in the custody of his mother Mary and stepfather Christopher Martin. Christopher Martin had married the widow Mary Prower in Great Burstead, co. Essex, England, on 26 February 1606/7. Solomon did not sign the Mayflower Compact, indicating he was under the age of twenty-one; this puts his birth somewhere roughly between 1600 and 1606.

Solomon, like his stepfather, had some run-ins with the church authorities in Great Burstead. In 1620, just months before the voyage of the *Mayflower*, Solomon Prower was presented to the archdeaconry court for "refusing to answer me at all unless I would ask him some question in some other catechism." The catechism in question was set down in the *Book of Common Prayer*, which the Puritans rejected.[225]

The voyage and first months in the New World were catastrophic for the Martin family: they all died. Solomon's death occurred on December 24, just days after the Pilgrims had begun exploring the area within Plymouth Harbor. A couple weeks later, his stepfather died, and his mother Mary died the first winter as well, although her exact death date is not recorded.

JOHN RIGSDALE

AND HIS WIFE ALICE

Almost nothing is known about John and Alice Rigsdale. William Bradford, when writing his *Mayflower* passenger list, grouped John and Alice Rigsdale in a list that included other Leiden residents, suggesting the couple may have been a part of the Leiden congregation. However, there are no known Leiden records that mention them.

Only one marriage record between a John Rigsdale and an Alice has been found in English records thus far: John Rigsdale to Alice Gallard on 17 November 1577 at St. Mary, Weston, Lincolnshire. If these are indeed the *Mayflower* passengers, then they can be counted as amongst the oldest passengers on the ship, probably in their mid sixties.

On 11 November 1620, John Rigsdale was one of the men who signed the Mayflower Compact. He left behind no other record. According to William Bradford, "Thomas Thinker and his wife and son all died in the first sickness. And so did John Rigsdale and his wife."

THOMAS ROGERS

AND HIS SON JOSEPH

Thomas Rogers was born about 1572, presumably in the vicinity of Watford, co. Northampton, where he married Alice Cosford on 24 October 1597. Thomas and Alice had five or six children recorded in the parish registers there between 1599 and 1613, including son Joseph who was baptized there on 23 January 1602/3.[226]

Sometime after 1613, Thomas and Alice Rogers and their four surviving children, Joseph, John, Elizabeth, and Margaret, moved to Leiden and joined the Separatist church there. Thomas Rogers purchased a house on *Barbarasteeg* in Leiden from a baker, Jan Bloemsaet, about 1616. He became a citizen of Leiden on 25 June 1618, and is called a camlet merchant.[227] Camlet was a luxury fabric of Asian origin that was originally a combination of camel's hair and silk.

When Thomas Rogers prepared to sell his house in 1619 in preparation for his voyage to America, he discovered there was still an outstanding lien on the property, so he sued Jam Bloemsaet and bondsman Gerrit Gerritsz.[228] On 1 April 1620, he finally sold his house for the price of three hundred guilders to Mordecheus Colven.

Thomas Rogers brought his eldest son Joseph with him on the *Mayflower*, but left behind in Leiden his wife Alice and three children John, Elizabeth, and Margaret. After arrival, Thomas signed the Mayflower Compact, but died the first winter, leaving behind his seventeen-year-old son Joseph at Plymouth, and his wife and three children back in Leiden. Alice and the children are found enumerated amongst the poor people of Leiden in the 1622 poll tax, living at the time in the back part of the house belonging to Anthony Clements.[229]

Joseph Rogers received two acres in the 1623 division of land, one for himself and one in right of his father; and in the 1627 division of land he was joined with the family of William Bradford and received a share in the "heifer of the last year which was of the great white-back cow that was brought over in the *Anne*, and two she-goats."

About 1629 or 1630, Thomas Rogers's children and other church members still in Leiden were brought over at the expense of the Plymouth Colony. Joseph became a freeman in Plymouth in 1633, and was taxed the lowest tax rate, nine shillings. He was taxed nine shillings again in 1634. Shortly thereafter, he moved north to Duxbury. In 1635, he received permission to operate a ferry across the Jones River, and in 1640 he was appointed the constable of Duxbury. With wife Hannah, he had eight children, most of them born in Duxbury. About 1647, he moved his family to Nauset, now Eastham, where on 1 June 1647 he was appointed the lieutenant in charge of training the men there in the use of their arms. He continued his duties throughout the next couple of decades, and was on the Plymouth Colony's Council of War in 1658. He died in January 1677/8 and is buried in the Old Cove Burial Ground in Eastham.

HENRY SAMSON

Henry Samson came on the *Mayflower* as a sixteen-year-old boy. He was baptized on 15 January 1603/4 in Henlow, co. Bedford, England, the son of James and Martha (Cooper) Samson.[230] Henry's mother Martha was the sister of Ann Cooper, who was married to Edward Tilley. It was Edward and Ann Tilley who brought young Henry on the *Mayflower* with them. The exact circumstances remain unknown—perhaps Henry had been apprenticed out to his uncle. Henry's parents and other siblings remained behind in Henlow, although Edward Tilley's brother John and his family, and a cousin, Humility Cooper, also came on the *Mayflower*. Henry would get a brief mention in his father's will of 1638, receiving £5.[231]

Henry Samson was too young to sign the Mayflower Compact. His aunt and uncle both died the first winter, as did John and Joan Tilley, leaving behind just his one-year-old cousin Humility, and John and Joan's thirteen-year-old daughter Elizabeth. It is unclear who took care of Henry for the next few years. He and cousin Humility received shares next to each other in the 1623 division of land on "the north side of the town next adjoining to their gardens which came in the *Fortune*." In the 1627 division of cattle, Henry and Humility were grouped with the William Brewster family, suggesting he was living with them. Their share in the cattle division consisted of "one of the four heifers came in the *Jacob* called the Blind Heifer and 2 she-goats."

Henry Samson became a freeman in Plymouth in 1635, and married Ann Plummer there on 6 February 1635/6. He was a volunteer for the colony in the Pequot War of 1637, but the war ended before Plymouth managed to get its troops organized. Henry and Ann moved shortly thereafter to Duxbury, where he had been granted land next to Henry Howland on 1 January 1637/8. Two years later, in April 1640, he was granted additional land that had formerly been a common, "lying at the head of his lot, . . . provided that a highway be left for cattle to pass to and fro[m] the common." Later, in November, he was granted another fifty acres "with some meadow."[232]

Beginning in the 1640s, Henry Samson began to fulfill some of his public-service duties. During his life, he was on six grand juries between 1641 and 1663, and twelve petty juries between 1644 and 1670. He was an arbiter in 1648, a surveyor in 1649 and 1650, and constable for Duxbury in 1661.[233]

In 1669, Henry Samson was on a coroner's jury assembled by John Alden to investigate the death of John Paybody. The jury concluded: "That he riding on the road, his horse carried him underneath the bow of a young tree, and violently forcing his head unto the body thereof, brake his skull, which we do judge was the cause of his death."[234]

In 1665 and 1667, Henry was allowed by the Plymouth Court to seek out land for his children. Between about 1638 and about 1654, Henry and Ann had had nine children. It is not known exactly when Ann died, but it was sometime after 1668, when she and Henry sold off some of their land at Nemasket. Henry would later sell off some of his Dartmouth properties in 1682 and 1684.

Henry Samson made out his will on 24 December 1684, and it was proved on 5 March 1684/5.[235] In his will, he divides his remaining Dartmouth landholdings between his eldest sons Stephen, John, and James. He gives James and Caleb one shilling each, and gives his daughters Elizabeth, Hannah, Mary, and Dorcas one shilling each as well. He gives "my daughter now the wife of John Hanmore" ten shillings, but fails to mention her name—a name which has not been found in any other record.

George Soule

George Soule came on the *Mayflower* as a manservant or apprentice to Edward Winslow. Nothing specific is known about George Soule's English origins, although there are several Soule families in England using the name George, including at Tingrith and Flitwick, co. Bedford; Ashperton, co. Hereford; Redmarly d'Abitot, co. Worcester, and Sudbury, co. Suffolk, among others. The most commonly published claim is that he was from Eckington, co. Worcester. However, my recently published research into the Soule records of Worcester has shown that all three or four George Soules living in the region can be accounted for, with records showing they could not have been the *Mayflower* passenger. The most promising candidate to date seems to be George Soule from Tingrith, co. Bedford.[236]

On 11 November 1620, George Soule signed the Mayflower Compact, indicating he must have been twenty-one years old—but since he was a servant, he was under twenty-five years old. This puts his birth between 1595 and 1599.

In the 1623 division of land at Plymouth, George Soule received one acre "on the south side of the brook to the baywards," apparently next to Francis Cooke and Isaac Allerton. About 1626, George Soule married a woman named Mary. It is presumed his wife was Mary Buckett, the only known Mary in Plymouth who was then unmarried. George and Mary Soule and their first son Zachariah are named in the 1627 division of cattle, where they were joined with the Warren family.[237] They were allotted a share of "one of the 4 black heifers that came in the *Jacob* called the Smooth-horned Heifer, and two she-goats."

He became a freeman at some point prior to 1632/3, and was taxed 9s. in both the 1633 and 1634—the lowest tax rate, indicating he did not then have any significant estate. But he did have at least one cow:

in July 1633, the Plymouth Court made "orders about mowing of grass," and George Soule was assigned to "mow for a cow near his dwelling house." Stephen Hopkins and Thomas Clark were appointed to mow where they did last year, "except George Soule's cow, as before appointed.[238]"

George seems to have lived a fairly ordinary life. He acquired various properties through the years, which he would distribute amongst his children as he got older. He was never involved in any legal disputes, and he performed public service on various occasions.

In 1637, he was assigned "a garden place . . . on Duxbury side, by Samuel Nash's, to lie to his ground at Powder Point." And in 1638, "one acre of land is granted to George Soule at the watering place . . . and also a parcel of Stony Marsh at Powder Point, containing two acres." The land at the "watering place" in South Plymouth was sold the next year, presumably because he was then living in Duxbury and had little use for property in south Plymouth. He was then granted a meadow at Green's Harbor (now Marshfield) in 1640.[239]

In 1637, George Soule began his public service by volunteering to fight in the Pequot War.[240] However, the war was over before the Plymouth company could get organized. In 1640, he was on a committee to grant land—a committee he would be on again in 1645.[241] He was on at least five grand and petty juries, the first in 1642 and the last in 1662.[242]

On 20 October 1646, "Anthony Thatcher and George Soule were chosen a committee to draw up an order concerning disorderly drinking [i.e., smoking] of tobacco." The law they came up with was as follows[243]:

> Whereas there is great abuse in taking of tobacco in very uncivil manner in the streets and dangerously in outhouses such as barns, stalls, about haystacks, corn stacks, and other such places, it is therefore enacted by this court, that if any person or persons shall be found or seen hereafter taking tobacco publicly in the open streets of any town, (unless it be soldiers in the time of their training) or in and about barns, stalls, haystacks, corn stacks, hay yards, or other such places or outhouses, that every such person or persons so offending shall forfeit and pay to the town's use, for the

first default 12d., for the second 2s., and so for every such default afterwards 2s., and it shall be lawful and by this act warrantable for the constable of every township without further warrant, upon sight or information thereof to detain his or their goods for it as do refuse to pay it upon his demand and to be accountable to the treasurer of what he receives yearly at the election court.

George and Mary Soule seem to have made a respectable Puritan home, building up some modest landholdings, having a large family of children, participating in public service, and never being involved in any criminal or civil court matter. But the records seem to show that some of their nine children (Zachariah, John, Nathaniel, George, Susanna, Mary, Elizabeth, Patience, and Benjamin) were a little harder to control, and were by Puritan standards rather undisciplined.

Son Nathaniel Soule seems to have been the biggest troublemaker of the brood. On 5 March 1667/8, Nathaniel was summoned to appear in court to "answer for his abusing of Mr. John Holmes, teacher of the church of Christ at Duxbury, by many false, scandalous and opprobrious speeches." He was sentenced to make a public acknowledgment of his wrong, to find sureties for his good behavior, and to sit in the stocks. But "at the earnest request of the said Mr. Holmes," the part of his sentence involving the stocks was remitted. In his public apology, Nathaniel Soule says he hopes this "may be a warning to me whiles I live to take heed that I no more so falsely and wickedly speak as I have done of the said reverend man, nor of any other." His father George and brother John were both bound for £10 for Nathaniel's good behavior. Nathaniel himself was bound for £20, and paid a fine of 10s.[244]

But three years later, on 5 June 1671, Nathaniel Soule was fined £5 for "telling several lies which tended greatly to the hurt of the Colony in reference to some particulars about the Indians.[245]" And then, on 1 March 1674/5, Nathaniel was sentenced to be whipped at the post for "lying with an Indian woman," and was also ordered "to pay ten bushels of Indian corn to the said Indian woman towards the keeping of her child.[246]"

George Soule's daughter Elizabeth Soule also had several run-ins with the Plymouth Colony authorities. On 3 March 1662/3, the

Plymouth Court fined Nathaniel Church and Elizabeth Soule £5 each, for committing fornication. Elizabeth Soule then sued Nathaniel Church for £200 "for committing the act of fornication with her . . . and for denying to marry her." The jury awarded her £10 damages, plus court costs.[247] But on 2 July 1667, Elizabeth Soule was whipped at the post "for committing fornication the second time.[248]" Although the man involved was not named, she did marry Francis Walker very shortly thereafter.

George Soule, the father, died about 1679. He had made out his will on 11 August 1677, and mentions "my eldest son John Soule and his family hath in my extreme old age and weakness been tender and careful of me and very helpful to me." He made son John his executor, and gave him nearly all his estate. But just two years later, in a codicil to his will, dated 20 September 1677, George Soule added this: "if my son John Soule . . . or his heirs or assigns or any of them shall at any time disturb my daughter Patience or her heirs or assigns or any of them in peaceable possession or enjoyment of the lands I have given her at Nemasket alias Middleboro and recover the same from her or her heirs or assigns or any of them, that then my gift to my son John Soule shall be void; and that then my will is my daughter Patience shall have all my lands at Duxbury and she shall be my sole executrix of this my last will and testament and enter into my housing, lands, and meadows at Duxbury.[249]" To put the youngest daughter ahead of the eldest son to inherit a father's estate, that would have been a significant humiliation. John Soule must have behaved himself after father George's death: he received his inheritance of the Duxbury estate, and twenty years later his sister Patience and her husband John Haskall sold off the Middleboro property they had received from George Soule.

George Soule's estate at his death included a dwelling house, orchard, barn, upland, meadow land, bedding and clothing, a gun, books, a chest and chair, two sheers, a trammel and wedge, old lumber, and £3 worth of debts due to the estate—in total, his estate was valued at £40 19s. George Soule had a number of small debts as well, which provide an interesting look at some of the late seventeenth century expenses: he owed money to various individuals for plowing in wheat and peas, reaping rye and peas, weeding, and for "getting and bringing home 3 loads of hay." Among other things, he owed money for "1 lock for a barn door," ten yards of canvas, buttons and silk, blue linen, brown-colored thread, four yards of red cotton, three hundred shoe nails, twenty yards of canvas, serge for a pair of britches, and one pair of sheets. He also owed someone eight shillings for making a fence between the orchard, and he owed £2 to someone for making a stone wall about the orchard. Funeral charges were rated at £1. Interestingly, the estate inventory (which was drawn up by son John Soule) includes a debt for "diet and tendance since my mother died which was three year last December, except some small time my sister Patience dressed his victuals."

MYLES STANDISH

AND HIS WIFE ROSE

According to Nathaniel Morton, writing in his 1669 book *New England's Memorial*, Myles Standish was "a gentleman, born in Lancashire, and was heir apparent unto a great estate of lands and livings, surreptitiously detained from him; his great grandfather being a second or younger brother from the house of Standish." Surprisingly, in spite of Standish's apparent status and family wealth, his name has not been found in any English record prior to his joining the *Mayflower* voyage.

Although Standish had always been identified as from Lancashire from the seventeenth century onward, in 1920, T. C. Porteus published a theory that Standish was actually from the Isle of Man, and this was followed up by later research by G. V. C. Young, who published his theories and supporting documents in a series of three books in the 1980s.[250] However, nothing conclusive was ever found, and therefore the Lancashire origins must still be considered the most probable. In 1999, Helen Moorwood published a five-part article in the *Lancashire History Quarterly*, with counter arguments to the Isle of Man theories, attempting to reassert Standish's origins in Lancashire.[251]

Traditionally, Myles Standish's birth has been placed about 1584. In the late nineteenth century, a supposed portrait of Myles Standish came to light, with an inscription that indicated his age was thirty-eight in 1625, which would place Standish's birth at about 1587. The authenticity of the portrait has been debated, but it seems reasonable that it could be authentic.

Portrait of Myles Standish made in 1625. Reprinted from *Memorial History of Boston* (Boston, 1880).

Standish, at a relatively young age, joined the army of Queen Elizabeth, where he started out as a drummer. Supposedly, during the nineteenth century, there existed a document that was Myles's commission to the rank of lieutenant. Unfortunately, this document has been lost, having never been transcribed or put into print. Standish may have attended the Rivington Grammar School in Chorley, Lancashire, though the records of pupils do not exist for the time period he would have attended. Standish, at his death, owned a book entitled *Allegations against Bishop Pilkington of Durham*, who was the founder of the Rivington Grammar School.

According to Captain John Smith (the same one that was rescued by Pocahontas in Virginia), Myles Standish was "a bred soldier in Holland." Nathaniel Morton, writing in 1669, confirms this by adding, "In his younger time he went over into the Low Countries, and was a soldier there, and came acquainted with the church at Leiden."

It is generally assumed that Standish was one of the 4,350 English troops under Sir Heratio Vere that attacked the Spanish in the Netherlands in 1601; if that was the case, he would have only been about twelve or fourteen years old, perhaps still a drummer. Dr. Jeremy Bangs of the Leiden American Pilgrim Museum has noted there is a hospital record in Leiden that reports the October arrival and November 1601 death of a "Myls Stansen." It has been suggested the death could have been a clerical error that should have been a discharge rather than a death; others have suggested this could be the father or close relative with the same name. Or it could just be a coincidence, with no relevance whatsoever.

Woodcut of a 17th century English soldier. Reprinted from Gervase Markham, *A School for Young Soldiers* (London, 1615).

Whatever the case, the Pilgrims' church congregation was not formed in Leiden until 1609, so Standish must have been in Holland much later than the battles of 1601 and 1602. Perhaps he was stationed there after the April 1609 truce was signed between the Netherlands and Spain.

In Leiden, Myles Standish appears to have struck up a close friendship with the Pilgrims' pastor, John Robinson. Robinson, in a letter dated 1623, wrote to Governor Bradford that he should "consider of the disposition of your Captain, whom I love." Myles Standish, in his will of 1656, gave £3 to Mercy Robinson "whom I tenderly love for her grandfather's sake."

When the Pilgrims made the decision to remove their church to somewhere in Northern Virginia, they needed someone who could take charge of the defense of the colonists (from the Spanish, French, and Dutch, as well as the Indians), and organize the militia. One possibility they considered was Captain John Smith, who had lots of experience in Virginia. But he charged too much for his services, and he had little sympathy for their religious views; the Pilgrims also thought they could just read his books to learn from his experiences. So, they chose someone closer to their church and community, someone they knew: Myles Standish.

After arriving and anchoring off the tip of Cape Cod and signing the Mayflower Compact, Myles Standish was put in charge of the various explorations that were sent out to seek a place to build their colony. Right after the signing of the Mayflower Compact, on the morning of November 11, the Pilgrims set ashore "15 or 16 men, well armed, with some to fetch wood." On November 13, they brought their shallop ashore to begin reassembling it, and the women were brought ashore to do laundry.

On November 15, "sixteen men were set out with every man his musket, sword, and corselet, under the conduct of Captain Myles Standish, unto whom was adjoined for counsel and advice, William Bradford, Stephen Hopkins, and Edward Tilley." Shortly into their walk up the Cape Cod coastline, from modern-day Provincetown toward Truro, the men saw "five or six people with a dog coming towards them," and quickly determined they were Indians. The Indians, seeing the armed Englishmen, ran into the forest. The Pilgrims followed their footsteps for about ten miles before nightfall, but could never meet up with them. The next day, they went in search of the Indians, and in search of fresh water (strangely, they had failed to bring any water with them!) They would happen upon fresh water about midday, and "sat us down and drunk our first New England water with as much delight as ever we drunk drink in all our lives." They then explored the Pamet River area, finding nearby an old Indian house, and dug up a basket full of thirty-six ears of Indian corn that had been buried, "some yellow, and some red, and others mixed with blue." They took it. Finding other mounds, they began to dig those up as well, hoping for more seed; but most of what they ended up digging were graves.

For the next exploration, a larger group of thirty-four men were organized, taking out both the shallop and the ship's longboat. The exploration was technically led by the *Mayflower's* master Christopher Jones, "for we thought it best herein to gratify his kindness and forwardness," but Captain Myles Standish was undoubtedly a leader of the exploration as well. They headed back to the Pamet River, which they nicknamed Cold Harbor, and explored up both creeks. Finding little, they returned to Corn Hill and found some more mounds to dig up, from which they got more corn seed. That night, about half of the weakest people went back to the *Mayflower* with Master Jones, leaving eighteen men to continue the exploration the next day. The eighteen that remained behind encountered a larger, more sumptuous grave the following day, which they dug up, and found mats, trays, bows and arrows, mats, red powder, and "the bones and skull of a man." The skull had "fine yellow hair still on it," and they also found a sailor's canvas cassock, a pair of breeches, a knife, and other things which made them believe it may have been a European sailor of some kind. They returned to the *Mayflower*, having still not found a place suitable to build a colony.

The third major expedition was set out on December 6, again with about eighteen men, led by Myles Standish. They sailed first to what is now Welfleet Harbor, where they espied several Indians cleaning a large fish along the shoreline, but the tide prevented them from making any kind of intercept. The next night, the Pilgrims took up their lodging around what is now modern-day Eastham. In the middle of the night, they heard strange howls, which some thought were wolves; early the next morning, about 5:00 AM, they heard the same noise, but this time it was an attack by the Nauset. "Withal their arrows came flying amongst us . . . In the meantime, Captain Myles Standish, having a snaphance ready, made a shot, and after him another; after they two had shot, other two of us were ready, but he wished us not to shoot, till we could take aim, for we knew not what need we should have, and

there were four only of us, which had their arms there ready."
Eventually, the gunfire scared off the attackers, and the Pilgrims went
on their way, circling around the cape. Toward the late afternoon, the
seas picked up, and their rudder broke from its hinges. And a little
while later, the mast broke into three pieces, forcing them to paddle
and steer with just a few oars. They managed to beach themselves on
an island that night, and the following morning they kept their Sabbath
there. On Monday, they explored Plymouth Harbor and determined
it was the best place to settle.

About two weeks into building some of the first structures onshore,
Standish and five others went out an a brief expedition to see if they
could meet any of the Indians, of which they had seen none since their
attack on Cape Cod. They could not find any to meet with.

Another month passed as construction at Plymouth proceeded,
and the First Winter began to take its toll. Myles Standish's wife Rose
died on 29 January 1620/1. William Bradford noted in his journal
history:

> But that which was most sad, and lamentable, was
> that in 2 or 3 months' time half of their company died,
> especially in January and February, being the depth of
> winter . . . so as there died sometimes 2 or 3 of a day, in
> the aforesaid time, that of 100 and odd persons scarce
> fifty remained: and of these in the time of most distress
> there was but 6 or 7 sound persons; who to their great
> commendations, be it spoken, spared no pains, night
> nor day, but with abundance of toil and hazard of their
> own health, fetched them wood, made them fires,
> dressed them meat, made their beds, washed their
> loathsome clothes, clothed and unclothed them. In a
> word did all the homely and necessary offices for them,
> which dainty and queasy stomachs cannot endure to
> hear named; and all this willingly and cheerfully, without
> any grudging in the least, showing herein their true love
> unto their friends and brethren; a rare example and
> worthy to be remembered. Two of these 7 were Mr.
> William Brewster their reverend Elder, and Myles
> Standish their captain and military commander (unto

whom myself, and many others were much beholden in our low, and sick condition) and yet the Lord so upheld these persons, as in this general calamity they were not at all infected either with sickness or lameness.

On February 16, Myles Standish and Francis Cooke were out cutting wood and gathering thatch for houses. Upon returning from a lunch break, they found all their tools had been stolen by some Indians. The next day, the colonists decided it was time to formally elect Myles Standish as captain, but the ceremony was interrupted when several Indians showed themselves at the top of a hill about a quarter mile away "and made signs unto us to come unto them," to which "Captain Standish and Stephen Hopkins, who went towards them, only one of them had a musket, which they laid down on the ground in their sight, in sign of peace, and to parley with them, but the savages would not tarry their coming: a noise of a great many more was heard behind the hill, but no more came in sight."

The Pilgrims decided it was best to bring ashore the canon and some other artillery to increase their defenses, and continued constructing their dwellings. A month later, they resumed the ceremony to appoint Standish as the military captain, but the ceremony was again interrupted. To everyone's astonishment, an Indian walked right into the colony and walked right toward the fort where everyone was meeting, "where we intercepted him, not suffering him to go in, as undoubtedly he would, out of his boldness." Then, to everyone's further surprise, "he saluted us in English, and bade us welcome." They learned his name was Samoset, and that he was just visiting the region from Maine where he had learned some broken English from the fishing vessels that traded there. From him, Standish learned that their nearest neighbors, led by Massasoit, were about sixty strong, and that the Nauset, whom they had encountered while exploring on Cape Cod, were about one hundred strong. They learned that the Nauset were very hostile toward Europeans because a number of them had been kidnapped by an English captain, Thomas Hunt, in 1614, and taken to Spain, where they were sold as slaves. Samoset noted that one of them, an Indian named Tisquantum, had made his way out of Spain into England, where he learned English, and had returned a couple of years before the Pilgrims with Captain Thomas Dermer. Samoset was sent off the next day, with promises to return with some of Massasoit's men, including Tisquantum, to meet and trade beaver skins.

On March 22, the Pilgrims again began their ceremony to appoint Myles Standish as their militia captain, and for the third time it was interrupted by the coming of Indians. This time, it was Samoset and Squanto, and they had brought with them Massasoit himself, and his brother Quadequina. Myles Standish and William Brewster went out to Town Brook and met Massasoit and escorted him to Governor John Carver's house. Carver and Massasoit formed a mutual defensive alliance together, promising to defend one another from each other's enemies.

The following year, Massasoit's neighbors, the Narragansett, sent a messenger with a rattlesnake's skin stuffed full of arrows to Plymouth—a symbolic gesture of hostility. Standish ordered the messenger be detained until the meaning of the message was better understood. After Squanto advised them of the meaning, they released the messenger—Myles Standish concluded that he was acting in the capacity of a messenger, and that holding him would be a violation of the Law of Arms. Governor Bradford had the rattlesnake's skin stuffed with bullets and returned with the message that the Pilgrims would not initiate hostilities, but that they were not afraid and would be well prepared. Bradford and Standish decided it would be best to initiate construction of a fort and walls to enclose the town. The men were divided into four squadrons, and everyone had a specific place to go when an alarm was sounded. They established a nightly watch, and procedures to ensure the town remained on guard even in the event of a fire.

By March 1622, the walls around the town were complete, and thoughts turned to trading with the Indians. In April, Standish, along with Hobomok and Squanto and ten other men, made a voyage to the Massachusett Indians to the north "where we had good store of trade." By summer, Standish saw the completion of the fort itself, which was a two-story flat-roofed structure where several canon were mounted and ready for service—either in defending from Indian attack, or for signaling (or shooting at) ships in the bay.

In July 1622, two ships with passengers arrived at Plymouth—the *Charity* and the *Swan*—sent out by Thomas Weston, one of the primary investors in the Pilgrims' joint-stock company. Weston had sold out his shares, and was going to establish a competing colony to the north in the Massachusetts Bay, in a location called Wessagussett. But in the meantime, his less-than-savory colonists took up an unwelcome residence at Plymouth and ate through much of the colony's store of food (just "borrowed," on credit, of course), before eventually making their way to set up their own colony. It took just a few months for the poorly managed colonists to work through their food supplies and trade goods—so some of the colonists began to take their food from the Indians by thievery. In November 1622, the Plymouth and Wessagussett colonists decided to send out a joint trading expedition to some Indian groups to the south of the cape. Standish led the expedition, but it was forced back twice by poor weather, at which point he fell sick with a bad fever. Governor Bradford took his place. The voyage was fraught with disaster, as Squanto died shortly into the voyage, and the boat wrecked in a storm and much of the trading goods had to be temporarily left in the custody of some local Indians while the men went by land back to Plymouth to get another boat to provide assistance in bringing everything home.

Captain Standish led the return voyage to retrieve the goods, and there found the Indians were becoming less friendly and hospitable. While at one of the Indian villages, some of the trade goods were stolen, and Standish threatened the local sachem with retaliation if the goods were not returned. The goods were found, and returned. At an Indian village called Mattachiest, again, some beads were stolen, and Standish had the sachem's house surrounded until the goods were returned.

Later at Manomet, Captain Standish witnessed a visit by Wituwamat (the leader of the Indians near the Wessagussett Colony) to the local sachem, Canacum, and he began to feel something was brewing when many of the Indians began behaving uncharacteristically. Although Standish was the "best linguist amongst us," he was not able to make out any of the conversation between Wituwamat and Canacum. Unbeknownst to Plymouth, many of the Indians, angered by the Wessagussett colonists' behavior, were conspiring together to expel the English from the region. There were apparently plans to take Standish's life during the night that weather enforced him to stay within an Indian house at Manomet; but Standish's bout of insomnia apparently foiled the attempt.

While Standish was returning with the trading goods, Edward Winslow had been dispatched to visit a reportedly sick Massasoit. Winslow ended up playing the unexpected role of doctor, and provided Massasoit with various English medical treatments (including chicken broth) that ended up working a miracle and curing Massasoit. As Winslow departed, Massasoit related the Indian conspiracy to Winslow. Massasoit urged Plymouth to kill the Indian leaders in charge of the conspiracy (in particular, Wituwamat). Within a few days of hearing about the conspiracy, a man from Wessagussett named Phineas Pratt arrived by foot at Plymouth, having run the whole way through the snow from the Massachusetts Bay. He related the terrible state of the colony, and that he too had discovered (from the slip of an Indian woman's tongue) that there was a conspiracy afoot to kill all the Englishmen at Wessagussett and Plymouth. After hearing all these things, Governor Bradford—in consultation with his assistants— ordered Captain Standish to take as many men as he desired, and return with the head of Wituwamat, the leader of the conspiracy.

When Standish arrived at the Wessagussett colony, he found the situation dire. They were scavenging for ground nuts and shellfish, having sold or traded away nearly everything they had for small amounts of corn from the Indians. There was no hope to save the colonists, so he offered to give them enough food and supplies so that they could sail to Maine, where they could catch fishing vessels home. But Captain Standish had orders to get Wituwamat's head first.

One of the Indian leaders, a pniese named Pecksuot, came to realize that Captain Standish had come to kill all the Indians, and began to taunt him: "tell him . . . we know it, but fear him not . . . he shall not take us at unawares." According to Edward Winslow, "they would whet and sharpen the points of their knives before his face, and use many other insulting gestures and speeches . . . Also Pecksuot being a man of greater stature [height] than the Captain, told him though he were a great Captain, yet he was but a little man . . . [and] though I be no Sachem, yet I am a man of great strength and courage." Captain Standish bore the insulting patiently that day. The next day, however, Standish saw his opportunity. Pecksuot and Wituwamat were both together with another man and Wituwamat's younger brother. Standish had the door shut behind them, and he grabbed a knife from around Pecksuot's neck. After "much struggling," Standish killed

Pecksuot; the other Englishmen killed Wituwamat and the other man, and would hang the younger brother of Wituwamat later that day. After the fight, Hobomok congratulated Standish: "Yesterday Pecksuot bragging of his own strength and stature, said, though you were a great Captain, yet you were but a little man; but today I see you are big enough to lay him on the ground."

Standish sent word to another group of Englishmen to kill all the Indian men that were there, and so they killed two. Standish took a few men out on a short expedition and killed another, but one escaped and alerted the other Indians to what was happening. Standish, "still seeking to make spoil of them and theirs," took a group of his men on a march to locate the remainder of the Indians. On their way, they encountered a group of Indians on their way to the fight. Standish and his men took a small hill; hiding behind trees, the two groups exchanged arrows and gunfire. One of the Indian leaders took aim at Standish, but the Captain managed to get a shot off and broke his arm, causing him to flee into the swamp. Standish "dared the sachem to come out and fight like a man, showing how base and woman-like he was in tonguing it as he did: but he refused and fled."

After his march, Standish returned to Wessagussett, and released the Indian women that had been taken captive, where "he would not take their beaver coats from them, nor suffer the least discourtesy to be offered them." Most of the Wessagussett colonists took their shallop off to Maine to seek passage home with the fishing vessels; a few returned with Standish to become residents of Plymouth. The head of Wituwamat was brought back to the Plymouth fort and stuck up on a stake to serve as a warning to other Indians who might want to conspire against the English. Cutting off the head of a convict and displaying it publicly was something that was regularly practiced by the English—in London, the severed heads were displayed at the London Bridge.

Although Standish's actions were viewed as reasonable and necessary by the colonists, many of their backers in England, and even their pastor John Robinson in Leiden, thought he had gone overboard. Robinson, in a letter to Governor Bradford, wrote:

> Concerning the killing of those poor Indians, of
> which we heard at first by report, and since by more

certain relation. Oh, how happy a thing had it been, if
you had converted some, before you had killed any;
besides where blood is once begun to be shed, it is seldom
staunched of a long time after. You will say they deserved
it, I grant it; but upon what provocations, and
invitements, by those heathenish Christians? Besides
you being no magistrates over them, were to consider,
not what they deserved, but what you were by necessity
constrained to inflict. Necessity of this, especially of
killing so many (and many more it seems they would, if
they could) I see not. Methinks, one or two principals
should have been full enough, according to that
approved rule: the punishment to a few, and the fear to
many. Upon this occasion, let me be bold to exhort you,
seriously to consider of the disposition of your Captain,
whom I love; and am persuaded, the Lord in great mercy
and for much good, hath sent you him, if you use him
aright. He is a man humble, and meek against you, and
towards all in ordinary course. But now if this be merely
from an human spirit, there is cause to fear that by
occasion especially of provocation, there may be wanting
that tenderness of life of man (made after God's image)
which is meet.

William Bradford, in a letter to the investors back in England,
simply wrote, "As for Captain Standish we leave him to answer for
himself; but this we must say, he is as helpful an instrument as any we
have, and as careful of the general good, and doth not well approve
himself."

In 1623, the ship *Anne* arrived, and onboard the ship was a woman
named Barbara, whom Standish married very shortly thereafter. It
seems probable that Standish may have arranged for Barbara's coming,
as it would be highly improbable for a single woman to travel to
Plymouth unaccompanied.

Also onboard the *Anne* was a passenger named John Oldham, and
the following year arrived Rev. John Lyford. Bradford recalled that
when Lyford first came to them, "he saluted them with that reverence,
and humility, as is seldom to be seen, and indeed made them ashamed,

he so bowed and cringed unto them, and would have kissed their hands, if they would have suffered him." But it was not long before Oldham and Lyford "grew very perverse, and showed a spirit of great malignancy, drawing as many into faction as they could; were they never so vile, or profane, they did nourish and back them in all their doings: so they would but cleave to them, and speak against the church here; so as there was nothing but private meetings and whisperings amongst them."

When Governor Bradford noticed that Oldham and Lyford were taking an unusually long amount of time to write some letters to send home on a ship that was then in Plymouth Harbor, he got suspicious of their activities. As the ship was preparing to depart, Bradford made one last visit out, where he opened and read their letters. He found Oldham and Lyford were writing slanderous and treasonous accusations against the Plymouth church and government. Bradford made copies of the letters, and added his own annotations and rebuttals, and then sent them on—holding on to the originals as evidence. Ironically, some of the letters indicated that Lyford himself had opened and annotated some of Edward Winslow's letters. Bradford shared the letters with a few of his closest advisers at Plymouth, probably Allerton and Brewster, but otherwise kept them secret so that he could "better discover their intents, and see who were their adherents." In one of the letters, Lyford admitted that after the ship left, they intended to force a reformation in the church, and begin administering the sacraments. And in a letter written by John Oldham, he wrote that Captain Standish "looks like a silly boy, and is in utter contempt."

Oldham's dislike for Captain Standish boiled over a few weeks later. Watch duty was a service that every man in Plymouth had to perform. But on this occasion, when Standish called Oldham to his watch, he refused. He "fell out with the Captain, called him a rascal, and a beggarly rascal, and resisted him, drew his knife at him; though he offered him no wrong, nor gave him no ill terms, but with all fairness required him to do his duty." When Bradford came to quiet the situation, Oldham blew up even further, calling them "all traitors and rebels, and other such foul language as I am ashamed to remember." After spending time in prison, and some "slight punishment," he was let go upon his further good behavior.

A short time later, Oldham and Lyford and a few others pulled out of Plymouth's Sunday services, and established their own separate meeting. That was the last straw. Bradford had them brought to court and presented them with conspiracy and disturbing the peace. Both were eventually sentenced to banishment.

In early 1625, Myles Standish was called upon again to defend the interests of Plymouth. In 1623, the Plymouth Colony obtained a patent from the Council of New England for exclusive fishing rights to Cape Anne, and the following year they constructed a fishing pier there. The fishing voyage that year was ultimately a failure, and the pier went unused in 1625. One Master Hewes, funded by West Country merchants, found the pier abandoned and took it over for his own use. When the company of New Plymouth discovered it had been usurped, they sent Captain Standish to reclaim it. As William Hubbard later reported it:[252] "The dispute grew to be very hot, and high words passed between them; which might have ended in blows, if not in blood and slaughter." Hewes barricaded himself and his men on the fishing stage, their escape cut off by Standish and his men who were on land. Hubbard noted that "Capt. Standish had been bred a soldier in the Low Countries, and never entered the school of our Savior Christ, or of John Baptist, his harbinger; or, if he was ever there, had forgot his first lessons, to offer violence to no man, and to part with the cloak rather than needlessly contend for the coat, though taken away without order. A little chimney soon fired; so was the Plymouth captain, a man of very little stature, yet of a very hot and angry temper. The fire of his passion soon kindled, and blown up into a flame by hot words, might easily have consumed all, had it not been seasonably quenched."

The situation was diffused with mediation from Roger Conant and William Pierce, and finally came to closure after the ship's crew agreed to help Mr. Hewes construct his own fishing stage instead of using the one built by Plymouth.

In the autumn of 1625, Standish was appointed to travel back to London to act as the Pilgrims' agent there to oversee the sale of their beaver and otter furs (which they estimated at the value of £277), and to procure additional English trade goods that could be used for further trade with the Indians. Bradford noted in a letter to Robert Cushman that Standish was the person "whom we have thought most meet for sundry reasons to send at this time. I pray you be as helpful to him as you can; especially in making our provisions, for therein he hath the least skill."

The timing of the voyage, however, proved most unfortunate. Bradford noted: "By reason of the great plague which raged this year in London, of which so many thousands died weekly, Captain Standish could do nothing either with the Council of New England, or any other hereabout, for there were no courts kept, or scarce any commerce held, the city being in a sort desolate by the fervent pestilence, and flight of so many. So as he was forced to return; having by the help of some friends (with much ado, and great both trouble and peril to himself) procured a convenient supply which he brought with him to save our greatest necessities.[253]"

Captain Standish returned in April 1626 by a fishing vessel, and then sent a message to Plymouth that he had arrived. Plymouth sent out its shallop to pick him up. He brought bad news—not only of the plague, but also of the death of Robert Cushman and their pastor John Robinson in Leiden. He also brought news of the death of King James I, and the ascension of King Charles I. And for trade goods, he could only gather enough funds to procure £150 worth, and that was at 50 percent interest.

In 1628, Captain Standish's services would be needed by the colonists once more—this time not against the Indians, but against an Englishman. Thomas Morton had taken up residence in the Massachusetts Bay, collecting around him a number of runaway servants. He renamed his settlement Merrymount, set up a maypole, and entertained Indians with dances. All this irked the staunchly religious Pilgrims; but Morton was outside of their jurisdiction, and they had no legal authority to do anything other than complain to the appropriate authorities in London. But Morton would eventually step over the line when he began trading guns to the Indians— something prohibited by a proclamation of King James. When Thomas Morton refused to surrender himself to Plymouth authorities for justice, they appointed Standish to arrest him by force. Of course, Thomas Morton's side of the story was much different, and is recorded in sarcastic tone in his book *New English Canaan*:

> The Separatists envying the prosperity, and hope of
> the plantation at Merrymount . . . conspired together

against Mine Host . . . and made up a party against him; and mustered up what aid they could; accounting of him, as of a great monster.

According to Morton, "Captain Shrimp" and his appointed "nine worthies" accidentally stumbled upon him at the town of Wessagussett and arrested him there. "Much rejoicing was made that they had gotten their capital enemy." Morton continues, adding, "The conspirators sported themselves at mine honest host, that meant them no hurt; and were so jocund that they feasted their bodies, and fell to tippling [drinking], as if they had obtained a great prize." But Morton pretended to be so grieved that he could not eat or drink. Standish, or rather Captain Shrimp, appointed six men to watch after Morton that night. But those men were unable to keep the watch, and Morton snuck out. He shut the door after him "with such violence, that it affrighted some of the conspirators." Morton imagined what happened next: "The word which was given with an alarm was, 'O he's gone, He's gone, what shall we do, he's gone?' The rest (half asleep) start up in a maze, and like rams, ran their heads one at another full butt in the dark."

Their grand leader Captain Shrimp took on most furiously, and tore his clothes for anger, to see the empty nest, and their bird gone . . . now Captain Shrimp thought in the loss of this prize (which he accounted his masterpiece), all his honor would be lost forever.

Thomas Morton returned to his home at Merrymount, and gathering his servants around him, prepared to defend himself. "Now Captain Shrimp, the first captain in the land (as he supposed), must do some new act to repair this loss, and to vindicate his reputation, who had sustained blemish, by this oversight." Morton was ready to give Standish and his men "such a welcome, as would have made him wish for a drum as big as Diogenes' tub, that he might have crept into it out of sight." Unfortunately for Morton, his servants proved incompetent—one was "a craven" and one was so drunk he ended up stabbing himself in the nose. Morton himself claims he could have "played upon them out at his port holes for they came within danger like a flock of wild geese, as if they had been tailed one to another, as colts to be sold at a fair . . . So much worthy blood . . . would have issued out of the veins of these 9 worthies of New Canaan."

Captain Standish offered Morton safety and good treatment if he came out unarmed. Morton refused, insisting that he was willing to give up, but wanted to keep his arms, claiming "they were so needful at sea, if he should be sent over." According to Morton, Standish agreed to the terms (that he would be allowed his gun for the voyage back to England), but as soon as he opened the door to surrender, "Captain Shrimp, and the rest of the Worthies stepped to him, laid hold of his arms, and had him down, and so eagerly was every man bent against him . . . that they fell upon him, as if they would have eaten him: some of them were so violent, that they would have a slice with scabbard and all for haste . . . Captain Shrimp and the rest of the nine Worthies, made themselves (by this outrageous riot) masters of Mine Host of Merrymount, and disposed of what he had at his plantation."

The next five or six years of Captain Standish's life were fairly quiet. He and wife Barbara were raising their young family, having had children Charles (about 1624, died young), Alexander (about 1626), John (about 1627), Myles (about 1629), Lora (about 1631), Josias (about 1633), and a second Charles (about 1635). He remained an assistant in Plymouth's government, and one of the purchasers and undertakers for the colony and its debt. In the 1627 division of cattle, he, along with his wife Barbara and children Charles, Alexander, and John, was allotted shares in the "red cow which belongeth to the poor of the Colony to which they must keep her calf of this year being a bull for the company," along with two female goats. A few months later, Standish bought out the six shares of the red cow owned by Edward Winslow, and two shares belonging to Abraham Pierce—giving Standish full ownership of the red cow.

In 1633 and 1634, Standish was taxed eighteen shillings, a relatively low tax that suggests that he did not then have any significant estate. About 1634, Standish began to establish a temporary residence to the north of Plymouth, helping to establish a town, Duxbury, which is thought to have been named after his ancestral home in Lancashire. Over the next few years, he and others (including John Alden) removed to Duxbury, though they continued to be involved in Plymouth's government.

In 1634, John Alden had been a witness to the trade dispute at Plymouth's Kennebec trading post. John Hocking of the Piscataqua settlement had established a trading post up the Kennebec River, intercepting trade that Plymouth Colony was legally entitled to. When Hocking refused to move, John Howland and several others from Plymouth attempted to forcefully remove him. Hocking shot and killed Moses Talbot, and was himself then shot and killed. Though the incident happened within Plymouth Colony's legal jurisdiction, the larger Massachusetts Bay Colony decided to overstep its jurisdiction. They arrested John Alden who was then in the Bay Colony trading. John Alden had just been a witness to the incident, but the Bay Colony held him until the magistrates there could hear the dispute. Plymouth, justifiably, was outraged that the Bay Colony would intermeddle with their affairs, and sent Myles Standish to procure Alden's release from prison (not militarily, but diplomatically). Standish succeeded in his mission to release Alden from custody; but the Bay Colony insisted that he bound himself to appear at the next court session, so that the magistrates could judge the merits of Plymouth Colony's patent that allowed them to defend their trading on the Kennebec. In the end, the Plymouth and Bay colonies agreed to have a neutral hearing on the matter—but when the Piscataqua representatives failed to show up or contest the issue, the matter was dropped.

The following year, Plymouth's trading post at Penobscot was attacked and taken over by the French. This was the second time that the Penobscot trading post had been attacked; the French had previously raided it, stealing as much as £500 of goods, to Plymouth's substantial loss. This time, the Plymouth colonists hired a "ship of force," a three-hundred-ton English vessel outfitted with numerous cannon. The master of the ship was to receive £700 of beaver if he succeeded, and nothing if he failed. Along with the ship, Plymouth also sent Captain Standish with their shallop, with twenty men under his command, to aid in the attack and to take command once the house was retaken. Standish also carried the beaver which was to be used as payment.

Unfortunately for Plymouth, the master of the ship proved incompetent, and refused to take any advice from Captain Standish. Instead, he "began to shoot at distance like a madman," and by the time he got close enough to actually be able to do any damage, he had run out of gunpowder. Unable to continue the attack, he withdrew and asked Captain Standish where he could get more powder. Standish took the shallop to a nearby plantation and procured gunpowder for him. In the process, Captain Standish received intelligence that instead of attacking the French, the ship's master was intending to attack the shallop and steal the beaver that was intended to be his payment for overthrowing the French. Standish, upon learning this, took the shallop and the beaver, and returned to Plymouth to prevent its being stolen.

In 1636, the Pequot Indians in Connecticut killed John Oldham while he was there trading—the same man who had called Standish a "silly boy" and eventually got expelled from Plymouth. The Bay Colony mounted a poorly organized and unsuccessful retaliation; they killed one Indian and burned a couple wigwams, but otherwise effected no purpose other than to enrage the Pequot. In early 1637, the Pequot retaliated by attacking Connecticut settlers "and slew sundry of them (as they were at work in the fields) both men and women." They also assaulted Saybrook Fort. The men and women of Connecticut then asked the Bay Colony for assistance in defending themselves and retaliating. The Bay Colony, in turn, asked Plymouth to provide volunteers and share in the costs of putting out an expedition. Plymouth, still raw over previous disputes with the Bay Colony, took the opportunity to redress all their past grievances, and refused to consider the offer until their general court session came up. By the time Plymouth's court finally organized forty volunteers under the command of Lieutenant William Holmes, the Massachusetts Bay had already massacred the Pequot.

Captain Myles Standish, strangely, is not mentioned in any of the court records, firsthand accounts, or writings of Bradford, in relation to the Pequot War. He does not appear to have played any part in it; perhaps he was ill, unavailable at the time, or otherwise disinclined to assist. Standish had not left the picture entirely, however. In 1640, the company of New Plymouth thought of sending him to England to assist in closing out the business, but they eventually decided it was not necessary.

Sometime in the early 1640s, a sachem by the name of Miantonomo led an attack on Massasoit, then named Woosemaquin. The Plymouth Colony, ever since the peace treaty of 1621, was obligated to protect and defend Woosemaquin and his people, so it sent Captain Standish "with a few men, not above 20, who sent a message over the bay of salt water which parts Woosemaquin from them [the Narragansett], either to make restitution of his goods so injuriously taken, or else to expect him to fetch them with a vengeance to their cost." Standish's threat worked: Miantonomo returned "every particular that could be demanded, even to a wooden dish."

With the disposal of the Pequot in 1637, the Narragansett became the most powerful Indian nation in the region, and began to seek and usurp powers and territory from its neighbors. The Connecticut, New Haven, Plymouth, and Bay Colonies had established an organization, the United Colonies of New England, to address concerns of mutual interest, such as defending the colonies from Indian threats. In 1645, in violation of peace agreements made with the English, the Narragansett began to attack a sachem named Uncas, who had long been an ally of both Plymouth and the Massachusetts Bay and had greatly assisted in the overthrow of the Pequot. The Narragansett had also begun to forge relations with the powerful Mohawk, long the bane of the Dutch settlers in New York. The commissioners of the United Colonies decided it was time to act to defend Uncas and their Indian allies from the Narragansett. They authorized three hundred troops to be commissioned—forty of which were to come from Plymouth.

The situation escalated quickly, and Plymouth's forty men were ordered to organize as quickly as possible and go to Seekonk "lest any danger should befall it." Plymouth's men arrived at Seekonk "well armed all with snaphance pieces, and went under the command of Captain Standish." While there, Standish observed some of the Englishmen of the Providence colony (not a member of the United Colonies), who "received the Indians into their houses familiarly, who had put themselves also into a posture of arms . . . [H]e sent to Providence, and required them to lay aside their neutrality, and either declare themselves on the one side or other: for the war being once begun, he would not bear with their carriage in entertaining, furnishing, and relieving the common enemy, but would disarm them." The residents of Providence were not too happy with Standish's threatenings, and listed it as one of their many objections to the United Colonies in a publication entitled *Simplicities Defence Against Seven-Headed Policy*, published later that year in London. But just as war was about to break out, the Narragansett sent representatives to Boston, and signed a new peace treaty, temporarily ending the dispute.

In 1653, Captain Standish was again called up to duty when there was intelligence received that there could be a war with the Dutch forthcoming. The United Colonies decided that Plymouth would be responsible for supplying sixty men. The Plymouth Court decided that "The commanders chosen and appointed to go forth on the said expedition, in case there shall be occasion, are Capt. Myles Standish for captain, Lieutenant Thomas Southworth for lieutenant, and Hezekiah Hoare of Taunton for ensign." However, their services would not be needed.

Captain Myles Standish did not only serve the Plymouth Colony in the capacity of military captain, however. He also took an active role in the government itself. He was an assistant to the governor for as early as court records exist, and continued in that capacity until his death, with only a few years of absence. He was also elected treasurer in 1644, and from 1646-1649, and again from 1651-1655. He was, of course, appointed as a member of all the councils of war that were organized, including those in 1642, 1643, and 1653. In 1653, for the court session held in May, he was the acting governor.

On 3 October 1656, Captain Myles Standish died. Plymouth Colony's secretary, Nathaniel Morton, writing in 1669 in his book *New England's Memorial*, eulogized him as follows:

> This year [1656] Capt. Myles Standish expired his mortal life. He was a gentleman, born in Lancashire, and was heir apparent unto a great estate of lands and livings, surreptitiously detained from him; his great-grandfather being a second or younger brother from the house of Standish. In his younger time he went over into the Low Countries, and was a soldier there, and came acquainted with the church at Leiden, and came over into New England, with such of them as at the first set out for the planting of the plantation of New Plymouth, and bare a deep share of their first difficulties, and was always very faithful to their interest. He growing ancient, became sick of the stone, or stranguary, whereof, after his suffering of much dolorous pain, he fell asleep in the Lord, and was honorably buried at Duxbury.

An iron pot originally owned by Myles Standish. Photo courtesy of the Pilgrim Hall Museum.

Myles Standish made out his will on 7 March 1655/6.[254] He asked to be buried "as near as conveniently may be to my two daughters Lora Standish my daughter, and Mary Standish my daughter-in-law." He gave a third of his estate to "my dear and loving wife Barbara Standish." He gave to his four sons, namely Alexander, Myles, Josias, and Charles, £40 apiece, giving son Alexander a double share of the land. He appointed "my loving friends Mr. Timothy Hatherley and Capt. James Cudworth" his supervisors, and named wife Barbara and sons Alexander, Myles, and Josias his joint executors. He then made two special bequests, namely giving £3 to Mercy Robinson "whom I tenderly love for her grandfather's sake," and forty shillings to "my servant John Irish Junior . . . always provided that he continue till the time he covenanted be expired."

The last segment of Myles's will has been the most intriguing and difficult for modern-day researchers looking for Standish's origins and family in England (generally, unsuccessfully). He writes:

"I give unto my son and heir apparent Alexander Standish all my lands as heir apparent by lawful decent in Ormistick Borsconge Wrightington Maudsley Newburrow Crawston and the Isle of Man and given to me as right heir by lawful decent but surreptitiously detained from me, my great grandfather being a 2cond or younger brother from the house of Standish of Standish."

The estate inventory of Myles Standish is equally interesting. His dwelling house and lands in Duxbury were valued at £140. For livestock, he owned four oxen, two mares, three young horses, ten cattle, eleven sheep, and fourteen swine. As would be expected for a military captain, he owned quite a few firearms, including one fowling piece, three muskets, four carbines, two small guns, one sword, one cutlass, and three belts. Standish owned a sizeable library, and unlike most Plymouth residents, a large number of his books were not related to religion. He owned a history of the world, a Turkish history, a German history, a Swedish history, *Chronicles of England, Countrey Farme* (a how-to farming guide), a history of Queen Elizabeth, *Physicians Practice* (a medical text), Rambart Dodoens' *New Herball* (for identifying plants and their medicinal uses), *The French Academy* (essentially a self-help book on morality), Caesar's *Commentaries*, Homer's *Illiad*, and Barriffe's *Artillery*. He did own some religious titles as well, including a large collection of religious tracts by Jeremiah Burroughs, John Dod's treatise on the Lord's Supper, and John Calvin's *Institutes of Christian Religion*, among others.

ELIAS STORY

Elias Story was one of two menservants brought on the *Mayflower* by Edward Winslow, the other manservant being George Soule. George Soule signed the Mayflower Compact on 11 November 1620, but Elias Story did not—indicating Elias was under the age of twenty-one. However, he was likely nearing the age of adulthood since he was referred to as a "manservant" instead of the other term that Bradford used, "servant boy," which indicated a youth.

No English records have been found which could indicate his origins. An Elias Story was baptized in 1614 in Kilburton, Yorkshire, but that is far too young to have been the *Mayflower* passenger nearing adulthood in 1620. There was a John Story who married a Margaret Smith in 1619 in Colchester, Essex, a city from which a number of Leiden Separatists had originated. The Story surname is also found in Great Burstead, Essex, where *Mayflower* passenger Christopher Martin hailed.

Elias Story died the first winter.

EDWARD THOMPSON

Edward Thompson holds the unfortunate distinction of being the first person to die after the *Mayflower* arrived in America. Edward Thompson was a servant to William White, and had not yet reached the age of twenty-one—indicated by the fact he did not sign the Mayflower Compact.

The English origins of Edward Thompson remain unclear, and given his enormously common name, it is unlikely anything conclusive can be determined unless he can be tied with an association to his master William White (whose English origins are also unknown).

Edward Thompson was the first *Mayflower* passenger to die after arrival at Cape Cod. He died on December 4, a couple of weeks before the Pilgrims had located and decided to settle at Plymouth.

EDWARD TILLEY

AND HIS WIFE ANN (COOPER)

Edward Tilley and Ann Cooper were married in Henlow, co. Bedford, England, on 20 June 1614, she having been baptized there on 7 November 1585, and he having been baptized there on 27 May 1588.[255] It is unusual for this time period to find instances where the wife is older than her husband, but Edward Tilley, as well as his brother John Tilley, married an older woman. The Pilgrim's pastor, John Robinson, himself, wrote in the "Of Marriage" chapter of his *Observations Divine and Moral,* that it was best for men not to marry older women.

Shortly after their marriage, Edward and Ann Tilley moved to Leiden, Holland, where they appear in a record there in 1616.[256] They are not known to have had any children.

In 1620, Edward and Ann Tilley came on the *Mayflower,* bringing with them Ann's sixteen-year-old nephew Henry Sampson and her niece Humility Cooper, then just about one year old.

Edward Tilley appears to have been an up-and-coming member of the congregation, and very early on he was eagerly participating in the exploration parties that were sent out after the *Mayflower* had arrived and anchored off the tip of Cape Cod. He was one of the signers of the Mayflower Compact on 11 November 1620, and later that day he was probably among the fifteen or sixteen men that were first set ashore to briefly explore the tip of Cape Cod. A few days later, on November 15, sixteen men, "every man his musket, sword and corslet" were sent out on a more comprehensive exploration of Cape Cod that would range from the tip of the cape down through the Pamet River near present-day Truro. One of the men on the expedition was Edward Tilley, specifically appointed along with William Bradford and Stephen

Hopkins to accompany and provide "advice and counsel" to the militia captain, Myles Standish. After marching along the sand for about a mile, they spotted some men that they initially thought might have been some of the *Mayflower*'s crew, but who proved to be Indians. The Indians ran into the woods, and the Pilgrim men followed after them for about ten miles through thickets and valleys, past small ponds and streams, before it became dark, and they made camp. They also found and dug up some sand heaps where the Indians had buried some of their corn seed for use the following year, and nicknamed the place Corn Hill. The Pilgrims made the decision to "borrow" the corn they dug up—justifying it by saying they would repay the owners as soon as it could be determined who the owners were.

Pamet river and Corn hill.

A second expedition was set out with thirty-four men later in November to do a more thorough exploration of the Pamet River and Corn Hill area, and we might presume that Edward Tilley was among them, although the names of those who went on the exploration were not recorded.

On December 6, the Pilgrims set out their third exploration of Cape Cod with about eighteen men, and this time Edward Tilley, along with brother John Tilley, was specifically named. The expedition got off to a bad start: even before the shallop could get beyond the sandy point at the tip of Cape Cod, they encountered "very cold and hard weather . . . in which time two were very sick, and Edward Tilley had like to have sounded with cold; the gunner also was sick unto death, and so remained all that day, and the next night." The expedition lasted several days. Near Eastham, they were attacked in the morning by a group of Nauset, but managed to escape unharmed. Rounding the cape, they eventually landed—nearly wrecking—on Clark's Island, and then started to explore the area of Plymouth. Finally, after more than a month of exploration, they had found where they would settle.

Edward Tilley, however, never did kick that illness he came down with just before the start of the third exploration. Certainly, wading to shore hip deep through ocean waves in freezing weather did not help matters. He died most likely in January, and probably of pneumonia; his wife died soon after as well.

JOHN TILLEY,

HIS WIFE JOAN (HURST), AND THEIR DAUGHTER ELIZABETH

John Tilley was baptized on 19 December 1571 at Henlow, co. Bedford, England, the eldest child of Robert and Elizabeth Tilley. John's younger brother, Edward, also came on the *Mayflower*.[257] John Tilley married Joan (Hurst) Rogers on 20 September 1596 at Henlow. Joan Hurst, youngest daughter of William Hurst, was baptized on 13 March 1567/8 at Henlow, making her a few years older than husband John Tilley. Joan had a daughter Joan, baptized on 26 May 1594, with her first husband, Thomas Rogers (no relation to the *Mayflower* passenger of the same name). But Thomas died shortly thereafter, and Joan then married John Tilley.

Surprisingly, little is known about John and Joan Tilley. Brother Edward is mentioned once in a Leiden record, but there has been nothing yet found to indicate John Tilley and his wife Joan were living in Leiden—although it is entirely possible. John and Joan Tilley had five children baptized in the parish of Henlow between 1597 and 1607, namely Rose (who died young), John, Rose (another), Robert, and Elizabeth. The fate of John, Rose, and Robert is not known; only daughter Elizabeth, baptized on 30 August 1607, came on the *Mayflower* with her parents.

John Tilley is briefly mentioned in the will of George Clarke of Henlow, dated 22 September 1607. The will mentions that Thomas Kirke, then dwelling with John Tilley, owed him money. A John Tilley, perhaps the *Mayflower* passenger, was living at Wooton, co. Bedford, when he made a deposition on 7 April 1613.[258]

John Tilley was one of the signers of the Mayflower Compact, and with his brother Edward participated in the early explorations of Cape Cod. John Tilley and his wife Joan both died the first winter, as did his brother Edward and sister-in-law Ann. Of the immediate family, only thirteen-year-old Elizabeth Tilley survived. At about seventeen years of age, Elizabeth married fellow *Mayflower* passenger John Howland, then probably about twenty-six years of age. John and Elizabeth Howland had ten children in Plymouth between about 1625 and 1649. Elizabeth's husband John died in 1672, and she lived a widow for an additional fourteen years. Elizabeth died on 22 December 1687 at Swansea. She made out a will, dated 17 December 1686 and proved 10 January 1687 '78.[259] One of the books she owned at her death was Pastor John Robinson's *Observations Divine and Moral*, which she gave to her daughter Lydia.

THOMAS TINKER,

HIS WIFE, AND THEIR SON

Very little is known about *Mayflower* passenger Thomas Tinker and his family. In fact, the names of his wife and son, whom he brought with him on the *Mayflower*, are not even known. William Bradford simply enumerates on his passenger list: "Thomas Tinker and his wife and a son." Bradford then recalls "Thomas Tinker and his wife and son all died in the first sickness."

Thomas Tinker's name occurs once in Leiden records, on 6 January 1617, when he became a citizen of the city, guaranteed by Abraham Gray and John Keble. He was called a wood sawyer. It has been reasonably proposed that this man may have been the same as the Thomas Tinker, carpenter, who married Jane White on 25 June 1609 in Thurne, co. Norfolk, England.

WILLIAM TREVOR

William Trevor was a seaman who was hired to stay in the Plymouth Colony for the entire first year. Although he was an adult, he did not sign the Mayflower Compact in November 1620 because as an employee of the company he was already contractually obligated to remain for a year.

William Trevor appears to have been to the region previous to the voyage of the *Mayflower*, which might explain why he was hired by the Pilgrims in the first place. In 1619, William Trevor was under the employ of Mr. David Thompson, and they visited some islands off what is now Dorchester, Massachusetts, which they viewed together with the Sagamore of Agawam. They took a liking to one particular island and took possession of it. According to the Sagamore of Agawam, he liked the island "because of the small river and then no Indians upon it or any wigwam or planting.[260]"

After returning to England, William Trevor then signed on to work for the Pilgrims and remain in Plymouth for a year, providing labor and his experience as a seaman which would be used for sailing the shallop up and down the coast to trade with the Indians. In 1621, William Trevor accompanied Myles Standish and others from Plymouth on a voyage to Boston Harbor to meet with and trade with the Massachusett Indians. There, they again visited the Islands that Trevor had been to just a year or two earlier. Myles Standish named the island "Island of Trevor," but Mr. David Thompson obtained a patent to the island, so it later became known as Thompson's Island.

In November 1621, the ship *Fortune* arrived at Plymouth with a supply of new colonists, but almost no new provisions or trade goods. Nonetheless, the Pilgrims filled the ship up, primarily with beaver furs that had been obtained in trade with the Indians, and sent it back to

England so that the company could cash in on its first revenue; but it was not to be. William Trevor and several others returned on the ship with the cargo. The *Fortune* set sail in December 1621, and upon approaching the English coast, it was overtaken by French pirates and forced in to the Ile d'Yeu, Poitou, where the captain, crew, and the few return passengers were stripped of all their goods and left with little more than their clothes and some old bacon. The loss was estimated to have been as much as £500—a disheartening loss for a company that desperately needed the revenue.

After being held for several weeks in the castle on the Ile d'Yeu by the Marquis de Cera, governor of the island, the ship *Fortune* was eventually returned to the stripped passengers and crew, and they were allowed to sail home to England where they would eventually file an official but fruitless complaint, attempting to recover their loss.[261]

Shortly after returning home, Robert Cushman, another passenger that was on the *Fortune* returning home, wrote the following in a letter to Governor William Bradford:

> By God's providence we got well home the 17 of February, being robbed by the Frenchmen by the way, and carried by them into France, and were kept there 15 days; and lost all that we had, that was worth taking, but thanks be to God, we escaped with our lives and ship . . . Mr. Weston hath quite broken off from our company, through some discontent . . . he hath taken a patent for himself . . . It is like he will plant to the southward of the Cape, for William Trevor hath lavishly told but what he knew, or imagined, of Capawack, Mohegan, and the Narragansetts.

It is not known what happened to William Trevor after he returned to England. As a seaman, it seems probable that he continued on and made other voyages with different companies; perhaps he was even involved in Thomas Weston's colony at Wessagussett that he helped encourage with his lavish descriptions.

He does show up again in the Massachusetts Bay Colony in April 1650, where he made a deposition before Increase Newell, about his knowledge regarding the ownership of Thompson's Island; Myles

Standish made a deposition a few months later, describing how he and Trevor had visited Thompson's Island shortly after their arrival in New England. Perhaps William Trevor even lived for a time in the Massachusetts Bay, although no other record of him is known.

JOHN TURNER

AND TWO SONS

John Turner was a long-time member of the Leiden church congregation, but despite that, very little is known about him. He is mentioned in only one Leiden record, on 27 September 1610, when he guaranteed the citizenship of Peter Boey and William Lisle. He was referred to as a merchant. Nothing is really known about his English origins, but he may have been among those who came to Leiden from Great Yarmouth, co. Norfolk, where there are several Turner families.

On 10 June 1620, John Turner delivered a letter from the Leiden congregation to their agent in London, Robert Cushman. Turner returned to Leiden a few days later with letters and firsthand information from Cushman. Whether he made other trips to London acting in the capacity of a courier is unknown.

According to William Bradford, John Turner came on the *Mayflower* with two sons, whose names are not given. Nothing is known about his wife. John Turner signed the Mayflower Compact on 11 November 1620, but neither of his sons signed the document, so they were certainly under the age of twenty-one.

John Turner and his two sons all died the first winter in Plymouth. According to William Bradford writing about 1651, John Turner had "a daughter still living in Salem, well married and approved of." Robert S. Wakefield noted that a "Lysbet Turner," orphan from England, is found in the Leiden poll tax of 1622.[262] In October 1635, an Elizabeth Turner witnessed a property deed between William Lord and John Woolcott of Salem, Massachusetts, and a few months later Elizabeth Turner joined the Salem church. Who Elizabeth Turner married in Salem remains unknown.

RICHARD WARREN

Richard Warren was one of the English merchants who signed on to actually make the voyage with the Leiden Pilgrims. His exact motivations are unknown, and given his apparent status, surprisingly little is actually known about him. Warren's English origins remained unknown until 2003, when Edward Davies published a set of articles in *The American Genealogist*.[263] Davies documented that the marriage of Richard Warren to Elizabeth Walker at Great Amwell, co. Hertford, on 14 April 1610, was that of the *Mayflower* passenger. He further showed that Richard Warren's wife Elizabeth was the daughter of Augustine Walker of Baldock, co. Hertford, where she was baptized in September 1583. In his will of 19 April 1613, Augustine Walker mentioned his daughter Elizabeth Warren, and her children Mary, Ann, and Sarah Warren. My searches for Richard Warren's parentage and birthplace in co. Hertford have come up inconclusive, but there is a promising Warren family living in the vicinity of Therfield.

By the time of the *Mayflower*'s voyage in 1620, Richard and Elizabeth Warren had five daughters: Mary, Ann, Sarah, Elizabeth, and Abigail. But Richard came on the *Mayflower* by himself, leaving his wife and daughters behind in England. Some husbands decided to bring their wife and children, such as Isaac Allerton and Stephen Hopkins; while others, like Richard Warren and Thomas Rogers, chose instead to leave their wife and children behind until better conditions could be established in the New World. It was clearly a difficult decision to make, and different families came to different conclusions.

Upon arrival in America, Richard Warren was one of the signers of the Mayflower Compact, and he participated in some of the early explorations of Cape Cod, looking for a place to establish their colony. After feeling the colony was now stable and well established, Richard

Warren sent for his wife Elizabeth and five daughters, and they all arrived at Plymouth in 1623 on the ship *Anne*. In the 1623 division of land, he received two acres of land "on the north side of the town next adjoining to their gardens which came in the *Fortune*," and five acres of land "on the other side of the town towards the Eel River."

He and Elizabeth had two more children—this time sons, Nathaniel and Joseph—who were born in Plymouth about 1624 and 1626, respectively. In the 1627 division of cattle, Richard and Elizabeth Warren, and their seven children, all received a share in the "one of the four black heifers that came in the *Jacob* called the smooth-horned heifer, and two she-goats."

Richard Warren died in 1628—the cause of his death, however, is not known. Nathaniel Morton recorded in his 1669 book *New England's Memorial* that "This year [1628] died Mr. Richard Warren, who hath been mentioned before in this book, and was an useful instrument; and during his life bore a deep share in the difficulties and troubles of the first settlement of the plantation of New Plymouth." Widow Elizabeth would substantially outlive her husband, dying on 2 October 1673, having surpassed ninety years of age.

WILLIAM WHITE,

HIS WIFE SUSANNA, AND THEIR SON RESOLVED

Through the years, William White has proven to be a very difficult passenger to research. Because there was an English wool-comber named William White in Leiden, Holland, who married Ann, the sister of *Mayflower* passenger Samuel Fuller, he is the man who is often assumed to have been the *Mayflower* passenger. William Bradford recorded on his passenger list that William's wife was named Susanna. Anna Fuller was born about 1578, and the widowed Susanna White remarried to Edward Winslow in 1621—if this were truly Anna Fuller, then she would have been seventeen years older than her husband, an unlikely circumstance.

There are, however, at least two William White's in Leiden, a wool comber and a tobacco merchant; but both appear to still be living in Leiden after the *Mayflower* departed. The wool comber is most likely the William White who witnessed the betrothal of Godbert Godbertson to Sarah (Allerton), widow of Degory Priest, on 25 October 1621—because Sarah had witnessed William and Anna's betrothal in 1613. And the tobacco merchant became a Leiden citizen on 8 December 1628.

A careful examination of William Bradford's passenger list shows that "Mr. William White" was included in a section listing all of the London merchants[264]—Mr. Christopher Martin, Mr. William Mullins, Mr. Stephen Hopkins, Mr. Richard Warren, and John Billington. Had William White been a member of the Leiden congregation, he would have been listed in that section of the passenger list, which includes Mr. John Carver, Mr. William Brewster, Mr. Edward Winslow, William Bradford, Mr. Isaac Allerton, Mr. Samuel Fuller, and John Crackston.

So it seems to me that William White should actually be counted as one of the London merchants, and that neither of the two William Whites living in Leiden were the *Mayflower* passenger of the same name. Unfortunately, William White is such a common name in England that it is extremely difficult to identify the correct man.

The cradle of Peregrine White. Photo courtesy of the Pilgrim Hall Museum.

William White and his pregnant wife Susanna came on the *Mayflower* with son Resolved, then about five years old. William signed the Mayflower Compact on 11 November 1620, and a couple weeks later Susanna gave birth to their son Peregrine onboard the *Mayflower*, while many of the Pilgrim men were out exploring for a place to settle.

William White died the first winter, on 21 February 1620/1. His widow Susanna remarried to *Mayflower* passenger Edward Winslow on 12 May 1621—the first marriage to take place at Plymouth. Edward Winslow's wife Elizabeth had also died the first winter.

Though deceased, William White is enumerated in the 1623 division of land, with five acres lying "behind the fort to the little pond." Edward Winslow received four acres in the division. Resolved and Peregrine White are both listed with their stepfather Edward Winslow and mother Susanna in the 1627 division of cattle, and moved with their parents to Marshfield about 1632.

Resolved was married on 5 November 1640 to Judith Vassall, daughter of William Vassall, and they resided in Scituate for over twenty years. Judith's father William died in Barbados in 1655; and a year later, Resolved and Judith traveled to Barbados to settle the estate and sell off Judith's inheritance. Resolved and Judith had about eight children in Scituate between 1642 and 1656; and about 1662, the family moved to Marshfield. Judith died and was buried on 3 April 1670 in Marshfield, and Resolved remarried to Abigail Lord, widow of William Lord. In 1676, Resolved fought in King Philip's War, and resided for a time in Salem before returning to Marshfield about 1684. Resolved

White was still living in 1690 when a note was written into William Bradford's manuscript history *Of Plymouth Plantation*, stating "Two persons living that came over in the first ship 1620, this present year 1690: Resolved White and Mary Cushman." He died within a few years, however.

ROGER WILDER

Roger Wilder is another one of the passengers about whom almost nothing is known. He came as a servant with the John Carver family. He was under twenty-one years old when he made the voyage, as he did not sign the Mayflower Compact on 11 November 1620.

William Bradford simply reported that "Mr. Carver and his wife died the first year, he in the spring, she in the summer. Also, his man Roger and the little boy Jasper died before either of them, of the common infection."

The name Roger Wilder is very uncommon. The only known baptism for a Roger Wilder between 1570 and 1620 is the Roger Wilder baptized on 28 December 1595 at Rotherwick, Hampshire. While this individual is too old to have been the *Mayflower* passenger, since distinctive names like Roger often run in families, this could suggest a general geographic location that could be investigated further.

THOMAS WILLIAMS

Thomas Williams appears to have been the man baptized on 12 August 1582 at Great Yarmouth, co. Norfolk, England, the son of John and Judith (Short) Williams.[265] Thomas and his younger sister Elizabeth (baptized 9 January 1591/2) left Great Yarmouth to join with the Separatist Church congregation that was then establishing itself in Leiden, Holland.

Thomas was a witness to his sister Elizabeth's betrothal on 11 March 1616 to long-time Leiden Church member Roger Wilson.[266]

Thomas Williams was listed by William Bradford as one of the adult men from Leiden who came on the *Mayflower*. He was one of the signers of the Mayflower Compact on 11 November 1620. Bradford simply noted that Thomas Williams "died soon after their arrival in the general sickness that befell."

EDWARD WINSLOW

Edward Winslow was born on 18 October 1595 and baptized two days later at St. Peter's, Droitwich, co. Worcester[267], the eldest son of Edward and Magdalene (Oliver) Winslow, and grandson of Kenelm Winslow of Kempsey, co. Worcester. It has been debated whether his family were gentlemen[268], but in any case, his family was fairly well-to-do. Edward's father held the office of under sheriff, and was involved in the salt-production trade. Winslow had a number of other younger brothers. Brother Gilbert Winslow would accompany Edward on the *Mayflower* in 1620; the other brothers, John, Josias, and Kenelm, all followed Edward to America over the next decade.

Between April 1606 and April 1611, Edward attended the King's School of Worcester Cathedral. Two years after leaving school, in August 1613, he was apprenticed to John Beale, citizen and stationer of London, for eight years; after an apparent legal dispute between Beale and the Stationers' Company, Winslow was reapprenticed for eight years beginning in October 1615. However, Winslow would apparently not fulfill his entire apprenticeship, as he removed to Leiden, Holland about 1617 and joined with the Separatist church there, helping William Brewster with his underground printing activities.[269]

Edward Winslow, called a printer of London, married in Leiden to Elizabeth Barker on 27 April 1618.[270] Elizabeth is said to have been from "Chatsum" in England. Some have speculated this was Chattisham, co. Suffolk. A search of Chattisham and neighboring parishes, however, did not reveal any noteworthy baptismal records.

Winslow quickly became one of the leading members of the Leiden church group exiled in Leiden. On 10 June 1620, he was one of the four men, along with Bradford, Fuller, and Allerton, who wrote a letter on behalf of the Leiden congregation to John Carver and Robert

Cushman, who were then in England negotiating the terms upon which the Pilgrims' would travel to America.

On the *Mayflower*'s voyage, Edward—then only twenty-five years old—brought his wife Elizabeth, and two servants, George Soule and Elias Story, and he also took custody of a young eight-year-old girl, Ellen More. Upon arrival, he was one of the first signers of the Mayflower Compact on 11 November 1620, and took part in all the early explorations of Cape Cod. He wrote a portion of the anonymously authored *Mourt's Relation*, describing these early explorations.

In the earliest years of the Plymouth Colony, Edward Winslow acted, in a sense, as the ambassador to the neighboring Indian groups. On 22 March 1620/1, the Pilgrims first met Squanto. That same day, Massasoit, the leading sachem in the region, with sixty men, came and stood on a hill nearby Plymouth. The Pilgrims were too afraid to send their governor John Carver to meet with him, so they sent Edward Winslow instead, "to know his mind, and to signify the mind and will of our governor, which was to have trading and peace with him." Massasoit admired Edward Winslow's sword and armor, and attempted to make a trade for it, but Winslow politely declined. He remained as a "hostage" with the Indians, as Massasoit crossed Town Brook to meet with the Pilgrims' governor. After Massasoit's meeting with Governor Carver, he returned and his brother Quadequina came to pay a visit—Winslow remained with the Indians for that visit as well. After Quadequina returned from his visit, Winslow returned to Plymouth.

Two days later, Edward Winslow's wife Elizabeth died—one of the last people to die during the first winter at Plymouth. Winslow remarried two months later to Susanna White, who had also been widowed the first winter after her husband William had died; her two children, Resolved and Peregrine White, joined the Winslow household.

Edward Winslow, along with Stephen Hopkins, made the Pilgrims' first diplomatic visit to Massasoit's home at Pokanoket, near modern-day Warren, Rhode Island, departing Plymouth on 2 July 1620. Later that month, he probably was one of the ten men that the Pilgrims' sent to Nauset to recover young John Billington who had gotten lost in the woods and had been taken by the Indians. The Pilgrims' made peace with the Nauset, paid off some debts (for the corn they stole the first winter), and returned the boy home.

In November 1621, the ship *Fortune* arrived, bringing more passengers to Plymouth. Winslow used the opportunity to send a letter back to a friend, possibly George Morton. In the letter, Winslow wrote the most detailed surviving account of the first Thanksgiving at Plymouth:

> Our corn did prove well, and God be praised, we had a good increase of Indian corn, and our barley indifferent good, but our peas not worth the gathering, for we feared they were too late sown, they came up very well, and blossomed, but the sun parched them in the blossom; our harvest being gotten in, our governor sent four men on fowling, that so we might after a more special manner rejoice together, after we had gathered the fruit of our labors; they four in one day killed as much fowl, as with a little help beside, served the company almost a week, at which time amongst other recreations, we exercised our arms, many of the Indians coming amongst us, and among the rest their greatest King Massasoit, with some ninety men, whom for three days we entertained and feasted, and they went out and killed five deer, which they brought to the plantation and bestowed on our governor, and upon the captain, and others.

Of the Indians, Winslow reported:

> We have found the Indians very faithful in their covenant of peace with us; very loving and ready to pleasure us: we often go to them, and they come to us; some of us have been fifty miles by land in the country with them; the occasions and relations whereof you shall understand by our general and more full declaration of such things as are worth noting, yea, it hath pleased God so to possess the Indians with a fear of us, and love unto us, that not only the greatest king amongst them called Massasoit, but also all the prices and peoples round about us, have either made suit unto us, or been glad of any

occasion to make peace with us, so that seven of them at once have sent their messengers to us to that end.

Winslow also gives future travelers to Plymouth some advice, presumably based on personal experience:

> [B]e careful to have a very good bread-room to put your biscuits in, let your cask for beer and water be iron-bound for the first tire if not more; let not your meat be dry-salted, none can better do it than the sailors; let your meal be so hard trod in your cask that you shall need an adz or hatchet to work it out with: trust not too much on us for corn at this time . . . build your cabins as open as you can, and bring good store of clothes and bedding with you; bring every man a musket or fowling-piece, let your piece be long in the barrel, and fear not the weight of it, for most of our shooting is from stands; bring juice of lemons, and take it fasting, it is of good use; for hot waters, aniseed water is the best, but use it sparingly: if you bring anything for comfort in the country, butter or salad oil, or both is very good; our Indian corn even the coarsest, maketh as pleasant meat as rice, therefore spare that unless to spend by the way; bring paper, and linseed oil for your windows, with cotton yarn for your lamps; let your shot be most for big fowl, and bring store of powder and shot.

Edward Winslow continued for the next several years to make diplomatic visits to the various Native American groups in the area. In March 1622, Edward Winslow was among the ten men who accompanied Captain Myles Standish on a trading voyage to the Massachusett Indians to the north. The governor then sent Winslow to Damariscove, in modern-day Maine, to seek trade with some of the English fishing vessels that came there each year; but although Winslow found many ships and received courteous entertainment from them, he was not able to procure any significant quantities of provisions. In June and July, it only got worse, as two ships, the *Charity* and the *Swan*, stopped at Plymouth. The passengers had been set out by

Thomas Weston to establish a colony in the Massachusetts Bay, but about sixty of them refreshed themselves at Plymouth for several weeks, stealing and damaging the corn crop, before they finally removed to establish their own colony. The two colonies, Plymouth and Wessagussett, sent out a joint trading expedition in November 1622, but Squanto suddenly died. Nonetheless, they managed a decent return in their trade for corn and beans, although not as well as they were hoping—the Indians complained about their ill treatment at the hands of the Wessagussett colonists, who had resorted to stealing Indian corn in their desperation for food.

In March 1623, word was received at Plymouth that Massasoit was very sick and near death. Governor Bradford sent Edward Winslow, with Hobomok as guide, to visit Massasoit in his sickness, and to see if he could make contact with the Dutch (they had heard rumors of a Dutch shipwreck). Along the way, they passed through the territory of a sachem named Corbitant, who had been "a hallow-hearted friend." There, they were informed that Massasoit had already died. Winslow, realizing that Corbitant was the likely successor, decided to visit him. Corbitant was not at home, but they then learned from others that Massasoit was actually still alive, although on the verge of death—so Winslow hurried to Pokanoket, where they found Massasoit's house packed full of people "in the midst of their charms for him, making such a hellish noise, as it distempered us that were well, and therefore unlike to ease him that was sick." Winslow recorded the meeting in his 1624 book, *Good News from New England*:

> [H]e desired to speak with me; when I came to him, and they told him of it, he put forth his hand to me, which I took; and he said twice, though very inwardly, *keen Winsnow*, which is to say, "Art thou Winslow?" I answered *ahhe*, that is, "yes;" he then doubled these words, *Matta neen wonckanet namen Winsnow*, that is to say, "O Winslow I shall never see thee again.

Winslow then took on the unpleasant duty of doctor:

> Then I desired to see his mouth, which was exceedingly furred, and his tongue swelled in such

manner, as it was not possible for him to eat such meat as they had, his passage being stopped up: then I washed his mouth, and scraped his tongue, and got abundance of corruption out of the same. After which, I gave him more of the confection, which he swallowed with more readiness; then he desiring to drink, I dissolved some of it in water, and gave him thereof: within half an hour this wrought a great alteration in him in the eyes of all that behind him; presently after his sight began to come to him, which gave him and us good encouragement. In the mean time I inquired how he slept, and when he went to the stool? They said he slept not in two days before, and had not had a stool in five; then I gave him more, and told him of a mishap we had by the way in breaking a bottle of drink, which the Governor also sent him, saying, if he would send any of his men to Patuxet, I would sent for more of the same, also for chickens to make him broth, and for other things which I knew were good for him, and would stay the return of the messenger if he desired . . . He requested me that the day following, I would take my piece, and kill him some fowl, and make him some English pottage such as he had eaten at Plymouth, which I promised . . . When the day broke, we went out (it being now March) to seek herbs, but could not find any but strawberry leaves, of which I gathered a handful and put into the same, and because I had nothing to relish it, I went forth again, and pulled up a sassafras root, and sliced a pice thereof, and boiled it till it had a good relish, and then took it out again . . . After this his sight mended more and more, also he had three moderate stools, and took some rest.

Winslow's chicken broth, English pottage, and his unspecified "confection" were thought by Massasoit and many of those around him to have saved his life. Massasoit's faithfulness toward the Pilgrims became all the stronger. Once he was well enough, he informed Winslow of a conspiracy by a number of the Indian groups to expel the English at both Wessagussett and Massachusett. On the way home,

Winslow stopped for a visit with Corbitant, and "had much conference with him." Winslow recalled of Corbitant:

> [H]e being a notable politician, yet full of merry jests and squibs, and never better pleased than when the like are returned again upon him. Amongst other things he asked me, If in case he were thus dangerously sick, as Massasoit had been, and should send word thereof to Patuxet for maskiet, that is, physic, whether then Mr. Governor would send it? And if he would, whether I would come therewith to him? To both which I answered yea, whereat he gave me many joyful thanks. After that, being at his house he demanded further, how we durst being but two come so far into the country? I answered, where was true love there was no fear, and my heart was so upright towards them that for mine own part I was fearless to come amongst them. But, said he, if your love be such, and it bring forth such fruits, how cometh to pass, that when we come to Patuxet, you stand upon your guard, with the mouths of your pieces presented towards us? Whereunto I answered, it was the most honorable and respective entertainment we could give them; it being an order amongst us so to receive our best respected friends: and as it was used on the land, so the ships observed it also at sea, which Hobomok knew, and had seen observed. But shaking the head he answered, that he liked not such salutations.
>
> Further, observing us to crave a blessing on our meat before we did eat, and after to give thtanks for the same, he asked us what was the meaning of that ordinary custom? Hereupon I took occasion to tell them of God's works of creation, and preservation, of his laws and ordinances, especially of the ten commandments, all which they hearkened unto with great attention, and liked well of: only the seventh commandment they excepted against, thinking there were many inconveniences in it, that a man should be tied to one woman: about which we reasoned a good time . . . This all of them concluded to be very well,

and said, they believed almost all the same things, and that the same power that we called God, they call Kiehtan. Much profitable conference was occasioned thereby, which would be too tedious to relate, yet was no less delightful to them, than comfortable to us. Here we remained only that night, but never had better entertainment amongst any of them.

In the 1623 division of land at Plymouth, Edward Winslow received four acres "on the north side of the town"—one for himself, one for his wife Susanna and her deceased husband William, and one for her son Resolved White. Edward and Susanna Winslow began building their family during the first decade at Plymouth. Their first child was born about 1622, but died an infant. About 1624, they had son Edward; 1626, son John; 1628, son Josiah; and 1630, daughter Elizabeth.

In September 1623, after the division of land, Edward Winslow was appointed to return to England on the *Anne*, which was loaded with clapboard and beaver skins. He was appointed to procure trading supplies and other things needful for the colony while in England. Winslow returned on the *Charity* in 1624, bringing "three heifers and a bull," and "some clothing and other necessaries."

In the 1627 division of cattle, Edward and Susanna Winslow, and their children and stepchildren were joined with Myles Standish's family, and they all received a share in the "red cow which belongeth to the poor of the colony to which they must keep her calf of this year being a bull for the company," and two female goats. The following January, Edward Winslow sold his six shares in the red cow to Myles Standish for five pounds and ten shillings, to be paid in corn at the rate of six shillings per bushel.

In 1631, Edward Winslow bought three acres of land from brother John Winslow, four acres of land from Francis Eaton, and two acres of land from Myles Standish, all adjoining lots. In the 1633 and 1634 tax lists at Plymouth, Edward Winslow was taxed £2 5s on both occasions. In the 1633 list, that was the second highest tax paid (behind Isaac Allerton), and in the 1634 list he was the most heavily taxed Plymouth resident—indicating he was also the wealthiest.

Although William Bradford was almost always elected governor of Plymouth, Edward Winslow did hold the office on a few occasions as well, namely in 1633, 1636, and 1644. He was assistant to the governor in most every other year. In 1635, Winslow made another trip on behalf of the company back to England, during which he submitted a petition to the Lords Commissioners for the Plantations in America. His petition requested protection from the encroachment of the Dutch in Connecticut and attacks by the French in Maine, and requested the colonies be given special rights to "defend themselves against all foreign enemies." However, the petition was blocked by Sir Ferdinando Gorges and Archbishop Laud; and when Winslow tried to get it reinstated, he ended up having to answer questions about their church—including accusations that the Pilgrims were marrying others outside of the Church of England. For these things, Winslow was arrested and held at the Fleet Prison, where he remained for about seventeen weeks before he managed to procure his release.

Edward Winslow was listed in the 1643 list of men able to bear arms, in the Marshfield section, indicating that by this time he had taken up residence in that town which was just north of Duxbury. However, the following year, 1644, he was again elected governor of Plymouth. In 1646, he made his next trip to England, following the English Civil War, and there he represented New England on various Parliamentary committees, before taking a position on an expedition sent out by Oliver Cromwell. He died at sea on 8 May 1655 between Hispaniola and Jamaica. The ship's clerk wrote the following after Winslow's death[271]:

Portrait of Edward Winslow painted in 1651. Reproduced from *History of Plimoth Plantation* (Massachusetts Historical Society, 1905).

> The eighth of May, west from 'Spaniola shore,
> God took from us our Grand Commissioner,
> Winslow by name, a man in chiefest trust,
> Whose life was sweet, and conversation just;
> Whose parts and wisdom most men did excel,
> An honor to his place, as all can tell.

Winslow's wife Susanna remained in America during his time in England. Winslow's will, dated 18 December 1654, leaves all his land and stock, and all future allotments and divisions, to his only surviving son Josiah, allowing wife Susanna her third part of the estate during her lifetime. He gave the poor of Plymouth and the poor of Marshfield £10 each. He gave all his linens to daughter Elizabeth, and a suit of apparel to each of his brothers.[272]

GILBERT WINSLOW

Gilbert Winslow was the younger brother of Edward Winslow. Baptized on 29 October 1600 in Droitwich, co. Worcester, he turned twenty years old during the voyage on the *Mayflower*. He was the only signer of the Mayflower Compact to have been under the legal age of twenty-one; perhaps he was an exception to the rule because of his family's higher social status.

Very little is actually known about Gilbert. In 1623, he received his share in the division of land "on the south side of the brook to the woodward," but he did not participate in the 1627 division of cattle. According to William Bradford, writing in 1651, "Gilbert Winslow after divers years abode here, returned into England and died there." No marriage record or any record of children is known. However, on 1 June 1663, the Plymouth Court noted: "The court do acknowledge Gilbert Winslow, deceased, who was one of the first comers, to have a right to land, and do allow his heirs to look out and propose to the court some parcel of land that the Court may think meet to accommodate them in.[273]" No further records relating to him have been found.

"ONE ELY"

According to William Bradford's list of passengers: "There were also other two seamen hired to stay a year here in the country, William Trevor, and one Ely. But when their time was out they both returned." As there are thousands of men in England with the surname Ely and its variant spellings, any attempt at identification would be almost certainly fruitless.

DOROTHY,

MAIDSERVANT OF JOHN CARVER

According to William Bradford, John Carver's family included "William Latham a boy, and a maidservant, and a child that was put to him called Jasper More." The name of John Carver's maidservant remained a mystery until a discovery was published by Neil D. Thompson in 1997 that brought to light her first name, Dorothy. It is actually a fairly complicated story.

In 1929, Charles E. Banks published a document he had found: an apprenticeship record dated 26 December 1626 at Bristol, England, which mentioned "Francis Eaton of the City of Bristol, carpenter, and Dorothy his wife"; and in the margins of the document was written "The Mr. at New England." However, many researchers assumed this was another man named Francis Eaton, since the *Mayflower* passenger was not known to have had a wife named Dorothy and was thought to have been married to Christian Penn by the time this document was made in 1626.

When the General Society of Mayflower Descendants revised and updated its volume on Francis Eaton in 1996, it included a paragraph that suggested this apprenticeship record did not belong to the *Mayflower* passenger. The next year, I posted a counter interpretation on my old "Mayflower Web Pages," predecessor to MayflowerHistory.com, giving my view that this apprenticeship document should not be counted out so easily; in fact, it had a lot going for it. The name Francis Eaton, after all, is extremely uncommon: there were no other Francis Eatons known to have come to America even through 1700, let alone by 1626. And the name of Francis Eaton's second wife was, in fact, unknown, and therefore could very well have been named Dorothy. William Bradford simply wrote that "his first wife died in the general sickness; and he married again and his second wife died, and he married third and had by her three children." His first wife was Sarah (who came on the *Mayflower* with him, and died the first winter). His third wife was Christian Penn, and they appear to have been married by 1626.

David Greene, editor of *The American Genealogist*, arrived at the same general conclusion that I had, and on a hunch that Francis Eaton's English origins might be discoverable in Bristol, hired Neil Thompson to undertake the research, which was later published in that journal.[274] The research proved successful: Francis Eaton's baptism record was discovered in the parish of St. Thomas, Bristol. This man had a younger brother Samuel, and the *Mayflower* passenger named his first son Samuel, further synching the identification.

So, it now appears that the 1626 document in Bristol, which mentions Francis Eaton's wife Dorothy, is actually a reference to the *Mayflower* passenger and his previously unidentified second wife.

But how do we know that Francis Eaton's second wife was John Carver's unnamed maidservant? William Bradford recorded that Carver's "maidservant married, and died a year or two after, here in this place." William Bradford's marriage on 14 August 1623 was recorded as having been the fourth marriage in Plymouth. The first marriage was in May 1621 between Edward Winslow and the widowed Susanna White. Who were involved in the second and third marriages at Plymouth? One of them was John Alden and Priscilla Mullins. The other was most likely Francis Eaton and Dorothy.

But how do we know that his wife was a *Mayflower* passenger, and not some other Dorothy who came on a later ship? The answer can be found in the Plymouth Colony's division of land that was recorded in 1623. Each passenger on the *Mayflower*, or their legal heir, was entitled to one acre of land. Francis Eaton received four acres. That would be one for himself, one for his wife Sarah, one for his son Samuel—all of whom came on the *Mayflower* with him. The fourth acre? It must have come from his second wife, and that second wife therefore must have been a *Mayflower* passenger. By process of elimination, the only female *Mayflower* passenger available for marriage was John Carver's maidservant. And the 1626 document tells us her name was Dorothy.

Dorothy died sometime probably in 1626, before Isaac Allerton left for Bristol on business. It is likely that Allerton was the one who brokered the above-mentioned apprenticeship. By the time he had returned, Dorothy had died, and Francis had remarried to Christian Penn, who had come to Plymouth on the ship *Anne* in 1623.

THE MAYFLOWER COMPACT

In ye name of god Amen. We whose names are underwritten,
the loyall subiects of our dread soueraigne Lord King Iames
by ye grace of god, of great Britaine, franc, & Ireland king
defendor of ye faith, &c

Haueing vndertaken, for ye glorie of god, and aduancemente
of ye christian faith, and honour of our king & countrie, a voyage to
plant ye first colonie in ye Northerne parts of Virginia. doe
by these presents solemnly & mutualy in ye presence of god, and
one of another, couenant, & combine our selues togeather into a
ciuill body politick; for our better ordering, & preseruation & fur=
theranco of ye ends aforesaid; and by vertue hearof to enacte,
constitute, and frame shuch iust & equall lawes, ordinances,
Acts, constitutions, & offices, from time to time, as shall be thought
most meete & conuenient for ye generall good of ye colonie: vnto
which we promise all due submission and obedience. In witnes
wherof we haue here vnder subscribed our names at cap=
Codd ye 11. of Nouember, in ye year of ye raigne of our soueraigne
Lord king Iames of England, franc, & Ireland ye eighteenth
and of scotland ye fiftie fourth An: Dom · 1620 ·

A copy of the text of the "Mayflower Compact," written by Gov.
William Bradford into his manuscript *History of Plymouth Plantation*.
The original Compact has not survived.

The 1623 Division of Land

The falls of their grounds which came first over in the *Mayflower* according as their lots were cast.

		The number of acres to each one
	Robert Cushman 1	
	Mr. William Brewster 6	
	William Bradford 3	
These lie on the	Richard Gardinar 1	
south side of	Francis Cooke 2	
the brook to	George Soule 1	
the baywards	Mr. Isaac Allerton 7	
	John Billington 3	
	Peter Brown 1	
	Samuel Fuller 2	
	Joseph Rogers 2	

These contain 29 acres

These lie on	John Howland 4
the south side	Stephen Hopkins 6
of the brook to	Edward 1
the woodward	Edward 1
opposite the	Gilbert Winslow 1
former.	Samuel Fuller junior 3

These contain 16 acres besides Hobomok's ground which lieth between John Howland's and Hopkins'.

This 5 acres lieth
behind the fort
to the little pond.

William White 5

These lie on the
north side of
the town next
adjoining to
their gardens
which came in
the *Fortune*

Edward Winslow 4
Richard Warren 2
John Goodman .... [damage]
John Crackston .... [damage]
John Alden .... [damage]
Mary Chilton .... [damage]
Capt. Myles Standish 2
Francis Eaton 4
Henry Sampson 1
Humility Cooper 1

The falls of their grounds which came in the *Fortune* according as their lots were
cast 1623. This ship came Nov. 1621.

<table>
<tr><td colspan="2">These lie to the sea,
eastward</td><td colspan="2">These lie beyond the first brook
to the wood westward.</td></tr>
</table>

William Hilton	1	William Wright &	
John Winslow	1	William Pitt	2
William Conner	1	Robert Hicks	1
John Adams	1	Thomas Prence	1
William Tench &		Stephen Deane	1
John Cannon	2	Moses Simonson &	
		Philip Delano	2
		Edward Bumpass	1
		Clement Briggs	1
These following lie		James Steward	1
beyond the 2 brook		William Palmer	2
		Jonathan Brewster	1
Hugh Stacey	1	Bennett Morgan	1
William Beale &		Thomas Flavell	
Thomas Cushman	2	& his son	2
Austin Nicholas	1	Thomas Morton	1
Widow Ford	4	William Bassett	2

| 15 acres | 19 acres |

The falls of their grounds which came over in the ship called the *Anne*, according as their lots were cast. 1623.

	Acres		These to the sea eastward. Acres.
James Rande	1	Francis Sprague	3

These following lie beyond the brook to Strawberry Hill.

Edmond Flood	1	Edward Burcher	2
Christopher Connant	1	John Jenny	5
Francis Cooke	4	Goodwife Flavell	1
		Manessah & John Faunce	2

These butt against the swamp and reed-pond
George Morton &		This goeth in with a corner by the pond.	
Experience Mitchell	8	Alice Bradford	1
Christian Penn	1	Robert Hicks his	
Thomas Morton junior	1	wife & children	4
William Hilton's wife		Bridgett Fuller	1
& 2 children	3	Ellen Newton	1
		Patience & Fear Brewster,	
		with Robert Long	3
		William Heard	1
		Mrs. Standish	1

These following lie on the other side of the town towards the Eel River.

Mary Buckett adjoining to		Robert Ratcliffe beyond the	
Joseph Rogers	1	swamp & stony ground	2
Mr. Oldham & those joined			
with him	10	These butt against Hobb's Hole	
Godbert Godbertson	6	Nicholas Snow	[damaged]
Anthony Annable	4	Anthony Dix	[damaged]
Thomas Tilden	3	Mr. Pierce's 2 servants	[damaged]
Richard Warren	5	Ralph Wallen	[damaged]
Bangs	4		

South side		North side	
Stephen Tracey three acres	3	Edward Holman 1 acre	1
Thomas Clarke one acre	1	Frances wife to William Palmer	1 acre
Robert Bartlett one acre	1	Joshua Pratt &	
		Phineas Pratt	2

THE 1627 DIVISION OF CATTLE

1. The first lot fell to Francis Cooke and his company joined to him, his wife Hester Cooke.
3. John Cooke
4. Jacob Cooke   To this lot fell the least of the 4 black heifers
5. Jane Cooke   came in the *Jacob*, and two she goats.
6. Hester Cooke
7. Mary Cooke
8. Moses Simonson
9. Philip Delano
10. Experience Mitchell
11. John Faunce
12. Joshua Pratt
13. Phineas Pratt

2. The second lot fell to Mr. Isaac Allerton and his company joined to him his wife Fear Allerton.
3. Bartholomew Allerton
4. Remember Allerton   To this lot fell the Great Black cow came in the
5. Mary Allerton   *Anne* to which they must keep the lesser of the two
6. Sarah Allerton   steers, and two she goats.
7. Godbert Godbertson
8. Sarah Godbertson
9. Samuel Godbertson
10. Mary Priest
11. Sarah Priest
12. Edward Bumpass
13. John Crackston

3.   The third lot fell to Capt. Standish and his company joined to him
2.   his wife Barbara Standish
3.   Charles Standish
4.   Alexander Standish
5.   John Standish
6.   Edward Winslow
7.   Susanna Winslow
8.   Edward Winslow
9.   John Winslow
10.   Resolved White
11.   Peregrine White
12.   Abraham Pierce
13.   Thomas Clarke

To this lot fell the Red Cow which belogeth to the poor of the Colony to which they must keep her calf of this year being a bull for the Company. Also to this lot came two she goats.

4.   The fourth lot fell to John Howland and his company joined to him
2.   his wife Elizabeth Howland
3.   John Howland Junior
4.   Desire Howland
5.   William Wight
6.   Thomas Morton Junior
7.   John Alden
8.   Priscilla Alden
9.   Elizabeth Alden
10.   Clement Briggs
11.   Edward Doty
12.   Edward Holman
13.   John Alden

To this lot fell one of the 4 heifers came in the *Jacob* called Raghorn.

5.   The fifth lot fell to Mr. William Brewster and his company joined to him.
2.   Love Brewster
3.   Wrestling Brewster
4.   Richard More
5.   Henry Sampson
6.   Jonathan Brewster
7.   Lucretia Brewster
8.   William Brewster
9.   Mary Brewster
10.   Thomas Prence
11.   Patience Prence
12.   Rebecca Prence
13.   Humility Cooper

To this lot fell one of the four heifers came in the *Jacob* called the Blind Heifer and 2 she goats.

6.   The sixth lot fell to John Shaw and his company joined
1.   to him
2.   John Adams
3.   Eleanor Adams   To this lot fell the lesser of the black cows
4.   James Adams   came in the *Anne* which they must keep the biggest
5.   John Winslow   of the 2 steers. And to this lot was two she goats.
6.   Mary Winslow
7.   William Bassett
8.   Elizabeth Bassett
9.   William Bassett Junior
10. Elizabeth Bassett Junior
11. Francis Sprague
12. Anna Sprague
13. Mercy Sprague

7.   The seventh lot fell to Stephen Hopkins and his company joined to
2.   him his wife Elizabeth Hopkins
3.   Giles Hopkins   To this lot fell a black weining calf to which
4.   Caleb Hopkins   was added the calf of this year to come of the
5.   Deborah Hopkins   black cow, which fell to John Shaw and his
6.   Nicholas Snow   company, which proving a bull they were to keep
7.   Constance Snow   it ungelt 5 years for common use and after to make
8.   William Palmer   their best of it. Nothing belongeth of these two,
9.   Frances Palmer   for the company of the first stock: but only half the
10. William Palmer Junior increase.
11. John Billington Senior   To this lot there fell two she goats: which goats
12. Helen Billington   they possess on the like terms which others do
13. Francis Billington   their cattle.

8.   The eighth lot fell to Samuel Fuller and his company joined to him his wife
2.   Bridget Fuller
3.   Samuel Fuller Junior   To this lot fell a Red Heifer came of the cow
4.   Peter Brown   which belongeth to the poor of the colony and so is
5.   Martha Brown   of that consideration. (viz) these persons
6.   Mary Brown   nominated, to have half increase, the other half,
7.   John Ford   with the old stock, to remain for the use of the
8.   Martha Ford   poor.
9.   Anthony Annable   To this lot also two she goats.
10. Jane Annable
11. Sarah Annable
12. Hannah Annable
13. ~~Thomas Morton Senior~~
13. Damaris Hopkins

9. The ninth lot fell to Richard Warren and his company joined with
2. him his wife Elizabeth Warren
3. Nathaniel Warren   To this lot fell one of the 4 black heifers that
4. Joseph Warren   came in the *Jacob* called the Smooth-horned
5. Mary Warren   Heifer and two she goats.
6. Anna Warren
7. Sarah Warren
8. Elizabeth Warren
9. Abigail Warren
10. John Billington
11. George Soule
12. Mary Soule
13. Zachariah Soule

10. The tenth lot fell to Francis Eaton and those joined with him his
2. wife Christian Eaton
3. Samuel Eaton   To this lot fell an heifer of the last year called
4. Rachel Eaton   the White-bellied Heifer and two she goats.
5. Stephen Tracey
6. Triphosa Tracey
7. Sarah Tracey
8. Rebecca Tracey
9. Ralph Wallen
10. Joyce Wallen
11. Sarah Morton
12. ~~Edward Flood~~
12. Robert ~~Hilton~~ Bartlett
13. Thomas Prence

11. The eleventh lot fell to the Governor Mr. William Bradford and
2. those with him, to wit, his wife Alice Bradford and
3. William Bradford, junior   To this lot fell an heifer of the last year
4. Mercy Bradford   which was of the great white-back cow that
5. Joseph Rogers   was brought over in the *Anne*, and two she
6. Thomas Cushman   goats.
7. William Latham
8. Manasseh Kempton
9. Juliana Kempton
10. Nathaniel Morton
11. John Morton
12. Ephraim Morton
13. Patience Morton

12. The twelvth lot fell to John Jenny and his company joined to him,
2. his wife Sarah Jenny
3. Samuel Jenny   To this lot fell the great white-backed cow
4. Abigail Jenny   which was brought over with the first in the *Anne*,
5. Sarah Jenny   to which cow the keeping of the bull was joined
6. Robert Hicks   for these persons to provide for. Here also two she
7. Margaret Hicks   goats.
8. Samuel Hicks
9. Ephraim Hicks
10. Lydia Hicks
11. Phoebe Hicks
12. Stephen Deane
13. Edward Bangs

ENDNOTES

Abbreviations

(1) EHP. Henry M. Dexter, *England and Holland of the Pilgrims* (London, 1906).
(2) HCA. High Court of Admiralty records, kept at the Public Records Office, England.
(3) MD. *Mayflower Descendant*, periodical published by the Massachusetts Society of Mayflower Descendants.
(4) MQ. *Mayflower Quarterly*, periodical published by the General Society of Mayflower Descendants.
(5) NEHGR. *New England Historical and Genealogical Register*, periodical published by the New England Historical and Genealogical Society (NEHGS).
(6) PCR. Nathaniel Shurtleff and David Pulsifer, eds., *Records of the Colony of New Plymouth*. 12-volumes.
(7) PRO. Public Records Office, England.
(8) TAG. *The American Genealogist*.

Although not specifically cited as a source for any given end note, special note is due for Robert C. Anderson's *Great Migration Begins* (3 volumes; Boston: NEHGS, 1995), and *Pilgrim Migration* (Boston: NEHGS, 2004), which were consulted regularly to ensure I did not overlook records of interest. Additionally, I have not used end notes to reference biographical material taken from the three most readily available historical sources: William Bradford's *Of Plymouth Plantation*, and the two main Pilgrim journals, *A Journal or Relation of the Beginnings and Proceedings of the Plantation Settled at New Plymouth* (London, 1622), and Edward Winslow's *Good News from New England* (London, 1624).

[1] Letter of Robert Cushman to Edward Southworth at Heneage House, London, preserved by William Bradford in his *History of Plymouth Plantation.*

[2] HCA 24/73/109, fol. 229.

[3] HCA 24/81, fol. 167 (219).

[4] HCA 24/75, No. 143. This mention of the *Mayflower's* forecastle and gunroom, never before published, is one of the only surviving descriptions that actually mentions specific rooms or areas onboard the ship.

[5] HCA 13/42, fol. 43-43d.

[6] HCA 13/42, fol. 45-45d.

[7] HCA 38/12 folio 156-157d.

[8] HCA 13/40, folio 235d-236d.

[9] HCA 13/40, folio 237-238, and folio 269d-271.

[10] HCA 13/40, folio 272d-274 (Haddon) and HCA 13/41, folio 51-51d (Fenton).

[11] HCA 13/40, folio 265-265d (Sr.) and folio 267d-268d (Jr.).

[12] HCA 24/73/27.

[13] HCA 24/73/37.

[14] HCA 13/40, folio 268d-269.

[15] HCA 13/40, folio 279-279d.

[16] HCA 24/74 No. 125, folio 195.

[17] HCA 24/75, No. 143.

[18] HCA 24/75, No. 250.

[19] HCA 38/12, folio 200; HCA 3/28, folio 132.

[20] HCA 3/28, folio 146.

[21] PRO CP 40/1863, rot. 1506.

[22] PRO E190/15/3 folio 7d-8.

[23] PRO E190/17/7 folio 24d-25.

[24] PRO E190/18/2 folio 27.

[25] J.R. Hutchinson, "The 'Mayflower', Her Identity and Tonnage," *NEHGR*, October 1916, p. 341.

[26] PRO E190/24/3.

[27] The most comprehensive study to date on the *Mayflower's* probable construction and layout is found in William A Baker, *The New Mayflower: Her Design and Construction* (Barre Gazette: Barre, MA, 1958).

28 Captain John Smith recorded his recommendations of what settlers should bring to the New World in his *General History of Virginia, New England and the Summer Isles* (London, 1624), at pp. 161-162.

29 A seventeenth-century description of the parts of a ship and their use can be found in Captain John Smith's *Seamans Grammar and Dictionary*.

30 John Clark's two depositions telling the story of his capture and time in Spanish custody can be found in Irene A. Wright, "Documents: Spanish Policy towards Virginia," *American Historical Review* 25(1920):448-479.

31 Charles Edward Banks, "Giles Heale and William Mullins," *Proceedings of the Massachusetts Historical Society* 60(1926-1927):144-150.

32 Higginson's journal is found reprinted in Alexander Young, *Chronicles of the First Planters of the Colony of Massachusetts Bay* (Boston: Charles Little and James Brown, 1846), pp. 215-238.

33 Winthrop's journal entries are reprinted in Richard S. Dunn and Laetitia Yeandle, *The Journal of John Winthrop 1630-1649* (Harvard University Press, 1996), pp. 13-28.

34 John Josselyn's journals are reprinted in Paul J. Lindholdt, *John Josselyn, Colonial Traveler* (London: University Press, 1988).

35 The various theories are nicely summarized in Alicia Crane Williams, "John Alden: Theories on English Ancestry," *MD* 39(July 1989):111-122, and 40(July 1990):133-136.

36 Deposition reprinted in *MD* 3:120-121.

37 Broadside reprinted in *MD* 34:49-53.

38 James W. Baker, "Some Pilgrim Fictions," *MQ* 71(March 2005):20-32, at pp. 23-26.

39 PCR 12:4.

40 PCR 12:9-13.

41 The will of William Mullins is reprinted in *MD* 1:230-232. All known wills and estate inventories belonging to the *Mayflower* passengers are also reprinted in full on the MayflowerHistory.com website.

42 William Bradford's *Letterbook*, reprinted in *Collections of the Massachusetts Historical Society*, 3(1794):27-76.

43 PCR 1:3-5.

44 *Winthrop Papers, 1498-1654* (Boston 1925-1992), 3:65

45 PCR 1:5-11.

46 PCR 1:12.

47 PCR 1:5.

48 Nichole K. Davi and Paul J. Krusic, "Dendrochronological Examination of Wood Samples from the John Alden House, Duxbury, Massachusetts," unpublished report prepared for the Alden Kindred of America in 2003.

49 Roland Wells Robbins, *Pilgrim John Alden's Progress: Archaeological Excavations in Duxbury* (Pilgrim Society, 1969).

50 The Kennebec trade incident is best described in a deposition that is found amongst the probate records of the Plymouth Colony. It is reprinted in C.H. Simmons, *Plymouth Colony Records: Volume 1, Wills and Inventories 1633 -1669* (Picton Press: Camden, ME, 1996), pp. 57-58. It is also discussed in Bradford's *Of Plymouth Plantation.*

51 PCR 1:51, 76, 91, 95.

52 PCR 2:16, 40, 72, 75, 94, 95, 104, 117, 123, 144.

53 PCR 8:189.

54 PCR 2:85.

55 PCR 2:96, 127, 144; 3:96.

56 PCR 2:153, 166; 3:7, 26, 28, 30, 48, 77, 96, 99, 114, 115, 117, 134, 135, 138, 162, 187, 214.

57 PCR 3:120.

58 PCR 3:195.

59 PCR 4:95, 5:141.

60 PCR 4:81-83.

61 PCR 5:245-246.

62 Plymouth Colony Land Records 3:330.

63 Plymouth Colony Land Records 3:194.

64 Plymouth Colony Land Records 6:53.

65 Plymouth Colony Land Records 5:427.

66 Plymouth Colony Land Records 4:65.

67 Broadside on the death of John Alden, reprinted in *MD* 34:49-53.

68 Estate Inventory of John Alden, reprinted in *MD* 3:10-11.

69 Leiden Archives 044 Reg. / ONA131 No. 185 (18 June 1618) [aged about thirty on 18 June 1618] and Thomas Letchford, *Note-book Kept by Thomas Lechford, Esq., Lawyer, in Boston, Massachusetts Bay, from June 27, 1638 to July 29, 1641* (Cambridge, 1885), pp. 189-190 [aged "about 53 years" on 26 September 1639].

70 Leslie Mahler, unpublished research, citing court minutes of the Blacksmiths' Company of London, v. 1-2, f. 115.

71 *Transactions of the American Antiquarian Society* 8:189, 259, and *New York Colonial Manuscripts: Holland Documents* 8:597.

72   Leiden Archives 006 Reg./ONA180fo.117v/8-1-1619 and 044 reg./ ONA131no. 185/18-6-1618.

73   Leiden Archives 044 reg./ONA131no. 185/18-6-1618.

74   Leiden Archives 006 reg./ONA180fo. 117v/8-1-1619 contract.

75   Letter of Edward Winslow to John Winthrop dated 1 July 1637, transcribed in *Collections of the Massachusetts Historical Society* 4th Series 6(1863):162-183.

76   *Records of the Colony and Plantation of New Haven from 1638 to 1649* (Hartford: Tiffany and Company, 1857), p. 116.

77   PCR 2:133.

78   *Records of the Colony and Plantation of New Haven from 1638 to 1649* (Hartford: Tiffany and Company, 1857), p. 309.

79   The will and estate inventory of Isaac Allerton is *MD* 2:155-157.

80   EHP, p. 601.

81   Ibid.

82   R.H. Winson, *NEHGR* 124:116-118.

83   Unpublished research on the Billingtons of Lincolnshire, performed by Paul C. Reed for David Greene.

84   Thomas Prince, *Chronological History of New England in the Form of Annals* (Boston 1736), citing a now-lost "register of Governor Bradford's, in his own hand, recording some of the first deaths, marriages and punishments, at Plymouth."

85   William Hubbard, *General History of New England* (Boston 1815, from a seventeenth century manuscript).

86   Thomas Morton, New *English Canaan* (Amsterdam 1637), reprinted Jack Dempsy, ed. (Scituate 1999), pp. 79-80.

87   "Ancestry of the Bradfords of Austerfield," *NEHGR* 83(1929):439-eoa, 84(1930):5-eoa.

88   Cotton Mather's short biography of William Bradford, found in his *Magnalia Christi Americana* (Boston, 1702).

89   Leiden Archives 163/RA67VVfo. 195/19-4-1619.

90   Cotton Mather in his *Magnalia Christi Americana* (Boston, 1702) reported that William Bradford's "dearest consort accidentally falling overboard, was drowned in the harbor." In 1869, a fictional story claiming Dorothy committed suicide appeared in *Harper's Weekly*, and from this many legends and family stories were created. See more in *MD* 29:97-102 and 31:105.

91   The letters of Emmanuel Altham are reprinted in Sydney V. James, ed., *Three Visitors to Early Plymouth* (Plimoth Plantation: Plymouth, 1963).

[92] William Bradford's poem, "A Word to New Plymouth," is reprinted in the *Collections of the Massachusetts Historical Society*, 1870, at pp. 478- 482.

[93] C.H. Simmons, ed., *Plymouth Colony Records: Volume 1, Wills and Inventories 1633 -1669*, pp. 331-337.

[94] The history of Scrooby Manor is described in more detail in EHP, especially at pp. 216-250.

[95] William Brewster's life is chronicled in much more detail in a nice biography, namely Mary B. Sherwood, *Pilgrim: A Biography of William Brewster* (Great Oaks Press: Falls Church, Virginia, 1982).

[96] EHP, p. 323-324.

[97] EHP, p. 392, citing the Act Books of the Ecclesiastical Causes Commission Court

[98] EHP, p. 401, citing Act Books, York Registry, of the High Court of Commissions

[99] C.H. Simmons, ed., *Plymouth Colony Records: Volume 1, Wills and Probates* (Picton Press: Rockport, Maine, 1996), pp. 113-125.

[100] Henry Dexter, "Elder Brewster's Library," *Proceedings of the Massachusetts Historical Society* (2nd Series) 5:37-85.

[101] Parish register transcripts of Crowhurst, Sussex [IGI batch C040911, FHL #504414].

[102] Caleb Johnson, "The Probable English Origin of *Mayflower* Passenger Peter Browne, and His Association with *Mayflower* Passenger William Mullins," *TAG* 79(July 2004):161-178.

[103] Thomas Prince, *Chronological History of New England* (Boston, 1736).

[104] International Genealogical Index, batch P008621, citing the parish registers of Worksop, FHL#0459652.

[105] William Mullins's will can be found transcribed in *MD* 1(1899):231-232, and on the MayflowerHistory.com website.

[106] Charles E. Banks, *English Ancestry and Homes of the Pilgrim Fathers* (Baltimore, 1929), p. 44.

[107] Jeremy D. Bangs, introduction to *Mayflower Families Through Five Generations: Francis Cooke*, pp. x-xi.

[108] EHP, p. 609.

[109] EHP, pp. 608-609.

[110] Ibid.

[111] Ibid.

[112] The date of 23 August comes from John Smith, *New England's Trials* (London, 1622).

113 Thomas Prince, *Chronological History of New England* (Boston, 1736).
114 Ibid.
115 Edward Winslow and others, *A Relation or Journal of the Beginning and Proceedings of the English Plantation Settled at Plymouth* (London, 1622).
116 John Smith, *New England's Trials* (London, 1622).
117 Nathaniel Morton, *New England's Memorial* (London, 1669).
118 James Chilton gives his age as sixty-three in a 1619 deposition, Leiden Archives ONA 180/239/30-4-1619.
119 Mrs. Russell Mack Skelton, "Copies of Wills of the Chilton Family," *MQ* 27:5-6.
120 Canterbury Cathedral Archives, The Canterbury Court of Quarter Sessions, CC/JQ/382/iv.
121 John G. Hunt, "Origin of the Chiltons of the Mayflower," *TAG* 38:244-245.
122 Michael R. Paulick, "The 1609-1610 Excommunications of *Mayflower* Pilgrims Mrs. Chilton and Moses Fletcher," *NEHGR* 153:408-412.
123 Nahum Mitchell, *History of the Early Settlement of Bridgewater, in Plymouth County, Massachusetts, including an extensive Family Register* (Boston: Kidder & Wright, 1840), p. 372.
124 Center for Kentish Studies, West Kent Quarter Sessions Records: Victuallers Recognizances QM/RLv/45.
125 Mary Chilton's baptism date is misstated as 30 May 1607 in *Mayflower Families For Five Generations* 15:3, and in Robert C. Anderson's *Great Migration Begins* 1:354, and Pilgrim Migration, pp. 105. I have verified the baptism date of 31 May 1607 with the original parish register.
126 Michael R. Paulick, "The 1609-1610 Excommunications of *Mayflower* Pilgrims Mrs. Chilton and Moses Fletcher," *NEHGR* 153:407, citing "Comperta and Dectecta Book," Sandwich Deanery 1585-1611, Canterbury Cathedral Archives, X.2.5 part 3 of 3 volumes f153v.
127 Leiden Archives, 1022/B41v/21-7-1615.
128 Leiden Archives, 008 reg./ONA180 fo. 239/30-4-1619.
129 Francis Cooke was included in a list of men able to bear arms in Plymouth, dated 1643. The men on this list were "from 16 years old to 60." This indicates Francis Cooke should have been born after August 1583. A marginal note, added probably in the late seventeenth or early eighteenth century by an unknown person into Bradford's manuscript, reports that Francis was "above 80" when he died in 1663, which would

mean a birth of before April 1583 (however, ages at death were often exaggerated somewhat). We would normally expect a man during this time period to be at least twenty-one years old when getting married, which for his June 1603 marriage would mean a birth before June 1582.

[130] The Leiden records relating to the Cooke, Mahieu, and de Lannoy families, as summarized on this page, are much more thoroughly presented in the excellent research of Jeremy D. Bangs, see his "The Pilgrims and Other English in Leiden Records: Some New Pilgrim Documents," *NEHGR* 143:195-212, and his foreword and summary of Francis Cooke found in *Mayflower Families for Five Generations: Francis Cooke* (Rockport ME, 1996), pp. v.-xi., and pp. 1-28.

[131] PCR 11:4-5.

[132] PCR 1:8.

[133] PCR 1:31.

[134] PCR 1:58-60.

[135] PCR 1:152.

[136] PCR 1:163.

[137] PCR 2:7.

[138] PCR 2:34, 40.

[139] PCR 2:84.

[140] PCR 2:160.

[141] PCR 3:169.

[142] PCR 1:86-87.

[143] PCR 2:132-133.

[144] PCR 2:134.

[145] PCR 4:153.

[146] Robert Leigh Ward, "The Baronial Ancestry of Henry Sampson, Humility Cooper and Ann (Cooper) Tilley," *The Genealgist* 6:166-186.

[147] EHP, p. 610.

[148] Robert S. Wakefield, "Pilgrim John Crackstone: A Search for His Ancestry and Posterity," *MQ* 40(November 1974), pp. 117-119.

[149] Parish registers of Stratford St. Mary, Suffolk, searched at my request by Simon Neal. See also, Caleb Johnson, "A Note on the English Origins of *Mayflower* Passengers John Crackstone and John Hooke," *The American Genealogist* 80(2005):100.

[150] There are a couple Edward Dotys found baptized in the vicinity of East Halton, co. Lincolnshire. The names used by Edward Doty match well with the names found in the East Halton family as well. Leslie Mahler

has examined some of the probate records in this area, but found nothing conclusive (personal correspondence and unpublished research).

[151] Thomas Prince, *Chronological History of New England in the Form of Annals* (Boston 1736), citing a now lost "register of Governor Bradford's, in his own hand, recording some of the first deaths, marriages and punishments, at Plymouth."

[152] The court record summaries are all taken from Shurtleff and Pulsifer, *Records of the Colony of New Plymouth in New England* (12 volumes), primarily the Court Orders found in volumes 1-2.

[153] Plymouth Town Records 1:16.

[154] C. H. Simmons, editor, *Plymouth Colony Records, Wills and Inventories*, pp. 287-289.

[155] Ibid.

[156] The Engish origins of Francis Eaton were discovered by Neil D. Thompson and published in "The Origin of Francis Eaton of the *Mayflower*," *TAG* 72(1997):301-304.

[157] Will of Christopher Cary, PCC 11/149 (Hele 60), dated 30 October 1615, proved 31 May 1626.

[158] The apprenticeship record was first noted by Charles Banks in his *English Ancestry and Homes of the Pilgrim Fathers*, and is discussed in more detail in Neil Thompson's article "The Origin of Francis Eaton of the *Mayflower*," *TAG* 72(1997):301-304.

[159] PCR 1:43.

[160] His marriage and the baptism records of his children are found nicely summarized by Robert S. Wakefield in "Pilgrim Moses Fletcher's Family," *MQ* 41(1975):45. Additional articles by Wakefield appearing in the *MQ* document some Dutch descendants of Moses Fletcher in Leiden through the fifth generation.

[161] The excommunication records relating to Moses Fletcher were first published by Michael Paulick, "The 1609-1610 Excommunications of Mrs. Chilton and Moses Fletcher - Mayflower Pilgrims," *NEHGR* 153:407-410.

[162] Leiden records relating to Moses Fletcher are summarized in *Henry Dexter, England and Holland of the Pilgrims* (London 1906), pp. 614-615. Robert S. Wakefield adds much new information about the descendants of Moses Fletcher in several articles, including "Pilgrim Moses Fletcher," *MQ* 38:89, "Pilgrim Moses Fletcher's Family," *MQ* 41:45-47, 126-129; and "The Search for the Descendants of Moses Fletcher," *NEHGR* 128:161-169.

[163] Francis H. Fuller, "Fullers of Redenhall, England," *NEHGR* 55(October 1901):410-416.

[164] Jeremy D. Bangs, *MQ* 51:58, citing Leiden Archives R.A. 79, L, fol. 172v.

[165] Francis H. Fuller, "Fullers of Redenhall, England," *NEHGR* 55(October 1901):410-416.

[166] Leiden Archives 1007/B4/4-11-1611.

[167] Leiden Archives 1002/A162v/4-12-1610.

[168] Leiden Archives 1010/B8/16-2-1612.

[169] Leiden Archives 1013/B18v/24-4-1613.

[170] Leiden Archives 1014/B21v/28-5-1613.

[171] Leiden Archives 1020/B30/31-5-1614.

[172] EHP, p. 615.

[173] Leiden Archives 1024/B44/3-10-1615.

[174] Leiden Archives 1032/B64/27-5-1617.

[175] Leiden Archives 1023/B43/25-8-1615 (Samuel Butler) and 1045/B89v/5-10-1619 (John Codmore).

[176] Samuel Fuller's letters are found in William Bradford's *Letterbook*.

[177] Parish registers of Harwich, co. Essex.

[178] Several lawsuits followed, the depositions of which contain a number of insights into the events surrounding the *Little James*. See HCA 13/44 folios 410-412, 414d, 415d-416d (Stevens and Fell vs. *Little James*) and HCA 24/81 folio 120-121 (Fletcher and Goffe vs. *Little James*).

[179] Sydney V. James, ed., *Three Visitors to Early Plymouth* (Plymouth: Plimoth Plantation, 1963), pp. 47-48.

[180] Leiden Archives, 1045/B89v/5-10-1619.

[181] Parish registers of Everdon, co. Northampton. Mary Barker was the widow of Edward Barker, who was buried on 11 December 1603. She had married Edward on 12 February 1595 at Everdon; her maiden name was Berrett.

[182] Caleb Johnson, "A Note on the English Origins of *Mayflower* Passengers John Crackstone and John Hooke," *The American Genealogist* 80(2005):100.

[183] Leiden Archives, 006 reg./ONA180fo. /8-1-1619.

[184] Ernest Martin Christensen, "The Probable Parentage of Stephen Hopkins of the *Mayflower*," *TAG* 79(October 2004):241-249.

[185] Caleb Johnson, "The True Origin of Stephen Hopkins of the *Mayflower*," *TAG* 73(July 1998):161-171.

186 The narrative that follows, about the *Sea Venture* and events in Bermuda, is based on two primary source accounts, one by William Strachey and one by Silvester Jourdain. These accounts were reprinted in Louis B. Wright, ed., *A Voyage to Virginia in 1609: Two Narratives* (Unviersity Press of Virginia: Charlottesville, 1964).

187 PCR 1:111-113.

188 John Howland's birth year has been traditionally set at 1592, based on the Plymouth Church record that states he died in 1672, above the age of eighty. However, an examination of Howland's life events, including the fact he was a manservant in 1620 (thus under the age of twenty-five) and married a girl who was born in 1607, strongly suggest Howland's age at death was exaggerated (a common occurrence).

189 Will of Humphrey Howland, reprinted in *Howland Quarterly* 28(July 1964), citing P.C.C. Twiss III.

190 The Howland indenture that seems to indicate a connection between the Thickens and Howland families of Stepney, co. Middlesex, is discussed in more detail in the *Howland Quarterly* 65(March 2000):1-7. The original indenture is currently in the possession of the Pilgrim John Howland Society.

191 C.H. Simmons, Jr., ed., *Plymouth Colony Records: Volume 1, Wills and Probates* (Picton Press: Rockport, ME, 1996), pp. 57-58.

192 PCR 1:70, 110.

193 PCR, Vol. 1, *passim*.

194 The will and estate inventory of John Howland are reprinted in *MD* 2:70-77.

195 PCR 1:10, 28.

196 C.H. Simmons, Jr., ed., *Plymouth Colony Records: Volume 1, Wills and Probates* (Picton Press: Rockport, ME, 1996), pp. 43.

197 PCR 1:14, 33, 40.

198 PCR 1:87, 101, 105, 106.

199 PCR 12:54-55.

200 Edward Everett Hale, Jr., ed., *Note-book Kept by Thomas Lechford, Esq., Lawyer, in Boston, Massachusetts Bay, from June 27, 1638 to June 29, 1641* (Picton Press: Camden, ME, 1988), p. 31.

201 PCR 8:187-196.

202 *Winthrop Papers* 4:445-446.

203 Thomas Prince, *Chronological History of New England in the Form of Annals* (Cambridge, 1736).

[204] Much of what is known about Christopher Martin's life in Great Burstead, co. Essex, was researched, documented and published by R. J. Carpenter in *Christopher Martin, Great Burstead, and the Mayflower* (London: Fact and Fiction, 1982, reprinted 1993).

[205] Carpenter, ibid., citing Essex Records Office Q/SR 180/10,11.

[206] Carpenter, ibid., citing Essex Records Office D/AEA 26 fol. 170.

[207] Carpenter, ibid., citing PRO CO 1 Vol. 2 No. 33. As this book was going to press, William Thorndale was preparing an article for *The American Genealogist*, "Christopher Martin of the *Mayflower* Was Not the Virginia Company Shareholder." He provides documents that indicate the same Christopher Martin was still doing business with the Virginia Company after the death of the *Mayflower* passenger of the same name.

[208] Carpenter, ibid., citing Essex Records Office D/AEA 31 Fol. 265 et. seq.

[209] Carpenter, ibid., citing Essex Records Office D/DP M907.

[210] EHP, p. 625.

[211] Leiden Archives, 009 reg./ONA182 fo. 157/10-5-1622

[212] Edward Arber, *Story of the Pilgrim Fathers* (London, 1897), pp. 246-247.

[213] Donald F. Harris researched, documented, and published most of what is currently known about the More family in Shropshire. See his article, "The More Children of the *Mayflower*: Their Shopshire Origins and the Reasons Why They Were Sent Away," *MD*, volumes 43 and 44, passim. Harris has also published a pamphlet, *The More Children of the Mayflower* (Churchwardens of St. James Parish: Shipton, Shropshire, 1999). David Lindsay has also published a book on Richard More, *Mayflower Bastard: A Stranger Among the Pilgrims* (New York: St. Martin's Press, 2002), which provides a nice, readable biography, but does become rather speculative in places.

[214] Records relating to William Mullins in co. Surrey are documented in my article "The Probable English Origin of *Mayflower* Passenger Peter Browne, and His Association With *Mayflower* Passenger William Mullins," *TAG* 79:161-178.

[215] Caleb Johnson, "The Probable English Origin of *Mayflower* Passenger Peter Browne, and His Association With *Mayflower* Passenger William Mullins," *TAG* 79:161-178, at pp. 176-177.

[216] Charles Banks, *English Ancestry and Homes of the Pilgrim Fathers* (1929), p. 73.

[217] *NEHGR* 111:320.

218 EHP, p. 630.

219 Leiden Archives 222/ONA129 no. 158/29-6-1617.

220 Leiden Archives 223/ONA129 no. 160/30-6-1617.

221 Leiden Archives 044 reg./ONA131 no. 185/18-6-1618.

222 Leiden Archives 045 reg./ONA131 no. 131/3-5-1619.

223 Leiden Archives 052a reg./RA79 M /9-4-1619.

224 PCR 2:131-132; 12:137.

225 R. J. Carpenter, *Christopher Martin, Great Burstead, and the Mayflower* (London: Fact and Fiction, 1982, reprinted 1993), p. 7, citing Essex Records Office D/AEA 31 Fol. 265 et al.

226 The English origins of Thomas Rogers were discovered by Clifford L. Stott and published in "The English Ancestry of the Pilgrim Thomas Rogers and His Wife Alice (Cosford) Rogers," *The Genealogist* 10(1989):138-149.

227 EHP, pp. 572-573.

228 Jeremy D. Bangs, "The Pilgrims and Other English in Leiden Records: Some New Pilgrim Documents," *NEHGR* 143(1989):195-212, at p. 207.

229 Ibid.

230 Robert Leigh Ward, "English Ancestry of Seven Mayflower Passengers: Tilley, Sampson and Cooper," *TAG* 52:198-208.

231 Ibid., at p. 207.

232 PCR 1:61 (Pequot War); 1:72 (Land 1637); 1:144 (Land 1640)

233 PCR, passim.

234 PCR 5:29

235 Henry Samson's will and estate inventory are reprinted in *MD* 2:142-144.

236 Caleb Johnson, "The Search for the English Origins of *Mayflower* Passenger George Soule: Part 1, Eckington, co. Worcester," *Soule Newsletter* 39(April 2005):28-32. Part II of the article, "Strenham, Redmarly d'Abitot, Dymock, Berrow, and Aspherton," is found immediately following, at pp. 33-38. Part III of the article, covering Tingrith and Flitwick, co. Bedford, will be published shortly in the *Soule Newsletter*.

237 It may be worth noting that the Warren family appears to have come from parishes in co. Hertford that are very near to the parishes of Tingrith, co. Bedford.

238 PCR 1:15, 56.

239 PCR 1:69, 83, 165; 12:45.

240 PCR 1:60.

[241] PCR 1:151, 2:88.

[242] PCR vol. 2-3, *passim.*

[243] PCR 2:108, 11:53.

[244] PCR 4:178-179.

[245] PCR 5:61.

[246] PCR 5:163.

[247] PCR 4:34.

[248] PCR 4:162.

[249] George Soule's will and estate inventory are reprinted in *MD* 2:81-84.

[250] T. C. Porteus, *Captain Myles Standish: His Lost Lands and Lancashire Connections* (Manchester University Press: London, 1920); G. V. C. Young, Pilgrim Myles Standish: First Manx American (Mansk-Svenska: Isle of Man, 1984); *More About Pilgrim Myles Standish: First Manx American* (Mansk-Svenska: Isle of Man, 1987); *Ellenbane was the Birthplace of Myles Standish: First Manx American* (Mansk-Svenska: Isle of Man, 1988).

[251] Helen Moorwood, "Pilgrim Father Captain Myles Standish of Duxbury, Lancashire," *Lancashire History Quarterly*, Volume 3 (1999).

[252] William Hubbard wrote a manuscript history of New England between the 1650s and 1680s, which was first published in 1815 under the title *The General History of New England.*

[253] This comment of William Bradford was recorded as a note following a letter dated 28 June 1625, found in his *Letterbook.*

[254] C. H. Simmons, Jr., ed., *Plymouth Colony Records: Volume 1, Wills and Probates* (Picton Press: Rockport, ME, 1996), pp. 313-316.

[255] Robert Leigh Ward, "English Ancestry of Seven *Mayflower* Passengers: Tilley, Sampson and Cooper," *TAG* 52:198-208.

[256] Jeremy D. Bangs, in *MQ* 52:7.

[257] Robert Leigh Ward, "English Ancestry of Seven *Mayflower* Passengers: Tilley, Sampson and Cooper," *TAG* 52 (1976):198-208.

[258] Robert Leigh Ward, "Further Traces of John Tilley of the *Mayflower*," *TAG* 60(1984):171-173, citing Pubs. Beds. Hist. Record Soc., 2(1914):50-51 [will of George Clarke of Henlow], and PRO Chancery Suits C21/T5/16 [deposition].

[259] Elizabeth Howland's will is reprinted in *MD* 3:54-57.

[260] "Four Depositions Relating to Thompson's Island," *NEHGR*, 9 (1855):248.

[261] PRO, State Papers Colonial, Vol. 5, No. 112.

262 Robert S. Wakefield, "Mayflower Passengers Turner and Rogers: Probable Identification of Additional Children," *TAG* 52:110-113.

263 Edward Davies, "The Marriage of Richard Warren of the *Mayflower*," *TAG* 78 (April 2003):81-86; and "Elizabeth (Walker) Warren and Her Sister, Dorothy (Walker) (Grave) Adams," *TAG* 78:274-275.

264 For more on Bradford's passenger list, see Caleb Johnson, "New Light on William Bradford's Passenger List of the Mayflower," *The American Genealogist* 80(April 2005):94-98.

265 Parish registers of Great Yarmouth, co. Norfolk.

266 Leiden Archives, 1026/B48v/26-3-1616.

267 The date of Edward Winslow's birth and baptism have been misstated in many sources, including Eugene Stratton, *Plymouth Colony: Its History and Its People*, and James Savage, *Genealogical Dictionary of the First Settlers of New England*. The dates given here were verified with the original parish registers of St. Peter's, Droitwich.

268 John G. Hunt, "The 'Mayflower' Winslows—Yeomen or Gentlemen," *NEHGR* 121 (1967):25-29, 122 (1968):175-178, 124 (1970):182-183.

269 Details of Winslow and Beale's London publishing activities are nicely summarized in Jeremy D. Bangs, *Pilgrim Edward Winslow: New England's First International Diplomat* (New England Historical and Genealogical Society, 2004).

270 Leiden Archives 1040/B75/27-4-1618.

271 The poem was recorded by Nathaniel Morton in his *New England's Memorial* (Cambridge, 1669), under the year 1655.

272 Edward Winslow's will is reprinted in *MD* 4:1-2.

273 PCR 4:40.

274 Neil D. Thompson, FASG, "The Origin and Parentage of Francis Eaton of the *Mayflower*," and David Green, "Notes on Francis Eaton of Plymouth," *TAG* 72:301-304, 305-310.